I'm Just A Fork-Lift Operator.
After All, What Do I Know?

January 2013

To Theresa;

Thank you for all you do for me/us. Thank you also for your interest in reading what I have learned in my faith journey with Jesus Christ. I hope and pray you enjoy your search for the truth in finding the narrow gate/path to eternal life.

Peace + Love,
Joe Traore
(The Fork-lift, operator)

I'm Just A Fork-Lift Operator.
After All, What Do I Know ?

Searching for the Truth

Finding the Narrow Path to Eternal Life

Joseph Traver

To order additional copies of this book, contact:
Xlibris Corporation
1-888-795-4274
www.Xlibris.com
Orders@Xlibris.com
88274

CONTENTS

THIS BOOK IS dedicated to my friend and fellow Christian Brother Forrest Habicht, a man whom I came to know and admire by and through our shared faith in Jesus Christ. The results of this book came about as a response to my friend urging me to do so. Of all the people I have ever met in my life, I consider my dear friend Forrest at the very top of the list when it comes to integrity, honesty, and sincerity. The kind of qualities he has shown me are the same ones I have tried to embrace in my life as I have walked the path of my faith as a follower of Jesus Christ. Furthermore, the results of this book came about as a result of many Saturday-morning telephone conversations in which Forrest and his wife, Joan, and I spent hours in fellowship and conversation about our faith as Christians.

I also want to dedicate this book to the wonderful ministry of the Mars Hill Network radio station, WMHR (102.9 FM), with general manager, Wayne Taylor. I truly believe if it hadn't been for this wonderful Christian radio station's ministry, I might have never heard about Jesus Christ and the good news message of the Bible.

I also want to dedicate this book to my wife, Estella, and my family (Stacia, Aubrey, and Machilia), who have endured the struggles through the years as I have been led by the Holy Spirit to spread the good news of Jesus Christ to a lost and dying world. What I have learned from my experience as a follower of Jesus Christ is that more often than not, the ones who are the closest to you can often be the ones who are the hardest to reach when sharing the gospel message (Matthew 10:36).

I also want to dedicate this book to a man by the name of Mark Baker, who helped me endure my time as a representative (steward and trustee) in the union as God molded and shaped me into being one of his watchmen. Only a handful of people understand the trials and tribulations that I endured, and Mark is one of those people. Mark is one of those people because he was right by my side as we endured these trials and tribulations together. I thank God for bringing a man of Mark's integrity into my life at a time when I really needed a true friend, who encouraged me in my (our) pursuit of the truth.

I also want to dedicate this book to two people by the names of Brian and Karen King. I truly believe that God brought these two people into my life at the proper crossroads of my faith journey as a follower of Jesus Christ. Karen especially gave me the encouragement and the support I needed as God began to open my eyes to the truth in regards to the Apostate Church age that exists in the world today.

I also want to dedicate this book to my fellow sisters in Christ by the names of Ella May (grandma) Potter and her daughter Robin Potter Butler. These two ladies have played a big part in my faith journey and have demonstrated a faith of not just talking the talk of faith in Jesus Christ but a life of walking the walk in obedience to the truth of God's word(s). They have faithfully demonstrated to me the cost that may/might be involved when you take up your cross and follow Jesus Christ each and every day.

I also want to dedicate this book to my Lord and Savior, Jesus Christ, who one day extended his hand to a lost sinner by the name of Joe Traver. With the help of the Holy Spirit's divine intervention, God opened my eyes to the realm of his kingdom, which begins with grace and love by and through complete faith in his Son, Jesus Christ.

INTRODUCTION

M Y INTENTIONS IN writing this book is solely to share with others what I have learned from the Holy Spirit as I have traveled down the path of my faith journey as a follower of Jesus Christ.

There's a saying that goes like this: "Opinions are like behinds—everyone has one." Well, this saying may sound a little strange to some, but in reality, in the world we live in, it is a wise saying. Why is it a wise saying, you ask, because everyone does indeed have an opinion. Just as everyone has a behind. In fact, it is at the heart of this saying that really drives the world we as human beings live in. It drives the world we live in because it is the opinions of each individual that ultimately leads us to what we believe, what we think, and how we as humans take what we believe and what we think and apply them to our everyday individual lives. Though we may not know it or realize it, it is within the framework of people's opinions that really does mold and shape our lives. It begins when we are born, and it carries on throughout our lives. I have learned this truth, and I hope before you're done reading this book, you may have a better understanding of what I'm saying.

Now before you start reading this book, I think it's important for you to know up front a few things about me. I am a simple man, a layperson if you will. I have no letters after my name. I didn't graduate from college. I didn't attend seminary or Bible school. I'm not some great theologian. I simply graduated from high school and spent 30 years as a blue-collar worker working as a forklift operator loading and unloading trucks and boxcars in a warehouse. I was also a member of the Teamsters union for thirty years, where I served as both a union steward and as an officer on the executive board in one of the locals of that union. I guess if there is one thing that could best describe for you what I'm really all about, especially as a professing Christian, I guess it would be 1 John 2:26 and 27.

These things I have written to you concerning those who try to deceive you. But the anointing which you have received from Him abides in you, and you do not need that anyone teach you; but as the same anointing teaches you concerning all things, and is true, and is not a lie, and just as it has taught you, you will abide in Him.

Now I know that you're probably asking yourself what it means. What could that possibly have to do with describing to me what you're really all about and why should I read this book? What gives you the right to think that you're so smart and that you have the answers I need for my life and possibly my faith journey as a Christian? Who do you think you are? The truth is I don't think I'm anybody special at all. In fact, it is this scripture reading that really tells a great deal to all those who truly believe in the Lord Jesus Christ. We read that God anoints a true believer. God does the anointing and not man. Far too often in the world of Christendom today, it is men who do the anointing and not God. There are many problems within the world of Christendom today, and I happen to believe that this is one of the key issues of our time. Not only is it a key issue of our time, I happen to believe that it's one of the enemy's best weapons. Enemy you say! That's right, enemy. At the core of every believer (and unbeliever, though they don't realize it) there lies the enemy of our souls, Satan himself, the evil one. The Bible describes him as an adversary who walks about like a roaring lion, seeking whom he may devour (1 Peter 5:8). The devil, meaning a slanderer who tries to malign people's hearts into total deception, so they cannot understand and grasp the things of God nor the truths found in His holy word. His main goal is to keep people from knowing the word of God, and if the modern-day church is any indication our adversary is doing a very good job of it.

1 John 2:26. These things I have written to you concerning those who try to deceive you.

Deception: the dictionary defines this word as (1) the act of deceiving or state of being deceived; (2) fraud or trick. (Common Dictionary)

In the world today, the word "deception" plays a major role in search for the truth. In the life of a true Christian, it lies at the very core of our walk with Jesus Christ. In fact, it is my true belief that deception has so much penetrated the walls of the modern-day churches of today that if the deception continues unchecked we will continue to see and feel the effects of that deception in both the church as well as the world outside the church. You see deception and anointing go hand in hand. If you don't have the true anointing of God, you won't be able to discern the truth from the lies. Many in the church today cannot discern who has the anointing and who does not. The reason this is taking place has a lot to do with what I discussed earlier about the devil.

Thirty years ago this year, I got the shock of my life. I say I got the shock of my life because that was the year that changed my life forever. I say it was a shock not to be misleading. I use the word "shock" because that's exactly what it was. It was a shock that woke me up to the reality of life. Some of those results I will be sharing within the contents of this book. If you read this book, you might be offended or get very confused by the words I'm going to share within these pages, especially if you don't have a good grasp of God's word. If you do find yourself getting offended or confused by the words I'm sharing, it is not my intention to do so. However, if you do find yourself getting offended, I might offer you this to ponder: maybe it's because of the opinions that have found their way into your life that are having a direct impact on the way your life is going. Maybe those opinions have formulated the way you're living and are therefore possibly leading you astray, especially if you claim to be a Christian and a follower of Jesus Christ. You see, the shock that changed my life was the shock of having Jesus Christ come into my life. Before 1982, my life had been formulated by opinions that weren't necessarily the ones that counted. In fact, what I have discovered since I became a Christian is that within the realm of opinions lies the truth. What I have discovered is that only within the pages of the Holy Bible can the truth be found and/or even known. I say that because of what Jesus said to one of his disciples in the New Testament, in John 14:5. The disciple known as Doubting Thomas asked Jesus how he and they could know which way was the right way. In other words, which was the right path for them to go in their lives? What opinions held the truth? Likewise in John 18:38, Pontius Pilate, who had the power to crucify Jesus, asked pretty much the same question of Jesus when he asked Jesus, "What is truth?" Pilate's question to Jesus was really the question about whose opinion mattered. What he was saying to Jesus was pretty much the same thing we hear in today's world. You have your opinion, and I have mine. The opinion Pilate had formulated in his mind was in reference to Jesus' answer to the question Pilate had placed before him. That opinion came about when he asked Jesus, "Are you a king?" The question Pilate placed before Jesus had come from the people (Jews) who were trying to use Pilate as a pawn in their plan to have Jesus killed, in the same manner the devil uses people today as pawns in his masterful art of deception. They had formulated in their opinion that Jesus was an evildoer and needed to be put to death. The problem they faced was that when Rome took over Judea and began direct rule the right to execute people was taken away from the Jews and given to the Roman governor (i.e., Pontius Pilate).

It is evident in their answer to Pilate when they said to him in verse 31, "It is not lawful for us to put anyone to death." You see, Pilate was being manipulated by opinion, and he didn't even know it. The chief priests had delivered Jesus to Pilate as a totally innocent person. Jesus had done nothing other than speak the truth to his own people; and now he stood before Pilate simply because he had proclaimed the truth of God with them, and they didn't like what the Son of God was telling them.

Well, maybe by now you're asking the same question that Pilate posed to Jesus. "What is truth? Whose truth, Joe? Your truth, my truth, the world's truth, or the church's truth? I want to know the truth! Where can I find the truth?" For you see, everyone is searching for the truth, and if they're not, then they should be. The problem lies not within the question of who knows the truth because someone has to know the truth. Who can that someone be? Within the pages of this book, it is my solemn hope and prayer that you will find the answer to that question. Within the pages of this book are my opinions, the opinions that have formulated my life and my faith journey with Jesus Christ for thirty years. They are the words my friend Forrest has asked me to share with others because he believes my opinion matters. He believes that because of my life experiences, I can make a difference in someone's walk with Jesus Christ in their search for the truth. Why does he believe it? He believes it because the words I'm sharing in this book are the ones I've shared with him. But then again, I'm just a forklift operator. After all, what do I know?

CHAPTER 1

The Journey Begins

For the Son of Man has come to save that which was lost.
—Matthew 18:11

EARLIER, I SPOKE about being shocked into the reality of life. The year was 1982. It was a year that I will never forget. I say it was a year I will never forget because that was the year that I was first introduced to the one true savior of this world, the Lord Jesus Christ himself, God's only begotten Son, the one who came to this planet called Earth to save that which was lost. Lost, you ask? What do you mean by lost? I'm not lost. I know exactly where I am, and I don't need anyone to save me. Save me from what? Question: Have you ever been lost? I mean have you ever been lost to the point where you didn't know where you are? Well, I have and I know from experience that it can be a very frightening experience; and if nothing else, it sure gives you something to think about. Please let me explain.

For years, one of my favorite pastime hobbies was in the sport of hunting. In fact, since I was a little boy, I had always enjoyed hunting. I was first introduced to hunting by my older brother at the age of fourteen. All throughout my childhood, I had always had a gun. My first gun was a BB gun, my second one was a Co2 pellet rifle, and my third one was a twelve-gauge shotgun that my father bought for me at the age of fourteen. At that time, in the state I live in, you could hunt for protected wildlife at the age of fourteen, but you couldn't hunt by yourself because you were considered as a junior hunter and therefore must be accompanied by a senior hunter who was over the age of sixteen. Maybe by now the law has changed, but that was how it was back then. That is where my older brother comes in because he was nine years older than me, and he would take me out hunting with him because he was a senior hunter. Since the time I began hunting, there weren't too many animals I hadn't hunted and/or killed. I hunted for such animals as rabbits, squirrels, pheasants, partridge, woodcock, raccoons, ducks, geese, and deer. Now there are many, many stories I could share with you about what I learned from my hunting experiences, but the ones I'm going to share are the ones that had such a profound impact on my life that I truly believe may help you as you travel down the path of your journey in search for the truth for your life.

One day, a bunch of us had made a decision to go deer hunting. Now I don't know how much you know about deer hunting, but this is usually the way it works. Deer are nocturnal animals. It means they are mainly active at night. They usually feed at night and rest during the day. The best time to hunt deer is in the early morning and late in the afternoon because that's when the deer are on the move. In other words, the deer are more likely to come to you instead of you having to go find them, and it's also the only time you can legally hunt them. Besides, have you ever tried to sneak up on a deer? Good luck because that's what you'll need. Well, anyway it usually gets light about 7:00 a.m. and gets dark at about 5:00 p.m. during hunting season. So what you usually do is everyone who goes hunting finds a place in the woods to sit, stand, or use a tree stand, and they wait for a deer to walk by and then they attempt to shoot the deer. This part of the hunt usually takes place in the morning and in the late afternoon just before dusk. If no one has any luck getting or seeing any deer in the morning watch, the hunting party usually starts what is called a drive. Usually this takes place around 10:00 a.m. and lasts throughout the day until it gets to be time to go to the afternoon watch at the end of the day when the deer start being active again. Depending on the area you are trying to cover, along with the number of people you have in the hunting party, the drive is set up to allow everyone to participate. Some of the hunters are used as watchers, and some are used as drivers. The watchers sit and watch for the deer, and the drivers push the deer toward the watchers in an attempt to shoot them. Now I had been hunting for many years and had gone through these hunting ritual multitudes of times. Throughout those years, I had been both a watcher and a driver many times. I have seen deer shot as well as shot deer myself as a result of these drives. However, the particular day I'm going to describe in this setting is a day that I will never forget. I say I will never forget because the experience I encountered that day was one that taught me an important lesson about this life as I walked the path of my faith journey in pursuit of the truth. Although I didn't know it at the time, the experience I was about to encounter was one that stayed in my mind for the longest time. It was an experience that I truly believe was a springboard that began to open my eyes to the fact that God did exist, and at that time he had no part in my spiritual life whatsoever.

We started our deer drive around 10:00 a.m., I was asked if I would be a driver instead of a watcher. I said that was fine although I was a little nervous about the position I was placed at in the drive. The position I was placed in just happened to be at the very end of the woods we were driving, and that particular area of the woods was not known to me. I had never hunted in that area before, and I really had no idea of the layout of the land we were driving. I thought to myself, the area we're driving is not really that big (at least I thought), so it's not a big deal and I should be fine. Wrong! As I was about to find out, it was a big deal because what I was about to endure would ultimately affect the rest of my life's journey, especially with regard to having a relationship with God and his Son, Jesus Christ.

As the drive began, I moved through the woods. Now it's important to know that as you're walking through the woods, it's very important to stay even in a direct line with the other people who are also drivers. It's important that you stay even with the person next to you; and in turn, they should stay in line with the person next to him so everyone remains in a straight line. If a deer does happen to move either in front or at the back of the drivers, no one will get shot if they decide it is safe enough to shoot at the deer. As we moved through the woods, I kept looking to my right to make sure I was staying even with the guy next to me as we walked toward the watchers. Now the area we were driving wasn't really that big, so the drive we were on shouldn't have taken more than thirty minutes or so. At first, I didn't have any problem keeping the guy next to me in my sight as we walked. But eventually I lost sight of him, and that's when my trouble began. Now I knew the road we were parked on was off to my right, so I figured if I kept walking to my right, I would eventually walk out on to the road. From there, I would simply follow the road back to where the cars were parked, and everything would be fine. That's what I thought! But that's not how it worked out. As I continued to walk, I thought I was moving to my right toward the road. However, as time went on (I figured at least an hour) it became quite evident to me that I was in serious trouble, and that I was lost. Now that day was very overcast and gloomy, which is usually the way it is at that time of the year in the state in which I live. At first, I was very calm. I knew that all I had to do was to find the road we were parked on, and everything would be all right. But the problem was I couldn't find the road. I also knew that the road was to the west of where we had begun the drive, so all I had to do was walk toward the west, and I would find the road. The other problem was that because it was so overcast, I couldn't determine which way was west. I knew the sun came up in the east and went down in the west. But unless the sun came out, there was no way for me to determine which way was west. As time went on, I became more and more fearful that I wasn't going to find my way out. Many things went through my mind as I tried to overcome the anxiety that existed within me as I continued to search for my way out of the woods and to safety.

I didn't have a watch on me so I couldn't tell what time it was. I knew I went into the woods on our deer drive around 10:00 a.m., but I had no way of telling what the time was. As time went on, I went from a calm attitude to a more serious attitude, and then into a panic mode attitude where I became very fearful for my life. I seriously believed I was not going to find my way out of the woods that day. And then something came into my mind that I didn't usually think about. I guess maybe it was because I didn't have nowhere else to turn, and at that time, I felt as though it was my last option. What was that last option? I prayed. That's right, I prayed. At the time, I thought it was a little silly to do. After all, I had nothing to lose. There was no one around (I thought). So what harm could it possibly do? Yeah. It may sound stupid to some, but when you're desperate (as I was), you're willing to try almost anything. I guess it's sort of like the old saying that goes, "There are no atheists in foxholes." Well, for me this was my foxhole, and this called for desperate measures. So I prayed something like this, "God, I don't know for sure why I'm praying this, but if you do exist, I'm asking you if you will help me out of this mess. Even though I probably don't deserve it, would you please help me find my way out of these woods? If you do, then I will promise to do what you want me to do for the rest of my life." Whatever that meant! How stupid of me to try and barter with God! To think that God owed me anything was really stupid. But do you know what? It worked! No sooner had I prayed that prayer when all of a sudden the sun came out. The overcast sky had cleared, and the sun was now showing me which way was west; and therefore, it was like God was guiding me to the road I was searching for. After I got my senses back from seeing the sun come out, right at that particular time I started moving (quite fast, I might add) in the direction of the sun. After I had traveled through the woods for a while, I came upon an old overgrown logging trail, which I knew from experience had to lead to a road. As I traveled down the path of the old logging trail, the overgrown weeds and vegetation that had grown on the path was getting less and less; and eventually, the old logging trail turned into a newer logging trail, which eventually led me out to the road I was searching for. The first thing I did was I got down on my knees and said, "Thank you God for helping me find my way out of the woods." Now whether there was a God that heard my prayer or not, I didn't really know. All I knew was that I had found the road, and there was no way in this world that I was going to leave that road again.

Now the next question for me was, in which direction do I start walking on the road? Do I walk to my right, or do I walk to my left? Well, after some careful thought, I decided to go to the right because I believed that all the time I was lost the road was to my right. So off I went walking down the road. After walking for a while, I came to an intersection where the road divided. One way led to the right, and one way led to the left. Which way do I go? Do I take the road to the right, or do I take the one to the left? What did I do? Answer: I did neither. I decided to walk back the way I came from because I was determined that in the area we were hunting, I never saw a road that went to the right. So back I went. As I began walking back toward where I had come from out of the woods, I heard a vehicle coming down the road behind me. It was the first contact I had encountered with another human being since I got lost. I had to get out of the middle of the road so I moved to the shoulder and turned to see who was coming. To my surprise and complete joy, it was two of the people who were part of my hunting party who were looking for me. I had been rescued, and I couldn't have been happier. The emotion I felt at that time is really too hard to put into words. I was indeed a happy camper, and my heart was literally pounding with joy within me.

After I got in the car, I learned that the time was about three thirty in the afternoon. I had come out of the woods approximately a mile and a half down the road from where I went in. I was lost for about five hours, and the reason I came upon the intersection I did when I came out of the woods was because I had walked so far through the woods that I had actually gone past the point where the two roads intersected. Although we had hunted in that area before, we had never hunted that far down the road, and that is why I didn't recognize that particular intersection when I walked up upon it. We went back to the place where we were hunting, and boy, was I wearing a big smile.

I had learned a great deal from my experience in the woods. It was a life-changing experience. How so, you ask? Well, for the answer to that question, you must move onto the next chapter. But I will tell you this much before you move on: you see, I was lost and the five hours I spent trying to find my way out of those woods had taught me a wonderful lesson about my life's journey, and I believe it is one that can help you as well.

What was the teaching? What can you learn from my experience? At the beginning of this chapter, I asked you a question. The question was, "Have you ever been lost?" Well, if you've never been lost, then you've never been saved. You may be reading this book, and you don't think there's anything wrong. But let me tell you. If you don't know who the Son of Man is, then you are indeed lost, and you don't even realize that you are. How do you know I'm lost, you ask? I know because I was once in your place. At one time, I didn't know who the Son of Man was nor could I have cared less. You see, I was as lost as you. That is if you who are reading these words don't know the Son of Man. Notice I didn't say if you don't know who the Son of Man is. Because there are many who know who the Son of Man is but they don't really know the Son of Man. That day in the woods I had no idea who the Son of Man was. I didn't realize it at that time, but I was not only lost in the woods. More importantly, I was in serious jeopardy of losing my very soul. In fact I was far more lost in my spiritual journey here on earth than I ever was in the woods those many years ago, and I didn't even realize that it was happening. How so, you ask? You see, the Bible verse I used at the beginning of this chapter is one that every person needs to come to grips with in this life. They need to come to grips with the reality that without knowing the Son of Man, they are indeed lost. Lost to what, you ask? Lost to the only thing that really matters in the journey of this life, and that is your eternal destiny.

Question: Where will you be one hundred years from today? You see, only the Son of Man has the answer to that question. Only the Son of Man can save you from what the Holy Bible refers to as death and Hades (Revelation 20:14). Only the Son of Man can save you from being cast into the Lake of Fire. Who is this Son of Man, you ask? Well, if you do your homework, you will find the phrase Son of Man is used approximately 192 times in the Bible and the Son of Man refers to none other than God's only begotten Son, Jesus Christ. But then again, I'm just a forklift operator. After all, what do I know?

CHAPTER 2

The Journey Continues

But even if our gospel is veiled, it is veiled to those who are
perishing, whose minds the god of this age has blinded, who do not
believe, lest the light of the gospel of the glory of Christ, who is the
image of God, should shine on them.
—2 Corinthians 4:3 and 4

IN THE PREVIOUS chapter, I shared with you a story about the
time I was lost in the woods while deer hunting. In this chapter,
I'd like to share another hunting story with you. Now the two hunting
experiences, though separate, were eventually tied together in my mind;
and these two experiences, though separate, became a major turning point
to the beginning of my faith journey as a follower of Jesus Christ.

If you remember when I was lost in the woods and became desperate
for help I actually made a covenant with God. How so, you ask? Well, if
you remember, the words I said to God, in prayer, went something like
this. "If you help me out of this mess, I promise to do what you want
me to do for the rest of my life." And if you also remember, it was at that
particular moment that the sun came out and ultimately led me out of the
woods to safety.

This hunting story goes something like this. Once again a bunch of
us guys decided to go deer hunting. Except this time we weren't hunting
with guns. We were hunting with bows and arrows. It is known as bow
hunting, and this type of hunting is usually done at the beginning of the
deer-hunting season. Usually the bow-hunting season opens about three or
four weeks before the gun-hunting season begins. In this particular story,
we had decided to go bow hunting on some state-owned property in the
southern part of the state in which I live. The area in which we were going
to hunt was about a two-hour journey by car.

Everyone in the hunting party decided to meet at a central location,
and then we would all travel together with one of the guys who had a
van, not a van like a regular family van, but a van that was only equipped

with two seats, a driver's seat, and a passenger seat. In other words, there were no other seats in the vehicle; and if you wanted to sit, you either sat on the floor of the van or you sat in a mobile seat, such as a lawn chair or something of that sort. The vehicle was more like a cargo van and was really meant more for transporting cargo rather than people. Because there were four of us in the hunting party, two sat in the regular front seats, and two of us sat in the back of the van in lawn chairs, which if you really think about it isn't so smart. But anyway, so off we went on our hunting journey leaving for our destination at around 5:00 a.m. in the morning. As we began traveling to our destination, it occurred to me that sitting in a lawn chair was not a very wise thing to do, but I wanted to go deer hunting, and after all, what could possibly happen? Well, little did I know that I was about to find out the answer to that question. In fact, it was within that particular question that I would ultimately learn an important lesson about the God of this universe. I would learn that when you make a promise to God, you are far better off to keep it than you are to not keep it. At least that's what I learned. How so, you ask? Please let me explain.

So off we went traveling in a cargo van with two guys in the front seats and two of us sitting in the back of the van in lawn chairs. The area we were traveling to hunt in was approximately sixty or seventy miles away. We anticipated that our driving time would be somewhere around an hour and a half to two hours. When we first started off on our travel, we were all having a conversation. We had only traveled for about a half hour and maybe twenty miles when for some unknown reason, something popped into my head and told me that we (the two of us sitting in lawn chairs) should lie down. Because we had gotten up so early, I justified our lying down to the guys in the front seats by telling them (and the guy sitting next to me) that we had a long way yet to travel so we might as well try to get some rest. The guy next to me concurred (thank God). So lie down we did. To this day, I don't fully understand why or how that thought came into my mind at that particular moment, but I truly believe that God had planted the thought, and I truly believe it actually saved my life. How so, you ask? Well, let me continue the story of our journey.

No sooner had we laid down (maybe five minutes) when we had to stop at an intersection for a red light when all of sudden we were hit from behind by another vehicle. Now from here, it's a pretty long story but the bottom line of this story is the man who hit us had been drinking. At least that's what the other guys in my hunting party told me. They knew he had been drinking because they could smell alcohol on his breath after he got out of his car. Notice I said it's what the other guys in my hunting party told me. You see, I never saw the guy who rear-ended us. In fact, I didn't see much of anything because I was injured and was bleeding profusely from the top of my head and needed to get to a hospital ASAP. I was told the man who hit us had seen I was bleeding and went to call for an ambulance (this incident took place before cell phones). After some time went by, one of the guys in our hunting party realized that the man who hit us just took off and had no intention of calling for an ambulance. By then, the police had come to the scene of the accident, and an ambulance was called and eventually came and took me to the hospital.

When I got to the hospital, they discovered that the top of my head had a big gash in it, and it required fifteen stitches to close it up. They stitched me up and eventually let me out of the hospital that same day. Now things had happened pretty fast, and we didn't really have much time to think about what happened until later that day. But this is what we think happened.

After we had laid down in the van, the guy hit us from the back. In the back of the van were the hunting bows we were going to use to hunt with. When the man rear-ended us, it allowed our bodies to move toward the back of the van. When my body moved to the back of the van, the sights on one of the bows went into my head and caused the injury (gash) to my head. What we also discovered was that the car that hit us was severely damaged. The car was a very big car, and the front end of that car was pushed in halfway to the windshield from the impact of hitting us. On the other hand, the van we were driving in had very little damage. Other than the injury to my head, we really didn't suffer too much at all, and even my injury wasn't really that severe.

By now you're probably asking yourself, "Okay, Joe, this is a very nice story, but what has this to do with your faith journey as a Christian and the scripture that you used at the beginning of this chapter?" You see, this story has everything to do with my faith journey. It has everything to do with it because within the framework of these hunting stories lies the truth of what I had to come to grips with in my personal life, not only within the secular world in which I lived but more importantly within the spiritual world that at that point I had no part in. Yes, I was living. I was breathing. I was in the carnal state of both body and mind, but with regard to my spiritual condition, which is the most important part of all; I was dead. How so, you ask? You see that when you're in the carnal mind-set. Meaning you are more set on the things of this present life than you are on the things of God then you are in a/the carnal mind-set. One of the best ways to describe this for you is found in the New Testament book of Romans chapter 8. Here, the Apostle Paul is speaking about walking in the Spirit versus walking in the flesh. A good example to use when thinking about this is by paralleling it with 1 John 2:16. How so, you ask, because they both speak about the two conditions we as human beings are in, if we're still in a carnal state. In other words, if we are only in a fleshly, worldly condition than we are, as the Apostle Paul says in verse 5 of Romans 8, "For those who live according to the flesh set their minds on the things of the flesh, but those who live according to the Spirit, the things of the Spirit." Likewise, Paul says in verse 8, "So then, those who are in the flesh cannot please God." The parallel verse I told you to use when considering this is from the words of the Apostle John in verse 16 of 1 John 2, which describes the things of the world as the lust of the flesh, the lust of the eyes, and the pride of life. We are further told in the end of that verse that these things, the lust of the flesh, the lust of the eyes, and the pride of life, are not, I repeat, are not of the Father (God) but are of the world. Question: If they're not of the Father (God), then who are they of? Who do they belong to? Answer: They are of the devil. Who is the devil, you ask? Well, that would take a lot more time to explain than we have in this chapter, but I will tell you this much: the Scripture refers to him as "the anointed cherub" (Ezekiel 28:14), or angel if you will; he is "the ruler of the demons" (Luke 11:15); he is the prince of the power of the air (Ephesians 2:2); and he is "the god of this world (age) (2 Corinthians 4:4), which just so happens to be the scripture I used at the beginning of this chapter.

You see, the scriptures I have been using up to now are all intertwined. How so, you ask? Well, the scripture I opened this chapter with speaks about the gospel message and how the message of God is veiled to those who are perishing. The word "veiled" in the dictionary means something that covers or conceals. In other words, it is impossible for anyone to understand the things of God if they are still in a carnal mind-set. His words and the way God operates are unknown and concealed to those whose minds have been blinded by the god of this world, who is the devil himself. You see, we were born with a sinful nature. In other words, from the time we were conceived in our mother's womb, we were adversaries (enemies) of God; and as I said, there is much to this whole topic. And before this book is finished, I hope much of this will become easier and much clearer for you to understand in your personal search for the truth.

Once again, you may be asking the question, "Okay, Joe. But what does this have to do with your faith journey?" You see, the story I shared about my hunting experiences had a lot to do with the solid foundation on which my faith in Jesus Christ was laid. That time I was lost in the woods was really the first time I had any contact with God. After all, everything was going okay in my life. I had no reason to have any contact with God. I thought I was in control of my life and therefore, my destiny was in my hands. I didn't need God. What I discovered from these experiences was that I had become my own god, and I was indeed blinded by the god of this world: the devil himself!

In my mind, the experience I had from being rear-ended by the man who had been drinking really put things in a different perspective. After all, I could have been killed. I hate to think about what might have happened if we hadn't lain down on the floor of the van at that specific time. I truly believe if we hadn't lay down, we would have probably been catapulted out the back door of the van and may have possibly broken our necks. For me, to only have the injury I had was truly a blessing of its own, and it really started me to think about what happens to me after I die.

I must have asked myself thousands of times, "Did God allow this accident to happen? Did God use this accident as a wake-up call? Was God mad at me because I had made a promise to him and didn't follow through? Is God taking me up on the promise I made to him back in the woods when I told him I would serve him for the rest of my life if he would just help me in my time of trouble?" Well, I don't know about you; but as for me, the answer was clear. God was sending me a message. What was the message? It's time to open your eyes to the truth. What truth, you ask? To the truth that he does exist, and that he was indeed seeking someone who was lost. And that someone was me! But I was still in darkness. How could I come to the light of the gospel message as the Apostle Paul wrote in the opening scripture of this chapter? Well, for the answer to that question, you'll have to move onto the next chapter as we continue on our search for the truth. However I will tell you this much before you do: the Bible uses the phrase "born again" to be able to see and understand the things of God (John 3:3). In Ephesians 6, the Apostle Paul commands us (true followers of Jesus Christ) to put on the whole armor of God, so that we (true followers of Jesus) may be able to stand against the wiles (tricks, schemes, and deception) of the devil.

I will also share with you that at this particular time of my faith journey, I had no idea what the heck it meant. I didn't know what I was looking for.

In other words, I felt something was happening to me, but I didn't quite know what it was or how to find it. I had no idea about what it meant to be born again. I knew nothing about the wiles of the devil. How about you? Do you know what I'm talking about? Do you know what it means to be born again? Do you know about the wiles of the devil? If you do, then maybe this book is not for you. But if you don't, then you might want to read on. But then again, I'm just a forklift operator. After all, what do I know?

CHAPTER 3

Finding the Right Path to Life

Because narrow is the gate and difficult is the way which leads
to life, and there are few who find it.
—Matthew 7:14

S O FAR IN my faith journey, you've heard about me being lost
in the woods and coming very close to being killed by a drunk
driver while pursuing the sport of deer hunting. We also learned that going
through these tribulations, or problems if you will, had begun to make
me look at things from a different perspective. We also learned that I felt
something was happening to me, but I didn't know quite what it was or
how to find it. I must also remind you that these stories I'm sharing with
you aren't necessarily in chronological order. These stories are ones that I
firmly believe God used simply as a means to establish in my mind the
truth of his existence as he attempted to soften my heart. As God (Jesus)
seeks us (Luke 19:10), one of the biggest obstacles he has to overcome is our
hardened hearts especially as we grow older and become more comfortable
in the way we live in this world. Because we are of a/the worldly mind-set,
our hearts are naturally hostile toward him, and it's only by softening our
hearts can his truths begin to be established in our lives (hearts). In other
words, we are still attached to the secular world we live in and are in reality
enemies of God (James 4:4). It is only through and by a truly softened
and humble heart can he begin to open up the pathway in our search for
the truths that is established in his word (Bible). It's like what the psalmist
says in Psalm 95, "For the Lord is the great God, And the great King
above all gods" (Notice the god here has a small g). Why does the psalmist
refer to one God with a big G and the other gods with a small g? Because
the psalmist knew there is but one true God, and he is to not only be
greatly praised (Psalm 96:4a), but he is also to be feared above all gods
(Psalm 96:4b). Now I know you're probably asking the question, "What
do you mean he is to be feared above all gods? Why would I want to fear
God (Jesus Christ)?" For you see, the basic theme of the Psalms is living

real life in a real world, where two dimensions operate simultaneously, the world that exists within the framework of the one true God (big G), and the world that exists within the framework of other gods (small g). It is at this point that the search for the truth must begin. I say it must begin because like the psalmist rightly wrote. The one true God must be feared because the search for the truth can only be found through the fear of God. Proverbs 1:7 says, "The fear of the Lord is the beginning of knowledge, But fools despise wisdom and instruction." Likewise the psalmist also says in Psalm 53:1, "The fool has said in his heart, 'There is no God,' The Apostle Paul also tells those in the church in Corinth to cleanse themselves from all filthiness of the flesh and spirit, perfecting holiness in the fear of God (2 Corinthians 7:1). Here, the Apostle Paul is admonishing Christians to not succumb to human (worldly) appetites, represented by both "flesh and spirit." Those who claim to be followers of Christ who expose their minds to false teaching cannot, I repeat, cannot avoid contamination by the devilish ideologies and blasphemies that assault the purity of divine truth and blaspheme God's name, which in the end really has a direct impact on not only defiling God's truths, but it also has a direct impact on our personal witnesses and integrity as Christians; not only as individuals but also in the true remnant collective universal body of God's kingdom (Christendom; Romans 11:5).

You see, the one thing I had to come to grips with in my journey was that I was a fool. I was a fool because I had spent the first thirty-two years of my life chasing the gods (little g) that the devil had placed before me. I had been deceived by the god of this world (2 Corinthians 4:4—the devil) and because of that deception, I was lost and headed for the very depths of hell itself. What I discovered was that once my eyes began to be opened to the truth, many of the things I had gone through became clearer. In other words, when I finally came to the point of believing that the Bible was indeed the inerrant word of God and made a decision to covenant with God by accepting his Son (Jesus Christ) as my personal Lord and Savior, the darkness I had been living in began to become clearer, and the veil of darkness that the devil had me under began to fade away. As the scripture I used in the opening chapter of this book had said, "the Son of Man has come to seek and to save that which was lost." You see, Jesus was seeking me and I had to find the proper path to find him. But to begin to find him, I first had to learn to fear him! For if I didn't fear him, I could and would never receive the knowledge I would need in my pursuit of finding true life which is Jesus Christ. Once again as Proverbs 1:7 says, "The fear of the Lord [God] is the beginning of knowledge, which brings us to the next stop in our search for the truth."

One of the most well-known sermons of all time was delivered by Jesus Christ in a sermon best known as the Sermon on the Mount found in the New Testament book of Matthew chapters 5 through 7. This sermon is a masterful exposition of the law and a potent assault on the religious elite of Jesus' day closing with a call to true faith and salvation. Christ expounded the full meaning of God's law, showing that its demands were humanly impossible. It closes off every possible avenue of human merit and leaves sinners dependent on nothing but divine grace for salvation. As we travel down the path in our search for the truth, I will be diving into some of this wonderful sermon from time to time; but for now, I'd like to take us toward the end of this famous sermon that was delivered by Jesus.

In Matthew 7:13 and 14, Jesus said, "Enter by the narrow gate; for wide is the gate and broad is the way that leads to destruction, and there are many who go in by it. Because narrow is the gate and difficult is the way which leads to life, and there are few who find it." Did you hear that? Did you hear what Jesus said? The way which leads to life is narrow and difficult, and there are few who find it. Question: What did Jesus mean when he said, "The way which leads to life is difficult and there are few who find it?" For me, when I first read this scripture in my search for the truth, the first thing I had to discover was what does the word "find" really mean, at least in the particular context that Jesus is speaking about here. So to the dictionary I went, and lo and behold, I discovered that one of the definitions used to describe the word "find" was this: to learn or obtain by search or effort; to recover (something lost). To recover something lost; to learn or obtain by search or effort, which began to tell me that with regard to my relationship with God, it was a two-way street. As God (Jesus) was seeking me, I also had to seek and find him. The second thing I had to establish was that the way which leads to life is difficult, and there are not very many who find their way to it. Who or what is representative of life? Jesus said in the New Testament book of John 14:6 that says, "He was the way, the truth, and the life." Jesus also said that no one (that's nobody) comes to the Father (God) except through him, which also told me that if Jesus did indeed represent true life then following him was, according to Jesus' own words, not going to be easy. It would be difficult! Not easy! Furthermore, not only did it tell me following Jesus would be hard and difficult, but also according to Jesus, there aren't very many who ever find their way to him, which also told me that if there are very few who ever truly find their way to him, then there must be many who never really know what true life really is. They never really know what true life is because they never really truly know the Lord Jesus Christ personally. How do I know that, you ask? I know it because of what Jesus said in the prior verse (Matthew 7:13), "Enter by the narrow gate; [meaning through/by Jesus Christ] for wide is the gate and broad is the way that leads to destruction, and there are many who go in by it." In other words, the road or journey that most people of/in this world today are traveling will ultimately lead them down the path of destruction. They are headed for the very depths of hell itself and unless the veil is removed from their eyes, they will spend their eternity in total separation from God. They will never get to see what God has prepared for those who have a personal relationship with his Son Jesus Christ. Now that is a pretty bold statement. In fact, that statement may be the one that makes you decide to stop reading this book. You may think that me saying that is rather crude or unloving or judgmental. Well, if you think that, then you're dead wrong. You're dead wrong because it is not my job to judge anyone, but it is my job—in fact, my duty—as a follower of Jesus Christ to share with others the truths God has allowed me to uncover in hopes it will bring them to accept his Son Jesus Christ and enhance their journey as they too search for the truth in their life. Furthermore, if you have a problem with that statement, then you may have a problem with many more as well.

You see, as I've traveled down the path of my journey as a Christian, I truly believe that the modern-day churches of today are literally jam-packed with people who truly believe their traveling on the narrow path that leads to heaven when in fact many are traveling on the wide path that leads to destruction (hell), and they don't even know that they are. How do you know that, you ask? Well, for the answer to that question, you'll have to travel to the next chapter of this book as we continue our search for the truth. However, I will tell you this much before you move on: earlier in this chapter, I asked you a question and that question was this: Why would I want to fear God? You see, we should fear him because in the final analysis of the journey in this life, he will be the one who makes the final decision of where we will end up—in heaven or in hell. I say he is the one who will make the ultimate decision of where you end up, but in reality, it is really you who makes the final decision. In other words, the decision you make will really make his job very easy. You really write your epitaph. You see, true salvation (deliverance from the power and the penalty of sin) cannot be obtained if you never have a fear of God. In fact, the words "salvation," "fear," and "trembling" are synonymous in God's word (Bible). I say that because of what is revealed in the truth of God's words in such scripture verses, like "work out your own salvation with fear and trembling" (Philippians 2:12); and "Even when I remember I am terrified, and trembling takes hold of my flesh" (Job 21:6); and "Serve the Lord with fear, and rejoice with trembling" (Psalm 2:11); and in Mark 5, "And He [Jesus] looked around to see her who had done this thing [she had touched him]. But the woman, fearing and trembling, knowing what had happened to her, came and fell down before Him and told Him the whole truth. And He said to her, 'Daughter, your faith has made you well. Go in peace, and be healed of your affliction.'" So you see, salvation, fear, and trembling do play a big part in our search for the truth. Oh, by the way, the story of the woman was one in which she had a physical ailment and had obviously tried to find a cure from what she had by visiting many physicians. But unfortunately, for her the illness, she had become worse instead of better (v. 27), that is until she met the physician who was and still is the ultimate physician of all time. Jesus is the ultimate physician who doesn't just cure the physical ailments in our lives but also (and most importantly) the spiritual. Because this woman had not lied but came and fell down at Jesus' feet and told him the whole truth, her faith had cured her of her illness. But even more than that, because of her faith, she could now live in peace. The woman had a physical ailment, and so does anyone who hasn't been cured by the great physician, Jesus Christ. The physical ailment I'm speaking of is the one that is found within the wide gate and the wide way that leads to destruction, the one that multitudes of people in this world are on. I know it to be true. I know it because I was once there. I was on the wide path that leads to destruction (hell), and I learned for myself the answer to one of the questions that I have placed before you in this book.

Why do I fear God? I fear him because he just so happens to hold the key to the gate of where I will spend my eternal future. Will I go through the narrow gate that leads to life (heaven)? Or will I go through the wide gate that leads to destruction (hell)? Why should I fear him? Why should you fear him? Why should anyone that's living in the world today fear him? For the answer to that question, I think it's most appropriate to let the one who is the author of the narrow gate and the wide gate answer that question for us. Jesus said, "Do not fear those who kill the body but cannot kill the soul [man]. But rather fear Him who is able to destroy both soul and body in hell" (God; Matthew 10:28). How about you? Do you fear him? Are you a fool, or are you wise? The choice is yours and yours alone.

As you search for the truth for your life, I truly believe it would be wise to remember once again the words of Proverbs 1:7, "The fear of the Lord is the beginning of knowledge, But fools despise wisdom and instruction." But then again, I'm just a forklift operator. After all, what do I know?

CHAPTER 4

"The Dash"

Born—Died

> Therefore we also, since we are surrounded by so great a cloud
> of witnesses, let us lay aside every weight, and the sin which so
> easily ensnares us, and let us run with endurance the race that
> is set before us.
> —Hebrews 12:1

AS WE'VE DISCOVERED in our search for the truth, there are two paths or two roads that we as human beings can take. According to Jesus Christ (God), we can choose the narrow path or the narrow road that will lead us to life (spiritual renewal), or we can choose the wide path or the wide road that will lead us to ultimate destruction (hell). For you see, there are only two ways to go, two choices to be made—the narrow road or the wide road. The question for us is which road do we want to go on? It is the question I had to answer for myself a long, long time ago, and it is an answer that you will have to answer for yourself as well.

In the last chapter, we learned that true salvation cannot be obtained unless you have a fear of God. In this chapter, we're going to take a look at another fear that we must consider if we're going to travel down the narrow road that leads to life. To do that, I'd like to start off our journey in this chapter with the following poem. There is much to this poem that really came at a pivotal time in my personal pursuit for the truth, and I think it is one that can help you as well. The name of the poem is titled "The Dash," and it goes like this:

I read of a man who stood to speak
at the funeral of a friend.
He referred to the dates on his tombstone
from the beginning . . . to the end.

He noted that first came his date of birth
and spoke the following date with tears,
But he said what mattered most of all
was the dash between those years.

For that dash represents all the time
that he'd spent alive on earth . . .
And now only those who loved him
know what that little line is worth.

For it matters not, how much we own;
the cars . . . the house . . . the cash.

What matters is how we live and love
and how we spend our dash.

So think about this long and hard . . .
Are there things you'd like to change?
For you never know how much time is left,
That can still be rearranged.

If we could just slow down enough
To consider what's true and real,
And always try to understand
The way other people feel.

And be less quick to anger,
And show appreciation more.
And love the people in our lives
Like we've never loved before.

If we treat each other with respect,
and more often wear a smile . . .
Remembering that this special dash
might only last a little while.

So, when your eulogy's being read
with your life's actions to rehash . . .
Would you be proud of the things they say
about how you spent your dash?

JOSEPH TRAVER

Now you're probably asking yourself, "What could this poem possibly have to do with the narrow path and the wide path? What does a eulogy have to do with me?" You see, it has everything to do with us! It has everything to do with us because if your eulogy's being read then that means you are dead. Dead, you say? Yes, dead, like not breathing. Now if you're like most people, you prefer not to talk about or discuss death. Speaking on the subject of death is an area that most people want to avoid. They say they will discuss it some other time but not today. And you know what? Most of the time, "sometime" never comes until one's eulogy is being read. Well, today we're going to discuss death because you know what? Death is as much a part of life as life itself. How so, you ask? I say so because when I last looked, the percentage of dying is 100 %. The figures are in, and it is a proven statistic that one out of every one will die. And it is to this very statistic that this poem really started to open my eyes to the fact that one day, I am going to die. It also started to open my eyes and my heart to some questions, like what will happen to me after I die? Is there life after death? Is there something beyond the casket? Is there more than just a marked tombstone? Is there more beyond the grave? Or does it all end when this life is over?

First of all, to even begin to unravel the mysteries surrounded by many of these questions, I think it's best if we start with the words from whom the Bible describes as one of the wisest men in all of God's word, the one known as the preacher, the one who was king over God's people, Israel. His name is King Solomon. He writes in the Old Testament book of Ecclesiastes in chapter 3, "To everything there is a season, A time for every purpose under heaven. And the first thing he mentions is; A time to be born, And a time to die: Which really adds credence to the statistic that 100% of the time people do die." Now there's much more wisdom that King Solomon shares within the book of Ecclesiastes, and I would strongly recommend that you check it out for yourself. However, there is some scripture that King Solomon shares that really started to bring things together in my mind and began to convict my heart. I say it began to convict my heart because the words I discovered opened my eyes to the fact that I had broken my vow to God. How so, you ask? Well, if you remember back in the first chapter, I had made a vow to God when I was lost in the woods while deer hunting. If you also remember, I had made a vow that if he would help me find my way out of the woods, then I would do whatever he wanted me to do for the rest of my life. The problem was I gave God lip service. I made a vow; but I never followed through with it, and I realized that I was a fool for making a vow to God and then not follow through with it. And you know what? As it turned out, I believe God was not happy with me. In fact, I truly believe he had to get my attention by allowing me to nearly be killed by the drunk driver that rear-ended us while on our way to go deer hunting. Why do I say I believe God was mad at me? I say it because of what it says in the fifth chapter of Ecclesiastes, "When you make a vow to God, do not delay to pay it; for He has no pleasure in fools. Pay what you have vowed—better not to vow than to vow and not pay." Question: If this was true and God was indeed mad or disappointed with me, could it be that there are other cases when or where God is disappointed or mad with others as well? For you see, the thinking in the modern-day world of Christendom (church) today is that God doesn't get mad. He doesn't get angry. After all, God is a God of love not anger. God loves us all no matter what we do, which brings us back to the poem, "The Dash" and also to the second fear we must understand if our search for the truth is going to continue to manifest itself to (within) us. And what fear is this, you ask? It is the fear that is spoken of in the word of God (Bible) found in Proverbs 8 (Solomon is also the author of Proverbs). Here, wisdom itself is speaking, and as we learned in the previous chapter of this book, wisdom is first born, or conceived if you will, within the boundaries or parameters of the fear of God. With that thought in mind, we now take a look at what wisdom tells us is a second fear where he says, "I, wisdom, dwell with prudence [caution and good judgment], And find out knowledge and discretion." The fear of the Lord (God) is to hate evil (vv. 12 and 13), which leads us to another scripture that says if we (true believers) love the Lord, then we must hate evil. You who love the Lord, hate evil (Psalm 97:10). So if we claim to love the Lord, then we must hate evil. I use the word "claim" because there are many who claim to love God, but they too, like I myself once did, only give God lip service. Which reminds me of the scripture that says from both the prophet Isaiah and Jesus Christ himself, "These people draw near to Me with their mouth, And honor Me with their lips, But their heart is far from Me. And in vain they worship Me, Teaching as doctrines the commandments of men" (Matthew 15:8, 9 and Isaiah 29:13).

Which begs the next question? What is evil? If I (we) must hate evil, then what is it? The word "evil" is described in the dictionary as such: morally wrong or bad, harmful or injurious, unfortunate or disastrous, an evil quality or conduct, harm or misfortune. The word "evil" is mentioned some 569 times in the Bible, while the word "love" is only mentioned 280 times. Do you think God was (is) trying to tell us something about evil?

Who is the author of evil anyways? Well, there is much to that study, and it is not one that we are going to tackle at this time. However, if you'd like to get a sneak preview of where and when evil first came on board, I can tell you to look in the twenty-eighth chapter of the Old Testament in the book of Ezekiel for some answers. I can also tell you that at the center of evil itself, you will always find the snare of pride. Snare, you say? Yes, I said snare. I use the word "snare" because it is one of the weapons that the devil uses in his arsenal to keep us from finding the narrow path to life (God; 2 Timothy 2:26). Which brings us back again to the narrow road or the wide road and my (our) search for the truth.

You see, the poem I'm sharing in this chapter very closely resembles a sermon I heard preached when God was first molding and shaping me into becoming a true Christian. The message was preached at a funeral I attended while God was in the process of renewing my mind. What do I mean by renewing my mind? Well, there is much to that story as well, but I will tell you this much: it is another necessary step that must take place in a person's life if they ever expect to find and travel on the narrow path that leads to life. I say it is another necessary step because the renewal of a person's mind is a requirement in finding what is good and acceptable and perfect will of God (Romans 12:2).

In the scripture I used at the beginning of this chapter, we are commanded to run with endurance the race that is set before us. We are also commanded to lay aside every weight, and the sin which so easily ensnares us. Why? Why are we commanded to do these things? Well, for the answer to that question, you'll have to go on to the next chapter. However, before you move on to the next chapter, I will tell you this much. The words contained within the poem, "The Dash" had such a profound impact on my life that not only did it impact the way I looked at death, but it also played a major role in my search for the truth and the narrow path. You see, most people don't realize it but it is the little line known as the dash that really is the most important line that a person will ever walk in this life. How so, you ask, because of what the words of the poem say to us. Listen once again where it says, "But he said what mattered most of all was the dash between those years. For that dash represents all the time that he'd spent alive on earth." The truth is, our lives really boil down to a little line that goes between the day we are born and the day we die. It is known as the dash, and it can usually be found on any tombstone and in any cemetery. After I heard that preacher share the story of the dash, I had a new and profound outlook on death. In fact, to this very day, I never enter a cemetery or look at a tombstone in the same manner as I had before. The questions that kept coming up in my mind time and time again are the same questions we took a look at earlier in this chapter. Is there more on the other side of death? Is there something beyond the grave? The answer to that question is a resounding "Yes, there is." There is hope beyond the grave! There is life eternal. But to find it, you must take the narrow path, and one of the conditions for finding the narrow path is to hate evil. Those are not my words, my friend. They are the words of the one who knows how to get you (us) on the narrow path. But then again, please keep in mind I'm just a forklift operator. After all, what do I know?

CHAPTER 5

Dead Man Walking

And you He made alive, who were dead in trespasses and sins,
in which you once walked according to the course of this world,
according to the prince of the power of the air, the spirit who now
works in the sons of disobedience.
—Ephesians 2:1, 2

IN THE LAST chapter, I shared a poem that began to get my attention with regard to me dying. It began to arouse my mind to the truth that one day I was going to die. In this chapter of our search for the truth, we're going to discover that I was already dead. Dead, you say? Yes, dead! Oh, I was walking, and I was breathing; but in reality, I was as dead as a man could get. And the worst part about it was I didn't even know it. How so, you ask? Well, let's uncover the answer to that question as we continue our search for the truth.

Thus far in my (our) journey, I've been uncovering some necessary steps that I learned I must go through if I was ever going to find the narrow road (gate) that God says we must find if we ever expect to find true life. You see, the one thing I had to understand was that with regard to my relationship with God, I was as dead as one can get in this life, because I was still walking on the wide path that leads to destruction. I say I was walking on the wide path that leads to destruction because as our opening verse of God's word said, "I was still walking in the trespasses and sins that were in my life and I was walking in the spirit of the prince of the power of the air, who is the devil himself." I was a son of disobedience because I was not walking in obedience to the word of God, but I was walking to my own beat if you will. I was the captain of my own ship (life). I was doing my own thing, and I was playing and walking on the wide road of disobedience that can only lead to one place, the path to destruction, again, as it says in God's word, "For wide is the gate and broad is the way that leads to destruction, and there are many who go in by it" (Matthew 7:13). I was living a life that was disobedient to God and his word. I was right in the very grips of the ruler of this age, and I was indeed one of the many who was traveling on the broad path that leads to ultimate destruction.

By now, you may be asking yourself, "What does the ruler of this age have to do with anything? What does the ruler of this age have to do with the truth? And what does the ruler of this age have to do with me finding the narrow path of life versus the wide path that leads to destruction?" Well, for the complete answer to that whole question, I would probably have to write another book; but for now, let's take a look at another piece of this puzzle in our search for the truth.

Earlier in this book, I wrote about a necessary step that must take place in a person's life if they ever expect to find the narrow path that leads to life. I say that because up to now I had been going through the beginning stages of the necessary process of having my mind renewed. I say that because the renewing of the mind is where the battle between good and evil really begins. It's where the rubber meets the road. It's where the bottom line of this life is really drawn. I use the word "battle" because that's really what life is; it's a battle between good and evil. The narrow road is the road traveled by those who are true followers of Jesus Christ (life), and the wide road is the road traveled by those who are in Satan's domain. There are only two choices. Now there are those who will say that this is insane and crazy. They will say, "I'm a good person. I'm not following Satan, and I don't need God! I don't try to hurt anyone. I mind my own business. I pay my taxes. I help my neighbor out when he or she needs help. I try not to break the laws of the land. All in all, I believe I'm a pretty good person. And if there is a heaven, I'm confident that I will go there when I die." Really, are you sure? For you see, you may think you're a good person. You may think there's nothing wrong with you. But believe me; if your mind isn't being renewed by God, then you are traveling on a dead-end road that will eventually lead to your destruction, besides God's word says in the New Testament book of Romans 3:12, "There is none that doeth good, no not one." It also says in the Old Testament book of Isaiah that "all we like sheep have gone astray; We have turned, every one, to his own way" (Isaiah 53:6). In other words, we are like sheep because we desire to live our own way and do our own thing, and because we do just that. We reap the fruit of what we have sown as it says in Proverbs 1:31-33, "Therefore they shall eat the fruit of their own way, And be filled to the full with their own fancies. For the turning away of the simple will slay them, And the complacency of fools will destroy them; "BUT WHOEVER LISTENS" to me [God] will dwell safely, And will be secure, without fear of evil." A parallel verse that really brings the words of Solomon home to our minds is found in the New Testament book of Galatians 6:8 where it teaches that "for he who sows to his flesh [wide road] will of the flesh reap corruption, 'but' he who sows to the Spirit [narrow road] will of the Spirit reap everlasting life." This leads us back to the words of Jesus with regard to the narrow way (gate) that leads to life.

By now, you may be asking yourself, "But what does this have to do with me?" You see, it has everything to do with you, if you're not listening to God! How so, you ask? Well, according to the scripture, if you're not listening to God then you're not safe and secure. You are eating the fruit of your own way; and according to the word of God, you are both simple (lacking in intelligence) and a fool. You are on the wide path instead of the narrow path. You too are like who I once was. You are dead, and you too don't even realize that you are. How so, you ask?

First of all, you must believe that the Bible is the inerrant word of God. In other words, you must believe that there are no errors within the Bible. The words contained within the Bible are the truth, the whole truth, and nothing but the truth. The Bible is very reliable and within its pages are the very foot prints and the very heart of Almighty God. They are His revealed words meant for those who truly love and wish to serve Him. If you remember, I shared with you earlier in this book that God sent his Son Jesus Christ into the world to seek and to save that which was lost (Luke 19:10). The lost spoken of here are those people who are walking in the course of this world and have not yet begun to have their minds renewed to the things of God that are found in his word. And until this process begins, they are indeed still dead in their trespasses and sins. They are simple! They are fools! And they are D-E-A-D! They are walking on the broad road that leads to destruction.

What is a trespass or sin, you ask? Well, the dictionary defines a trespass as to enter unlawfully or without permission upon the land of another; to intrude or encroach; to commit an offense; the act or an instance of trespassing. The word "sin" means a willful violation of some religious or moral principle; any wrong or evil act; live in sin, to cohabit (to live together as husband and wife without being legally married). Oh, is that one for the day we're living in or what? In other words, with regard to God's word contained in the Bible, a trespass and/or a sin is any violation, any defiance, or any disobedience to his word. You see, the problem lies in the fact that if you are not aware of what is and what is not a trespass or a sin, then you cannot possibly begin to know in what area of your life that you are in defiance of God's word. And according to God's word, you are still dead in those trespasses and sins and are a participant in the spirit of the sons of disobedience. In other words, you are a transgressor against God and his word (law), and you may not even realize that you are (1 John 3:4). I know I didn't. And I know it was only by the grace of God and him seeking me that I began to awaken from the dead and the course of this world in which I was walking. The course I was walking on was the one that was leading me to my eternal destruction. It was the course of this world that Jesus alluded to as the broad gate. It was the one that is traveled by the devil and his snares of deception. In 1 John 3:8, we are told "that he who sins is of the devil, for the devil has sinned from the beginning." Which if you did your homework from chapter 4, you would know some of the attributes of the devil that are spoken of in the twenty-eighth chapter of the Old Testament book of Ezekiel as well as in the Old Testament book of Isaiah 14.

Another thing for us to consider in our search for the truth is the one I spoke about in the last chapter with regard to the command to lay aside every weight and the sin, which so easily ensnares us so we can run with endurance the race that is set before us. The truth is, my friend, sin is in itself a snare. It is a weight that holds us down from finding the narrow path that leads to life. It is a weapon that is used by the devil in his arsenal as he attempts to keep us on the wide path of destruction, the wide path that keeps us dead in our transgressions against the God of the Bible and therefore in an evil state of mind. We will remain in the devil's snare until our minds are renewed, and therefore that weight will be a burden to our running our race on the narrow path. I am reminded of the scripture in Proverbs 29:6, "By transgression an evil man is snared, But the righteous sings and rejoices." Why do the righteous sing and rejoice? They sing and rejoice because they know they are traveling on the narrow path that leads to life, and they know they are free from the snare of the devil's trap that leads to destruction. They know they can run the race that is set before them. They know they are seen as righteous in the sight of God and therefore can run their race with complete confidence that God is well pleased with them as they run their race. How about you, my friend? Have you considered what path you're on? Has God began to awaken you from the dead yet? Has he spoken to your heart today? I hope he has, because if you remain in your trespasses and sins, you will never begin to find the narrow gate and the narrow way that leads to life, nor will you be able to run the race with confidence; because the devil will always have a grip on your life, and you will continue to be a son of disobedience.

As we close out this chapter, I'd like to take us to one of the prophets in the Old Testament. The prophet's name was Jeremiah. The word "prophet" means a person who speaks with divine inspiration, a person who foretells future events. Prophets were used by God throughout the Old Testament as he chooses. They were used by God to be his messengers. In other words, they spoke the words that God had instructed them to speak for him. In fact, most of the Old Testament is jam-packed with nothing but prophets. Jeremiah was known as the weeping prophet and/or the broken-hearted prophet. Jeremiah the prophet is traditionally credited with authoring the books of Jeremiah, 1 Kings, 2 Kings, and the book of Lamentations. I said Jeremiah was known as the Weeping Prophet or the Broken-hearted Prophet. He got that title because of his lamenting spirit. In other words, he was full of sorrow and deep regret. He was full of sorrow and deep regret because the words and warnings that God had called him to speak to the people of Israel went largely unheeded. In fact, God told Jeremiah that his words would fall on deaf ears. I say that because throughout the book of Jeremiah, you find the prophet warning the people of Israel to return to the ways (things) of God. You see, God's people had turned to idols. In other words, they had turned their hearts from the narrow path of life in God and had turned to the wide road of secularism and destruction that is found on the wide path. Jeremiah had warned them, but his warning fell on deaf ears.

By now you're probably asking yourself, "Okay, Joe, what does this story with regard to the prophet Jeremiah has to do with me?" You see, it has a great deal to do with you. I say that because sorrow and a lamenting heart have a great deal to do with finding the narrow road that leads to life. How so, you ask? Well, for the answer to that question, you'll have to move on to the next chapter; but before you do I will tell you this much: the shortest scripture verse in the entire Bible is the one found in the New Testament book of John 11:35 where it says, "Jesus wept." Why was Jesus weeping? Many thought He was weeping because His friend (Lazarus) had died, but in reality his tears weren't being poured out because of his friend's death because he knew that God was going to resurrect his friend back from the dead. But his weeping was meant for a fallen world that was entangled in sin. What sin, you ask? It was the sin of unbelief. How so, you ask? Look what Jesus said to Martha, the sister of him who had died (Lazarus), "Did I not say to you that if you would believe you would see the glory of God?"

The glory that Jesus was speaking of was the glory that God receives every time a person comes to true belief in his Son Jesus Christ. Every time a person believes, God gets the glory. He gets the glory because they are resurrected from the dead (narrow path). How do you know that, you ask? I know it because of Jesus' words in verse 42 when he says to God, "And I know that you always hear Me, but because of the people who are standing by I said this, that they may believe that you sent Me." What was Jesus referring to? He was referring to Martha's faith and also the faith of the people who were watching what was going on. Martha had given Jesus lip service, just like so many people in the world today. She told him she believed, but in fact, her faith was suspect. How so, you ask? She believed that her brother would rise in the last day, which is in reference to John 5:28 with regard to the resurrection at the end of time, but she didn't have faith that Jesus could raise her brother from the dead right then. You see, the point is, there are those who are dead right now, and you may be one of them. How so, you ask? Because of your unbelief, and if you don't believe that Jesus was indeed the Son of God, you are in serious trouble; for you are on the broad road that leads to destruction, and you are caught in one of the devils best snares, the snare of unbelief. There is one last point to make, and that is there are also many who think they're on the narrow road, but in fact they are on the broad road. That was the reason the prophet Jeremiah was known as the Weeping Prophet. He wept because he knew that unless the people of Israel would listen to his cries from God for repentance and turn from their wicked ways, God was going to destroy them. They were walking in the path of destruction, and they didn't even realize that they were. They thought they were safe and secure because after all, they were the people of God. They were a generation that was pure in their eyes and wouldn't listen to God's messenger. It reminds me of the scriptures that say, "Every way of a man is right in his own eyes, But the Lord weighs the hearts" (Proverbs 21:2). And also, "There is a generation that is pure in its own eyes, Yet is not washed from its filthiness" (Proverbs 30:12). From a secular viewpoint, there are many similarities between the nation of Israel in Jeremiah's time and the United States of America today. Also from a religious viewpoint, there are also many similarities between the two as well. So how about it, do you think we might just be a generation who thinks we're pure in our own eyes? I believe there is evidence that we just may be. But then again, please keep in mind I'm just a forklift operator. After all, what do I know?

CHAPTER 6

"Judge Not That You Be Not Judged." Are You Kidding?

Do not judge according to appearance, but judge
with righteous judgment.
John 7:24

A S WE CONTINUE our search for the truth, I think it's important that we take a look at one of the most misunderstood issues of the day in which we live. And that issue is regarding the issue of judging. I say it is one of the most important issues because it is an issue that can hinder us from ever finding the narrow road that leads to life.

In the last chapter, we found the prophet Jeremiah warning the people of Israel to turn their hearts back to the ways of God, but his cries for repentance had fallen on deaf ears. Failing to grasp the situation, the people asked, "Why has the Lord pronounced all this great disaster against us? Or what is our iniquity? Or what is the sin that we have committed?" How similar are the words of those who listen to the gospel (Bible) today but do not want to acknowledge that they are guilty and lost? Feeling that they have led a well-ordered and honest life, they forget that man's worst sin is to reject Christ and his work. In verses 11 and 12 of Jeremiah 16, we read what God had commanded Jeremiah to tell the people of Israel, "Your fathers have forsaken Me, says the Lord; (God) they have walked after other gods and have served them and worshiped them, and have forsaken Me and not kept My law. And you have done worse than your fathers, for behold, each one follows the dictates of his own evil heart, so that no one listens to Me."

Throughout Jeremiah's life, he kept expounding this message. In fact, in the twenty-fifth chapter of Jeremiah, verses 3 through 7, we read that Jeremiah had been pleading with the people since his ministry began in the thirteenth year of King Josiah's reign, "From the thirteenth year of Josiah the son of Amon, king of Judah, even to this day, this is the twenty-third year in which the word of the Lord [God] has come to me; and I have spoken to you, rising early and speaking, but you have not listened. And the Lord [God] has sent to you all His servants the prophets, rising early and sending them, but you have not listened nor inclined your ear to hear. They said, 'Repent now every one of his evil way and his evil doings, and dwell in the land that the Lord [God] has given to you and your fathers forever and ever. Do not go after other gods to serve them and worship them, and do not provoke Me to anger with the works of your hands; and I will not harm you. Yet you have not listened to Me,' says the Lord, 'that you might provoke Me to anger with the works of your hands to your own hurt.'"

Well, by now you're probably asking yourself, "Okay, Joe, this is a nice story but what could this possibly have to do with me and what can this possibly have to do with our search for the truth?" You see, it has a great deal to do with you, and it has a great deal to do with finding the truth because the other gods spoken of in this warning by Jeremiah represented the false gods found within their own hearts. And what are the false gods, you ask? They are the ones that are found on the wide path that leads to destruction (hell). How so, you ask? Well, for the answer to that question, let's go to the truth of God's word that is found in the New Testament book of Galatians 5 and 6, "For you see the works that provoked God to anger are the same ones that are found on the wide road [path]. They are the ones that keep people from inheriting the kingdom of God. They are the works of the flesh, the works of the flesh that lusts against the Spirit." What Spirit, you ask? The Spirit of God, the third person of the trinity, the Father, the Son, and the Holy Spirit. The Spirit of God that dwells in all true believers, the true presence of the indwelling Holy Spirit. The dictionary defines the word "indwell" or "indwelling" as such: to be or reside (within), as a guiding force. In other words, God's Spirit lives within someone and his Spirit then guides that person in the ways of God; therefore, if someone is walking (being guided by) in and by the Spirit (narrow path), they will not fulfill the lust of the flesh. The lust of the flesh is a trait or characteristic that is found in those who are walking on the wide path that leads to destruction (hell). The Apostle Paul puts it like this, "I say then; Walk in the Spirit, and you shall not fulfill the lust of the flesh. For the flesh lusts against the Spirit and the Spirit against the flesh; and these are contrary to one another, so that you do not do the things that you wish. But [and I want to emphasis the word 'but'] if you are led by the Spirit, you are not under the law" (Galatians 5:16-18). What law, you ask? God's law, the handwritten requirements (law) that was (is) against all humanity. In other words, every unredeemed human being is guilty before the one who created us, God, which takes us back to our last chapter where we learned from the Apostle Paul's letter in Romans the words, "There is none who does good, no not one" (Romans 3:12). Mankind is universally evil. Another place in God's word that affirms what the Apostle Paul was speaking about can be found in the Old Testament book of Psalms 14:1-3 where it says, "The fool has said in his heart, 'There is no God.' They are corrupt, they have done abominable works; There is none who does good." The Lord looks down from heaven upon the children of men (that's you and I, folks), to see if there are any who understand, who seek God. They have all turned aside, they have together become corrupt; there is none who does good, no, not one. The dictionary defines the word "corrupt" as "guilty of dishonest practices, as bribery; debased in character; decayed or putrid (very bad)." The word "abominable" is defined as "repugnantly hateful; very bad or poor, highly offensive, opposed or contrary, as in nature."

The fact is, my friends, none of us are good. All of us who draw a breath as human beings are considered as fools in God's eyes. With that being said, we are all guilty of death. Death, you say! Yes, death. Well, you say, everyone dies. Yes, as we've already discovered in an earlier chapter, the statistic for people dying is one out of every one. But the fact that everyone dies is not the end of the story. It's not, you ask? No, it's not, at least if you believe that there is a God. But you say if that's not the end of the story, then what comes next? What happens after I (we) die? Well, for the answer to that question, let's take a look at what the Bible says about that is found in the New Testament book of Hebrews 9:27 where it says, "And as it is appointed for men to die once, but after this the judgment." What judgment, you ask, God's judgment? There will come a time when you will be judged. Judged for what, you ask? Judged on how you have lived your life here on earth. Have you lived your life for yourself, or have you lived your life for God (Jesus Christ)? Have you lived your life on the narrow path or on the wide path? The truth is you're being judged right now! How so, you ask? Well, go back to our previous scripture from the Apostle Paul (Galatians 5:16-18) with regard to us either walking (living) in the Spirit (narrow road), or are you walking in the flesh? Because if you're walking in the flesh, then you are under the law of God, and you are bound for eternal destruction (wide road) after you die, which leads us back to the beginning of this chapter. "Judge not, that you be not judged." These words are the words of Jesus Christ found at the beginning of Matthew 7, which just so happens to be the words found in the same chapter as those Jesus shared with regard to finding the narrow path to life versus the wide path that leads to destruction.

You see, I could have used any of the Old Testament prophets to begin to open your eyes in our search for the truth about the issue of judgment, but I chose Jeremiah because as we learned in the previous chapter, he was known as the Weeping Prophet. Why was he weeping? He was weeping because he knew that God's judgment was going to fall on the nation Israel because of their idolatry, and no one was listening to him. In fact, it is said that Jeremiah preached his whole ministry and never once had one conversion. No one listened to him. The reason I chose Jeremiah is to show you that God is a God of judgment, and he expects us to live in obedience to him and to the words that are found in the Bible. There is much to the story that leads up to the prophet Jeremiah's time, but in a nutshell God made a covenant (agreement) with the nation Israel that goes all the way back to the old testament book of Genesis 12 with regard to a man by the name of Abram, which was later changed to Abraham. The covenant included God's protection and blessings because of Abram's faith in God. It also included a set of laws or commandments that God expected his chosen people to follow. Why did God have to set up a set of rules, you ask? Well, if you know anything about God, then you would know that he is holy. In fact, he declares it to be so within his word (Bible). "I am holy. I am holy" (Leviticus 11:44, 45). "I am holy" (1 Peter 1:16). But as God has declared himself to be holy, there is also another declaration that goes along with God's declaration of his holiness, and it pertains to you (us). And what is that, you ask? Well, take a look at what he says, "For I am the Lord your God. You shall therefore consecrate yourselves, and you shall be holy; for I am holy" (Leviticus 11:44). You shall therefore be holy, for I am holy" (Leviticus 11:45). Also, "Be holy, for I am holy." What? Did God say we are to be like him? Yes, he did. But you ask, "How can I be as holy as God? After all, he is God and I am not. Answer: You can't, not on your own. But that's why God came up with a plan, a plan so clever, a plan so ingenious, a plan so loving that to those who are blinded by the god of this age (Satan); it is to them a mystery, and they are not capable of seeing it (2 Corinthians 4:4). A mystery, you ask? Yes, I said a mystery. What mystery? Well, for the answer to that question, you'll have to move on to the next chapter, but I will tell you this much before you do. As I mentioned earlier, you must first believe that the Bible is the word of God. You must also believe that the words contained within its pages were written by actual people who were inspired by God to do so. And you must believe that unless you become as holy as God, you will by no means ever find the narrow path that leads to life. Remember one thing: I didn't say you had to be holy like God. He said it! You see in today's world we live in, speaking of judgment is not a very popular thing. I say it's not a popular thing because of what the opening scripture says to us about judging. The problem lies within the parameters of God's word. I say that because of what his word is speaking of. Jesus said in Matthew 7:20 that "by their fruits you will know them." We're not to judge others by the way people look on the outside (wide path), but we are to make judgments about their actions as it lines up with the truth of God's word on the inside (narrow path); which by the way, the inside is representative of the fruits of the Spirit (the Holy Spirit), which leads to life through God. And the outside is representative of the works of the flesh, which leads to destruction (wide path) through Satan. What kind of fruit are they producing, Godly fruit or satanic fruit? What is truly in their hearts? How can I know, you ask? Truth is, you will never truly know them or their fruits until and unless you have the power of God. What power, you ask, the same power that the prophet Jeremiah had. He had the power because he was in unison with God's word (heart). He was on the same page with Almighty God. The problem wasn't with Jeremiah; the problem was with those who wouldn't listen to his cry for them to repent from their evil ways and their evil doings (Jeremiah 25:5). They weren't in unison with God!

Question: Are you in unison with God? Are you on the same page as God? Would you like the power to be in unison with the God of this universe? I know I did! And I found it. I found the power to be in unison with Almighty God. How did I do it, you ask? I did it because the first place I started judging was within my own heart. And do you know what I found. I found a man who was producing the kind of fruit that comes from the god of this world, Satan himself. The works of the flesh was exactly where I was, and I knew I had to change the direction of my life. I was walking down the broad path that was leading me to my destruction (hell), and I finally realized that I needed God's power to help me find the narrow path/way to life. Again, you ask, but how did you do it? How did you find the power? I found it with the help of God's word that says in the New Testament book of John 1:12 and 13, "But as many as received Him, to them He gave the power to become children of God, to those who believe in His name: who were born, not of blood, not of the will of the flesh, nor of the will of man, but of God." You see, when I believed in his name, I received God's power not because I had blood running through my veins, not by willfully trying to keep myself from defiling my flesh by sexual purity, and not by doing good works or deeds in an attempt to impress God. I simply truly believed in my heart that in his name, he was indeed the God of the Bible. And because I did that, he was true to his word, and he did indeed lived up to his word by giving me the power to become one of his children. For you see, believing in his name is one thing, but what you do with the power he gives you in his name is quite another. I say that because even Satan believes in his name (God). He believes that God is real, and he knows that anyone who is a child of God is a threat to his kingdom and his domain here on earth. He knows you're a threat, and he will do everything in his power to trip you up by his skillful art of deception. How will he do that, you ask? He will do it by unleashing his spiritual hosts of wickedness that are amassed in the heavenly places (Ephesians 6:12). Where are the heavenly places, you ask? The heavenly places refer to the entire realm of spiritual beings (Ephesians 1:3 and 3:10) that wage war against the souls of men (1 Peter 2:11). Once you become a child of God, you become a target of/for Satan. But also not only do you become a target for Satan. You also become one of God's soldiers. Soldier you say? Yes, soldier (2 Timothy 2:3, 4). But you ask, "How can I fight an enemy I can't see?" Answer: You can't. You can't until you receive God's power. That's why you need the power of God. It's by and through that (his) power that you receive what is called; the whole armor of God (Ephesians 6:10). The armor of God that is necessary to be able to take a stand against the wiles of the devil (Satan) (Ephesians 6:11). And oh, by the way, the prophet Jeremiah was a soldier for God. But then again, please keep in mind, I'm just a forklift operator. After all, what do I know?

CHAPTER 7

Building a House of Perfection

Therefore you shall be perfect, just as your Father
in heaven is perfect.
—Matthew 5:48

FIRST OF ALL, I'd like to commend and also thank you for still being with me as we continue our search for the true things of this life. So far I've covered quite a bit of territory regarding what I have discovered in my own personal walk in finding the narrow gate/path that leads to life (heaven).

In our last chapter, we started discovering about what it means to walk in the Spirit. What Spirit? Whose Spirit? God's Spirit! We learned that if you walk in God's Spirit, then you will not fulfill the lust of the flesh. And if you are led by the Spirit, you are not under the law, which what we learned earlier, is a transgression and/or an offense against God and his rules, his commandments, his statutes, his word (Bible). So if we're not walking in the Spirit of God, then we are walking in the spirit of the ruler of this age, who is Satan himself. Why do I say that, you ask? I say it because it just so happens to be one of the key reasons it is so difficult to find the narrow way that leads to life. How so, you ask, because as human beings, we're in a never-ending war. Yes, I said war! What war, you ask? It's the war that is being fought between God and Satan, God's Spirit versus Satan's spirit. Good versus evil. How so, you ask? You see, Satan uses our flesh as a weapon against our very souls, which in turn keeps us from finding the narrow path of life. The Bible speaks of this in the New Testament book of Matthew 13:38, where it speaks of the world we live in as a field. It says that the good seeds are the sons of the kingdom (true believers), and the tares are the sons of the wicked one (Satan). In scripture, the wheat are known as true believers and tares are known as unbelievers. (Note: the Bible uses other words to describe believers, such as sheep, circumcised [Matthew 25:33 and Colossians 2:11-15] and unbelievers are described as goats, uncircumcised [Matthew 25:33 and Romans 4:11]) But there is much more to a tare than just an unbeliever. What is a tare? Well, a tare is probably a type of weed known as darnel. It can hardly be distinguished from wheat until the head matures. In an agricultural setting, sowing darnel in someone else's wheat field was a way for enemies to destroy someone's livelihood catastrophically. In the spiritual realm (Christendom), it pictures Satan's efforts to devastate the church by mingling his children with God's (wheat), in many cases making it nearly impossible for believers to discern the true from the false. So if you look at this as a truth for life, picture all through your life you will be dealing with people who are either tares or wheat. But you ask the question, "Why is this significant for my life's journey? And how will I be able to separate the wheat from the tares?" Good question! In fact, it is probably the most important question you can consider in this life because the answer to that question parallels what we learned in the last chapter about being as holy as God. And that is that not only are we to be holy like God, but we are also commanded to be as perfect as him, which begs the question, "how can we be as holy and perfect as God?" Answer: We can't. Not on our own. But (and again I want to emphasis the word "but") God can! God can make us holy, and God can make us perfect. How so, you ask? He can do it by and through belief in his only begotten Son, Jesus Christ. Why do I have to believe in his Son to be like him? Good question! The answer is because you can't do it on your own. You can't do it on your own because in order to be holy and perfect like Him, you need his Spirit. And without his Spirit, it is impossible to please him, or it is possible to find the narrow path that leads to eternal life (Hebrews 11:6). We can't because we as human beings were all born with the same problem. We were born as tares and not wheat. We were born with the nature of the world (sin/wide path) and not with the nature of God (righteousness/narrow path), which if you do your homework like I have, you will learn that if you want to be accepted by God (holy and perfect), you must truly believe in his Son, Jesus Christ. You must truly believe that because if you don't, then you will always remain on the wide path that leads to destruction (tare), and you will ultimately destroy your life, and you will spend your eternity (forever) in hell. What is hell, you ask? The dictionary defines hell as the place or state of punishment of the wicked after death, the abode (house) of evil and condemned spirits, any place or state of torment or misery. In other words, it is not a nice place for you or me to be. But the truth is, those who do not believe in God's Son, Jesus Christ, will have an understanding of what hell is like, because the reality is, they will be there. How about you, my friend? Will you be there? Are you on the wide road that is leading you to hell or are you on the narrow road that will take you to heaven? The journey begins with God's holiness and with God's perfection (truth).

Which takes us back to the opening chapter of this book where I used the scripture from the New Testament book of Luke 19:10, which says, "for the Son of Man has come to seek and to save that which was lost." You see, God sent his Son Jesus Christ here (earth) among us to save us. To save us from what, you ask? To save us from ourselves! To save us from the consequences of walking on the wide road of this life! To save us from the effects (corruption) produced from walking in the spirit of our flesh instead of the Spirit that leads to everlasting life. I guess one of the best ways to describe it is to share from the word of God where it says, "Do not be deceived, God is not mocked; for whatever a man sows, that he will also reap. For he who sows to his flesh will of the flesh reap corruption, but he who sows to the Spirit will of the Spirit reap everlasting life" (Galatians 6:7, 8). It is known as the doctrine or creed or belief of sowing and reaping. In forklift operator's lingo, it is known as "What goes around comes around." In other words, you get what you deserve. And I can think of no better example of describing the sowing and reaping analogy for you than to share the one I'm going to share. It is a story that I truly believe in my heart that God used as an example in my personal pursuit for the truth and in many ways are good examples for all of us as we continue our search for the truth.

"Bah, humbug!" Yes, I said, "Bah, humbug!" Now if I were to ask you the questions, "Who would you associate those words with? And who was best known for the use of those words? Could you answer those questions?" Well, if you've never read and/or seen a story with the title, A Christmas Carol, then you probably wouldn't be able to answer those questions. But for me, those words speak near and dear to my heart. I say they are near and dear to my heart because those words are forever embedded within the very core of the foundation of my faith journey as a believer in God's only Son, Jesus Christ. How so, you ask? Well, I'm glad you asked. I say I'm glad you asked because up to now, we've been taking a look at the things that will help us in our search for finding the narrow path that leads to life eternal versus the wide path that leads to destruction (hell). And this story is a classic tale of what it means to get what you deserve and to open up our eyes to what God's word says about the sowing and reaping of life.

Now if you know anything about the Christmas story (like I do), you would know that the words "Bah, humbug" were those used by the main character in the story whose name was Ebenezer Scrooge. The word "humbug" is an old term meaning "hoax" or "jest." While the term was first described in 1751 as student slang, its etymology (history of a particular word) is unknown. Its present meaning as an exclamation is closer to "nonsense" or "gibberish"; while a noun, a humbug refers to a fraud or imposter, implying an element of unjustified publicity and spectacle. The modern usage of the word is most associated with Ebenezer Scrooge as he declared Christmas to be a fraud, a hoax, and a scam. In forklift operator lingo, it was a bunch of bologna.

Now the Christmas Carol story is a story of greed, remorse, and redemption and was written in the year 1843 by an English novelist whose name was Charles Dickens (February 7, 1812-June 9, 1870). Ebenezer Scrooge was a stingy, miserly, penny-pinching, miserable, and mean-spirited old man with no love for anything but money. It was said that external heat and cold had little influence on Scrooge. No warmth could warm, no wintry weather could chill him. No wind that blew was more bitter than he. Nobody ever stopped him in the street to say with a joyful look, "My dear Scrooge, how are you? When will you come to see me?" No beggars would ask him for money, no children would ask him what time it was, no man or woman ever once in all his life ever asked Scrooge for directions to such and such a place. Even the blind men's dogs appeared to know who Scrooge was and when they saw him coming, would lead their owners into a doorway or an alleyway away from the presence of Scrooge. But what did Scrooge care? It was the very thing he liked—to edge his way along the crowded paths of life, warning all human sympathy to keep its distance from the heart of Ebenezer Scrooge.

You see, Scrooge had a serious problem. And one of the problems he had was that he didn't even realize that he had a problem at all, just like those who are traveling on the wide path of destruction that Jesus spoke about in his Sermon of the Mount message. What was his problem, you ask? It was a heart problem. It was the condition of his heart. He was on the wide path that was leading him to his destruction, and he didn't even know it. Scrooge had a serious problem, and he was about to find out just how serious the problem was. How so, you ask? Well, the story begins on Christmas Eve and though Scrooge didn't know it, he was about to be visited by three ghosts: the Ghost of Christmas Past, the Ghost of Christmas Present, and the Ghost of Christmas Future. But before he was visited by those three ghosts, his former business partner, whose name was Jacob Marley, had come to tell him about the three ghosts that were coming to visit him that night. But not only did he come to tell him about the three ghosts. He had come to warn him. Warn him, you ask? Yes, warn him. He had come to warn him not to follow the same path that he had traveled in his life. For you see, Scrooge's friend and business partner had died seven years earlier. In fact, the sign over Scrooge's business still bore Marley's name on it. Why did Marley come? Why did the three ghosts come? They came to show him what he has done, what kind of man he is now, and what his ultimate fate will be if he doesn't change. Will his eyes be opened to the truth about his life, or will he continue on the road toward an unmarked grave, a man forgotten? Through the experience he is about to encounter, Scrooge will have to reevaluate all he is, all he has done, and all that he can be. You see, when I first heard the Christmas story, there was something that resonated within the very walls of my heart. It resonated within me because by and through this story, I realized that in many ways, I too was like Mr. Scrooge. Oh, my heart in many ways might not have been as bad as Scrooge's; but I was in the same condition, and I too didn't even realize that I was. I had a heart problem, and it needed to be changed. It had to be changed and the story, A Christmas Carol, began to show me just how much. Now there's much to A Christmas Carol story, and I would strongly urge you to check it out for yourself. However, there are a couple of key points that I'd like to zero in on our continuing search for the truth.

Now I said that Scrooge's former business partner had come to warn him not to do the same things he had done in his life. What things, you ask? Well, when Marley first appeared to Scrooge, he came bound in a chain that was clasped about his waist. It was long and wound like a tail; and it was made (for Scrooge observed it closely) of cash boxes, keys, padlocks, ledgers, deeds, and heavy purses wrought in steel. It was as Marley in his own words put it, "The chain that I forged in life, I made it link by link, and yard by yard; I girded it on my own free will, and my own free will I wore it." Once again, Marley had come to warn his friend Scrooge that he was traveling down a path (wide) that would ultimately lead him to the same fate that had come to him if he didn't change his life's course. You see, those items Marley had bound around him in the chain were the things he clung to when he was alive. Those things were more important to him than the things of God. How so, you ask? You see, all those things Marley mentioned were things that had ultimately destroyed him. They destroyed him because those things were things that kept him from finding the narrow path to life eternal, and now he was cursed because of it. He had traveled his life on the wide path that leads to destruction, and he was indeed one of the many who travel down that wide path (Matthew 7:13).

He had lived his life exactly as the Bible had said regarding the sowing and reaping creed, and now he was paying the price. He was paying the price because he had sown to his flesh and therefore had corrupted himself and had in fact realized what he had done after it was too late. Instead of pursuing the desires of God, he had pursued the desires of the flesh. He had put his confidence in his worldly desires (Satan) instead of heavenly desires (God; Philippians 3:3). How do you know that, you ask? Well, let's take a look at what Marley says in his own words.

There comes a point in the conversation Scrooge was having with Marley when Scrooge tells Marley that he always was a good businessman, and Marley quickly rebukes Scrooge in a rage saying, "Business! Mankind was my business; The common welfare was my business; charity, mercy, patience, kindness, and compassion, were all my business. The dealings of my trade were but a drop of water in the comprehensive ocean of my business! It held up its chain at arm's length, as if that were the cause of all its unveiling grief, and flung it heavily upon the ground again."

"At this time of year," Marley said, "I suffer the most. Why did I walk through crowds of fellow-beings with my eyes turned down, and never raise them to that blessed Star which led the Wise Men to a poor abode [dwelling]! Were there no poor homes to which its light would have conducted me?"

The light which Marley was alluding to was the light that had led the wise men of long ago to a baby born in a manger in a little town of Bethlehem. Marley had finally seen the light that lies within true repentance and redemption. But unfortunately for him, it was too late. His life here on earth was over, and there was no second chance for him to, as Jacob Marley put it, turn his eyes toward the blessed Star that led to the one true light of the world, the baby, the Son of God, who is Jesus Christ.

You see, Marley had finally come to realize that the dealings of his flesh were the true "Bah, humbug" of his life. The dealings of his business were what drove his life, and they were in fact the true nonsense and fraud and scam. He was motivated by the love of money (flesh) instead of the things of God. Charity, mercy, patience, kindness, and compassion were his business; and he realized it when it was too late. He had gotten caught in one of the devil's snares/traps, the love of money, and the love of the almighty dollar. This according to God's word is the root of all evil. The New Testament book of 1 Timothy 6:10 says it like this, "For the love of money is a root of all kinds of evil." Notice it says "For the love of money is a root of all kinds of evil." It doesn't say money in itself is the root of all kinds of evil, but it says, "For the love of money 'is a root' of all kinds of evil"; it's a root. There are quite a few descriptions for the word "root" in the dictionary but the ones I'd like to zero in on are these: a quantity that, when multiplied by itself a specified number of times, produces a given quantity; to become fixed or established; the fundamental or essential part; the part of a plant that develops and spreads under the ground, anchoring the plant and providing it with water and nourishment from the soil; any underground part of a plant; to begin to grow; to become fixed or established. In other words, in forklift operator terms, Marley had received the reward he had forged in his life. The foundation (root) of his life was based on his business practices instead of his faith in Jesus Christ. How do I know that, you ask? Look what he says in his own words: "The dealings of my trade were but a drop of water in the comprehensive ocean of my business!" The drop of water he is referring to is regarding him spending all his time doing business transactions and making money instead of focusing on the things that really matter which was, according to Marley, the light of Jesus Christ. Marley realized that his business practices (love of money) were just a small part of his life, and that a life in Jesus Christ should have been the main focus of his life. He traveled his life on the wide path that led him to his ultimate destruction. And the worse part about it was he didn't even realize that he was traveling on that path.

How about you, my friend? Are the dealings of your life focused on the almighty dollar, or are they focused on the blessed Star, which led the Wise Men to the baby in the manger, who is Jesus Christ? I urge you to take a good look at your life because as I have walked down the narrow path of my life, I have seen what the love of money can do to people. Their lives can be destroyed, and the root of that evil can be embedded so deep within them that only the truth of God's Spirit can show them the way out, which takes us to our next step in our search for the truth. What is that next step, you ask? It is the step of faith which leads to the blessed Star of light in Jesus Christ that Marley spoke of. What faith, you ask? It is the same kind of faith that led those Wise Men to the baby Jesus those many, many centuries ago. It is also the kind of faith that had led Marley to understand that his own worldly flesh had led him down the road of destruction and as the second part of 1 Timothy 6:10 states; in their (Marley's) greediness, they have pierced themselves through with many sorrows. Marley had indeed felt the piercing of that sorrow he had inflicted upon himself by and through the evil that came from his love of money. And parts of those sorrows were wound about him like a tail. They were the chain that he had forged in his life and as Marley himself said, "I made it link by link, and yard by yard. I girded it on my own free will, and of my own free will I wore it."

As we have been looking at the narrow way that leads to life and the wide way that leads to destruction that Jesus spoke of, we are going to move on to another piece of the puzzle as we continue to search for the truth and also build a house (life) of perfection that is acceptable to God. What is that piece of the puzzle, you ask? It is the piece that includes what Marley had found after it was too late. You see, Marley had walked in the darkness of this life. He never found the light in the Lord that the New Testament book of Ephesians 5:8 speaks of where it says, "For you were once darkness, but now you are light in the Lord. Walk as children of the light [for the fruit of the Spirit is in all goodness, righteousness, and truth], finding out what is acceptable to the Lord" just as I spoke about in an earlier chapter with regard to myself. I too was walking in darkness for the first thirty-two years of my life. I could have wound up just like Marley (as well as multitudes of people), but by the grace of God, I found the light. Or should I say, the light found me. The light found me and I obeyed. What do you mean you obeyed, you ask? I obeyed the truth of God's word, and I began to build my house (life) on what the Bible refers to as the "rock." What is the rock? It is the rock that leads to one's salvation. It is the rock known as "the word of God," and it can only be found within the one true word of God which is the Holy Bible. In the gospel of John 1, we read these words, "In the beginning was the Word, and the Word, was with God, and the Word was God." He was in the beginning with God. All things were made through him, and without him, nothing was made that was made. In him was life, and the life was the light of men. And the light shines in the darkness, and the darkness did not comprehend it. Question: Who is the life and the light? It belongs to the one who said, "I am the way, the truth, and the life. No man comes to the Father, but by me" (John 14:6). Why couldn't Marley comprehend that? He couldn't because he was caught in the devil's snare, and the darkness of that snare couldn't penetrate the evil of his love for money. He was dead in his trespasses and sins, and he walked according to the course of this world. He was a son of disobedience, and he walked the wide path according to the prince of the power of the air who is old Satan himself (Ephesians 2:1, 2). And you know what? Marley wasn't the only one, and we're going to take a look at some more in our search for the truth. But then again, please keep in mind, I'm just a forklift operator. After all, what do I know?

CHAPTER 8

Mankind Is Our Business

For what profit is it to a man if he gains the whole world, and loses
his own soul? Or what will a man give in exchange for his soul?
—Matthew 16:26

IN OUR LAST chapter, we discovered that one of the characters in
the classic story, A Christmas Carol, written by Charles Dickens had
come to warn his former business partner Ebenezer Scrooge of his pending
doom unless he changed his ways. Unless he changed his ways, the same
fate Marley had endured was also waiting for Scrooge, which begs a couple
of questions for us to ponder as we continue on our journey in search for
the truth.

First, at least for me, whenever I read a story such as the one written by
Charles Dickens, I can't help but wonder where the person writing the story
or book is coming from. In other words, it's kind of like the story behind
the story. Meaning, like, from what perspective is the person writing the
story coming from? What is their angle? What is their outlook? What is
the message or viewpoint the person writing the story trying to convey to
me in that story? And one of the most important perspectives to look for,
whether it is in a book or in life in general, is the person writing or speaking
to me conveying a message that is best for me or best for them? In other
words, where is their heart? Is it centered—as Marley put it—on charity,
mercy, patience, kindness, and compassion? Is the root of what they're
trying to convey to me (us) based on goodness, righteousness, and truth? I
say that because one of the key things I have learned in my personal walk
on the narrow path of my faith journey is to seriously evaluate whatever is
going into my mind. I say that because the life of a Christian begins with
not only a changed heart, but it also begins with the renewing of one's
mind (Romans 12:2). It is also where the spiritual battles between God and
Satan are being fought, and the Holy Spirit (Ghost) of God will help you
overcome and defeat Satan's stronghold on your life if you allow God to do
just that (John 16:33).

You see, as I have done my homework and have studied some of the life of Charles Dickens, I discovered that Mr. Dickens was a compassionate man who was very concerned about the social issues of his day, including one of the same issues of our time: class inequalities. He often depicted the exploitation and repression of the poor and destitute and criticized public officials and institutions that not only allowed such abuses to exist, but flourished as a result. I would say that Mr. Dickens did a great deal in his life to address these issues and what the Bible refers to as the poor and the destitute among us in our society (Psalm 102:17 and Mark 14:7).

Question: Who are the poor and destitute among us today? Well, if we go back to the Christmas Carol story and think about the physical aspects of our society, you would be drawn to what Mr. Dickens referred to when Scrooge was approached by two men soliciting him for a monetary donation. Such a donation was to help those who were poor and destitute afford some food, drink, and the necessary funds to help sustain them and their families with the basic necessities of their existence of the physical life. Mr. Scrooge abruptly rebukes the two gentlemen by telling them he wanted to be left alone. Scrooge wasn't about to give the two gentlemen any of his money to help those who needed help. In fact, the two gentlemen reminded Scrooge that if the poor and destitute among them didn't get any financial help from those who could afford it, then many would die, in which Scrooge basically said, "Well then let them die." You see, in this specific case, the poor and destitute had to do with the physical aspects of life. The material things that human beings need to exist. Things like food, water, body comforts, etc. But if you take a look at Scrooge's life, he had the means to afford all the material things he needed to exist in the physical aspects of life but was lacking in the spiritual aspects; and like his partner Marley, he was traveling down the wide path that would ultimately lead to his destruction.

Well, by now you're probably asking yourself, "Okay Joe, this might be quite interesting but what could this possibly have to do with our search for the truth? You see, it has a great deal to do with our search for the truth because it further opens our eyes to the fact that there are two ways of looking at who are the poor and destitute among us. You see, Marley finally realized that he was duped and that he had lost his soul. If you read the story, you can hear it in his voice. You can hear the sadness, the sorrow, and the regret he was feeling. It reminded me of the scripture in the New Testament book of Luke 13 where Jesus says, "Depart from Me, all you workers of iniquity. There will be weeping and gnashing of teeth, when you see Abraham and Isaac and Jacob and all the prophets in the kingdom of God, and yourselves thrust out." You see, Marley had been a worker of iniquity in his physical life, and he knew it. He knew it because, as we learned in our previous chapter, his love for money had ultimately sealed his doom, and that was one of the reasons Marley had come to warn Scrooge not to follow in his footsteps. I truly believe the chains bound around Marley are like the one's depicted in the Bible in reference to those whose hands and feet are bound just before they are cast into what the Bible describes as hell (outer darkness—Matthew 22:13). In a way, I believe the author Charles Dickens placed a direct connection to what Marley was going through into a direct connection for us in our lives as well. The connection has to do with traveling on the narrow road to life or the wide road to destruction. For me, what Mr. Dickens had placed before me was what led me to the second question.

Would I (you) ever want to find myself in the same situation in which Marley found himself? If you take a good look at the scripture I used at the beginning of this chapter, you will see that I believe Marley knew the answers to those questions. But unfortunately for him, the answers had come too late. What are the questions, you ask? These are the ones that Jesus has placed before us in this scripture verse, "For what profit is it to a man if he gains the whole world, and loses his [their] own soul?" Or what will a man give in exchange for his soul? Answer to the first question: nothing! What do I mean by nothing? I mean nothing! The dictionary defines the word "nothing" as "no thing" or "not anything, no matter of any kind, a complete absence of something, a zero quality, to regard as insignificant." In forklift operator's terms, it means "notin', honey," "zippo," "not a darn thing," "notta." In other words, in this current world we live in today, there is not a thing worth more than a person's very soul. Not all the money in the world or all the tea in China is worth losing your own soul for. It reminds me of what God's word says in the New Testament book of 1 Timothy 6:7-9, "For you brought nothing into this world, and it is certain we can carry nothing out. And having food and clothing, with these we shall be content. But those who desire to be rich fall into temptation and a snare, and into many foolish and harmful lusts which drown men in destruction and perdition (spiritual ruin)."

Marley got caught in the snare of the desire to be rich, and it cost him his very soul; and now he was confronting Scrooge not to take the same path as him. But wait, there's the second question. How so, you ask? There's the question of what will a man give in exchange for his soul. Answer: Well,

I guess it depends on who's answering the question? I say it depends on who's answering the question because as I wrote earlier in this chapter, it all depends on perspective. How so, you ask? Well, in the case of Marley, it is quite evident from what he shares in the story, A Christmas Carol; he would have done things quite differently if he were given another chance. However, as we've discovered in our search for the truth, it was too late for him. For Marley, it was indeed too late. But you know what? It wasn't too late for old Ebenezer Scrooge. And do you know something else? It's not too late for you either. It's not too late because Scrooge was still alive; and if you're reading this book, so are you. Scrooge had been given a chance to change, and according to the Christmas Carol story, Scrooge did change. In fact, according to the story, Scrooge was even better than his word. It said that Scrooge became as good a friend, as good a master, and as good a man as any city, town, or borough in the world could have known. Question: Why was that? Why did Scrooge change? What compelled Scrooge to change his ways? Well, to answer that question, it once again comes down to perspective. And seeing this is my book, the perspectives I'm sharing are the ones that matter to me. They matter because as I shared earlier, they are the ones that have had such a profound impact on my life that I truly believe they can impact your life as well. But then again, if you've reached this far in this book, then I truly believe God has begun to plant his seed in you as you too continue your personal search for the truth in finding the narrow path that leads to life. It matters to God because unless God plants his seed in you, you will never be born again (John 3:3); and therefore you will never find the narrow path that leads to life nor will you ever see the kingdom of God (heaven).

(i.e., seed planting is found throughout God's word [Bible] and in many cases is referenced regarding the spiritual seeds sown within a person's heart and therefore are seeds grown within the line [hearts] of God's people)

Born again, you ask? What does it mean to be born again? Well, if you take another look at Christmas Carol story from a secular (worldly) view, which is exactly what happened to Scrooge. Scrooge had been born again because he had a complete change of heart. His heart was changed, and he began to see things in a whole new way. Exactly what happens when anyone (you) makes a/the decision to believe and obey what God has placed before us in his word (Bible), which leads us back to what we discovered in our last chapter regarding God's word being "the rock" which leads a person to salvation. Salvation! What is salvation, you ask? The dictionary defines "salvation" as the act of saving from harm or loss; the state of being thus saved; deliverance from the power and penalty of sin. In other words, we as human beings are lost and like Marley and Scrooge, we need to have our hearts changed, and that's exactly what the word of God does when we are born again. That is the number 1 key to unlocking the door that leads to the narrow path of life: to be born again. To be filled with the Spirit of God. Remember what God's word (the rock) says about the fact that God is a Spirit and those who want to worship Him must, and I want to emphasis, "must," worship in spirit and truth (John 4:24), which begs the question, "What is truth?" This takes us back to the introduction of this book where that same question was asked by Pontius Pilate to Jesus in John 18:38. If you recall, Jesus was being questioned by Pilate because Jesus had ticked off the religious high mucky mucks (forklift operator term) of that time, and they wanted Jesus dead. They wanted him dead, and they were using Pilate as their pawn to get their own way. Pretty much like Satan does in people's lives if they don't have God's spirit living within them. Why do I say that, you ask? I say that because of Jesus' response to Pilate. In verse 37, Pilate asked Jesus a question. The question was whether or not Jesus was a king in which Jesus tells Pilate that he was, but that his kingdom was not of this world (v. 36). What Jesus meant was that his kingdom is not connected to earthly political and national entities nor does it have its origin in the evil world system that is in rebellion against God. You see, Pilate was a part of the world system. Those who were trying to have Jesus killed were part of the world system as well. They were being controlled by the devil, and they didn't even know that they were. They should have known better, but the most ironic part of this whole thing is they didn't! They didn't and yet they were the religious elite. They were the cream of the crop when it came to the things of God. They were the Jewish religious leaders, and they had direct access to God's word and therefore God's truth, but they didn't get it. Jesus was the Jewish Messiah. Jesus was the promised and expected deliverer of the Jewish people foretold throughout the Old Testament, and yet they missed it. In fact, they missed it so much that they were responsible for putting to death their anticipated messiah. How could that have happened, you ask? It happened because they were of their father, "the devil." How so, you ask? Well, for the complete answer to that question, you'll have to move on to the next chapter in our search for the truth, but I can tell you this much. The answer to how the religious elite of Jesus' day missed the fact that Jesus was their messiah comes from the eighth chapter of John's gospel, where Jesus was speaking to those same religious elite where he tells them that God had sent him. The one true God of the universe had sent him to be the light of the world in which anyone who follows him would not walk in darkness but will have the light of life (i.e., narrow path, road). Ahhh! Where did we hear that word before? The light of life! We heard it from the lips of Marley where he was referring to the light of the baby Jesus laying in a manger in Bethlehem. He was referring to the very Son of God himself, who is Jesus Christ.

You see, Marley got it, even though it was too late for him. He got it! He understood that Jesus was the light of the world, and he understood that mankind was his business. Business, you say! Yes, I said business! Jesus' business was mankind. I spoke about that earlier in this book where I wrote that Jesus came to seek and to save that which was lost (Luke 19:10). God sent his own Son, Jesus Christ, into this world to save us from the power of the devil's (flesh) deceptions and Marley got it. The question is, have you? Have you got it, or are you like the religious elite of Jesus' day (Pharisees)? Oh, by the way, the Pharisees told Jesus that they only had one father and that was God (John 8:40), in which Jesus replies to them saying, "If God were your Father, you would love Me, for I proceeded forth and came from God; nor have I come of Myself, but He sent Me. Why do you not understand My speech? Because you are not able to listen to My word [i.e., the rock] You are of your father the devil, and the desires of your father you want to do. He was a murderer from the beginning, and does not stand in the truth, because there is no truth in him." Once again, Jesus said, "I am the way, the truth, and the life. No one comes to the Father except through Me. If you had known Me, you would have known My Father also; and from now on you know Him and have seen Him" (John 8:19 and 14:6).

Question: Do you want to know God? Do you want to understand God's speech (his word)? Do you want to know how to find the narrow path that leads to eternal life? There's only one way that that can happen. You must be born again. And in our next chapters, we're going to start looking at a man who was among the religious elite of Jesus' day and needed just that. He needed to be born again. He wanted to know more about God's kingdom, and I truly believe he knew his very soul was at stake, and he knew in his heart that only Jesus held the answers to his questions. But then again, please keep in mind, I'm just a forklift operator. After all, what do I know?

CHAPTER 9

Born Again

*Jesus answered and said to him, "Most assuredly, I say to you, unless
one is born again, he cannot see the kingdom of God."*
—John 3:3

IN OUR LAST chapter of our search for the truth, we started
taking a look at the question, "Who are the poor and destitute
among us today?" I say that because as I stated in our last chapter, the
question of who one considers as poor and destitute really boils down to
the word "perspective." In this chapter, we're going to start taking a look
at a man who, from his perspective, was right on the same page with God.
He thought he was on the narrow path that would lead him straight to
heaven, but what he discovered was that he was on the wrong path. He
was traveling on the wide path that would ultimately lead him to his ruin
and his destruction. The worst part about it was he was a man of God. He
was of the religious elite of his time. He was the cream of the crop as far as
religion and God goes. He was one of the religious mucky mucks (forklift
operator term), but yet, as he learned, he was not serving the one true God
of the universe; but he was serving the god of this world, the devil. He
was one of the poor and destitute among us and from his perspective, he
thought he was one of God's representatives. How about your perspective,
my friend? Are you serving God, or are you serving the devil? As I said, it
all depends on perspective.

Perspective: the dictionary defines the word "perspective" like this: the
art of depicting or drawing objects so as to give the impression of distance
and depth; the manner in which objects appear to the eye in respect to
their relative positions and distance; a broad view of events or ideas in their
true nature and relationships. Another way of looking at the question is
not only who are the poor and destitute among us today but also who were
the poor and destitute in the past as well? I say that because if we find out
who were the poor and destitute in the past, it might help us discover who
are really the poor and destitute among us today, which goes back to what

Marley discovered when he stated that mankind was indeed his business. In fact, not only was it his business, but it also is in fact all our business. I say it is all our business because in terms of mankind, the word "love" is at the very center of mankind, or humanity if you will. How so, you ask? I say it because of what the Bible teaches about the relationship we must have with mankind if we want to have a true relationship with God. If we truly love God, then we will truly love mankind (others). The Bible refers to mankind as our neighbors. In the New Testament book of Matthew 22, we find the words of God's Son (Jesus) when he was asked the question by one of the scribes (lawyer) saying, "'Teacher, which is the great commandment in the law?' In which Jesus replied; 'You shall love the Lord your God with all your heart, with all your soul, and with all your mind.'" This is the first and great commandment. And the second is like it. You shall love your neighbor as yourself.'" On these two commandments hang all the laws and the prophets. "Thus Jesus subsumes man's whole moral duty under two categories; love for God, and love for one's neighbors (mankind)."

Question: What is love? What does it mean to love someone or something? What did Jesus mean when he said that our love for God and our love for our neighbors (people) must coexist together. Who are our neighbors, and why should our neighbors have anything to do with our love for God (Jesus)? Well, the answer to those questions, I think we first have to establish what love is. I say that because from what I've witnessed in my life, I truly believe most people don't really know what the word "love" means. Furthermore, seeing I've been on both sides of the roads of this life (narrow path and wide path), one cannot fully understand what love really is until a person has been born again. Born again, you say. Yes, I said born again, born of God's Spirit, the indwelling of/by the Holy Spirit of God, the third person of the Trinity (the union or group of three) consisting of the Father (God), Son (Jesus Christ), Holy Spirit (comforter). Jesus referred to the Holy Spirit (also Holy Ghost) as the "comforter" (also referred to as the helper in John 14:26). In other words, the Holy Spirit is really God living within us, and the comforter helps you (anyone who is truly born again) understand the things of God (narrow path) instead of the things of the world (wide path). Now that doesn't mean that the comforter only helps you in the spiritual aspect (invisible things), but he will also help you discern or separate what is of God (narrow path) and what is of the world (wide path—devil). He helps you determine the things that are pleasing to God, and he also helps you determine those things that are not pleasing to him. He helps you determine those things that bring glory and honor to God, and he also helps you determine those things that do not bring glory and honor to him. How so, you ask? He does it by the means of the grief (Ephesians 4:30) that you feel when you do something that is against God's word (the rock). When a person is truly born again, God places his seal upon them (you); and they (you) become redeemed or placed back into God's favor and therefore no longer do they (you) walk in the darkness of this world (wide path). Now that doesn't mean that a person will never do anything that goes against God's word, but when they do, they will be grieved by the Holy Spirit that now lives within them. In other words, God's Spirit takes over your life, and his Spirit (the comforter/helper) now lives within you, and you begin life all over again. You are born again. The only difference is now you are controlled by God's Spirit (the comforter), and you now live in the light of God's truth. You become as we discussed in an earlier chapter: a son of God; and when you become a son of God, then you receive the power. What power, you ask, the power to overcome those things that would/will keep you from having a relationship with God. The power to overcome the sins and trespasses that keep you separated from him, those things that lead you to destruction on the wide path of life. In the New Testament, there are a couple scripture verses that really address this transformation or change (power) that takes place in a person's life once they are born again. This change takes you from traveling the wide path that leads to destruction (hell) and puts you on the narrow path that leads to life (heaven). This transformation (power) also starts to take away the fear that keeps us (you) as human beings in bondage. Bondage you say. Yes, I said bondage. You see, we are bound by fear and this is one of the enemy's (devil/Satan) greatest weapons. In comparison, if we are being controlled by God's Spirit (the comforter), we will walk in love; and therefore, we will have the power to overcome the bondage of fear. God's Spirit will equip us with the power to overcome the snare of fear by and through the power of love which is God's greatest attribute. It is his greatest attribute; and when a person is truly born again of God's spirit (comforter), they will have that characteristic as well. They will need that characteristic to overcome the wide path that everyone (human being) who isn't born again is on. They will need that characteristic because once they receive God's spirit (comforter) and become a son of God; they will come under direct attack of the wicked one. And that wicked one is no other than our adversary, the devil who walks about seeking who he may devour (1 Peter 5:8). This takes us back to a previous chapter where I spoke about putting on the whole armor of God. You see, unless a person is truly born again, they can't begin to see the spiritual battles that are being waged all around them (us). Also in an earlier chapter, I spoke about how the god of this world, the devil, has blinded people so they can't understand the things of God. He is an expert at the skillful art of deception. He is a liar and the ultimate deceiver; and unless a person is truly born again with God's Spirit (the comforter), they (you) will never be able to overcome the devil's deception. While God's Spirit is one of love, the devil's spirit is one of fear and deception. As we are told in 1 Peter 5:8, our adversary, the devil, roams about seeking whom he may devour, and we are commanded to resist him in the next verse (v. 9) How? How can we resist him (devil) by steadfast faith? By faith in Jesus Christ, which can only be achieved with and by the help of God's Spirit living within us (you, i.e., the comforter/helper)?

I think the New Testament books of John 14 and Acts 1 and 2 really describe the truths of the comforter the best. In fact, the 14th chapter of John was written to Jesus' followers (disciples) to comfort them as Jesus knew that his time on earth was drawing near. Jesus knew he was going to die, and he wanted to teach them that after his death his Father (God) would send the Holy Spirit to indwell in them. The Holy Spirit would energize the hearts and minds of the apostles in their ministries helping them to produce the New Testament scriptures. I say that because at this particular point of Jesus' time on this earth, the books of the New Testament had not yet been written. That's why it was so essential for God to send the comforter to Christ's apostles. It was essential because if the apostles didn't have the comforter (God Spirit) living within them, they could have never written the words that they wrote without the help of the comforter (i.e., God's Spirit). And if they had never written those words, people (disciples or followers of Christ) would not have known the heart of God Almighty nor would they have been able to find the narrow path that leads to life eternal (heaven). We would have been left in our trespasses and sins, and we would have never known the things (heart) of God nor would we as human beings had known how to get back into a right relationship with him. We don't have enough time to get into all of this in our search for the truth, but in a nutshell (forklift operator term), you can read more about this in the New Testament book of Acts 1 and 2. There is quite a bit there, but the gist of what we're looking at is found in chapter 1 verse 8 where Jesus told his followers (apostles/disciples) that they would receive power when the Holy Spirit (God's Spirit) has come upon them. The comforter, the helper, who is God's Spirit living within anyone who truly believes in his Son, Jesus Christ. You see, the key element to unleashing the comforter, the helper, God's Spirit in your life really boils down to one word: belief. Yes, I said belief, belief in the one true Son of God who was (and still is) Jesus Christ. As we've been searching for the truth in this book, so too were Christ's apostles searching for the truth as well. The truth is they couldn't know the truth at this point. They couldn't know the truth because the truth teller wasn't within them yet. How do I know that, you ask? I know it because of what Jesus told them in his words where he said in John 14:25 and 26, "These things I have spoken to you while being present with you. But the Helper, the Holy Spirit, whom the Father will send in My name [Jesus], He [comforter/helper] will teach you all things, and bring to your remembrance all things that I said to you." You see, Jesus knew that the apostles couldn't understand all the things Jesus was telling them, but he knew that the time would come when they would. And that time would come after Jesus ascended back from where he came, heaven. The Holy Spirit (comforter), when manifested within them, would energize the hearts and minds of the apostles in their ministry, helping them to produce the New Testament scriptures and thus fulfill their appropriate ministries. The disciples had failed to understand many things about Jesus and what he taught, but because of this supernatural working of God's Spirit (comforter/helper), they came to an inerrant (free from error) and accurate understanding of the Lord Jesus Christ and his work. Likewise in verse 29, Jesus told his followers, "And now I have told you before it comes, that when it does come to pass, you may believe." What was Jesus speaking about? He was speaking of a time after he was put to death that is known in the world of Christendom as the day of Pentecost, the day that the power of the Holy Spirit was released into all mankind so that all those who truly believe in the Son of God (Jesus Christ) may/might be saved. Saved from what, you ask? Saved from the wrath of God's judgment. What judgment, the judgment on all of those who reject God's Son, Jesus Christ (You can read more about this judgment in the New Testament book of Revelation, the last book of the Bible, which was written by the Apostle John while he was in exile on the small, barren island of Patmos, located in the Aegean Sea southwest of the city of Ephesus).

We'll be taking a look at this judgment a little later as we continue on our search for the truth, but for now it's important for you to know that there are multitudes of people in the world today who don't believe in God's judgment. They believe that the one true God of the universe is a God of love and not a God of judgment. However, that is not true, and I truly believe that that kind of thinking is exactly what the devil would have people believe. I believe in today's world that kind of thinking has been deeply fueled by the great deceiver himself, and multitudes of people are caught in that deception. Many think they are on the narrow path to heaven when they are really traveling on the wide path that will ultimately lead to their destruction. This is true in the secular world, and it is also true in the religious world today. What do I mean by the religious world? Well, for the answer to that question, I would have to write another book; but as far as this book is concerned, and as we continue on our search for the truth, when I refer to the religious world, I'm speaking of the world of Christendom or Christianity. In other words, I'm speaking of those who claim the name of Jesus Christ and claim to follow his teachings that are revealed to mankind by and through the Holy Bible (God's word), better known as Christianity, which is defined in the dictionary as the Christian religion, including the Catholic, Protestant, and Eastern Orthodox churches; the state (condition) of being a Christian. This begs another question. What does it mean to be a Christian? And why would I want to be a Christian and a follower of Jesus Christ instead of a member of some other religious group? And that, my friend, is a great question. In fact, that is one of the most important questions a person can or will ever ask themselves. How do you know that, you ask? I know it because that was probably the most important question I have ever asked myself. Why would I (you) choose and desire to be a Christian instead of being a member of some other religious organization? Why would I want to be a follower of this so-called Son of God by the name of Jesus Christ? Why would I follow and believe the teachings of this Jesus instead of some other person who is at the heart of those other religious sects? My friend, those are the most important questions you will ever ask yourself. They are the most important questions of our (your) life. In forklift operator terms, they are indeed the sixty-four-dollar questions of this life. Why? Because it is the answers to these questions that determine whether a person (you) will ever find the narrow gate/way that leads to life (heaven) or will you remain on the wide path/way that leads to destruction (hell). So what is the answer, you ask? Why would I want to follow this Jesus instead of others? Answer: Because he (Jesus Christ) is the only one who holds the key that unlocks the door to the pathway that leads to heaven. He (Jesus) is the only one that the God of this universe finds acceptable in his (God's) sight to atone for the transgressions or offenses or sins that we covered in a previous chapter. If you remember, we spoke about the fact that God is holy and perfect. He is holy and perfect, and no one can approach him unless they are holy and perfect as well. The problem lies in the fact that we as human beings are not perfect and holy, and God knows that. But because he knows that he gave us all a way of being able to approach him and that is by and through the sanctifying work of Jesus Christ. Question: What do I mean by the sanctifying work of Jesus Christ? Well, the word "sanctify" is defined in the dictionary as such: to make holy; to purify or free from sin; to give sanction to. In other words, once a person truly believes in his heart that Jesus Christ was (is) indeed the Son of God and that he (Jesus) died on a/the cross for their sins (transgressions against God's standards) and truly repents (asks for God's forgiveness), then that person is then considered by God as being sanctified (holy and perfect). And when this process of sanctification is conceived, then and only then, is a person seen as being holy and perfect in the eyes of God, and God then sets in place the indwelling of his Spirit (i.e., comforter/helper—Holy Spirit) in their lives. I think we can get a clearer picture of this as it is written in the New Testament book of 2 Timothy 2, where the Apostle Paul speaks about the seal that God places upon those who are truly his because of their belief in Jesus Christ. Beginning in verse 19 of chapter 2 we read, "Nevertheless the solid foundation of God stands, having this seal: 'The Lord knows those who are His,' and, 'Let everyone who names the name of Christ depart from iniquity (wickedness).'" But in a great house, there are not only vessels of gold and silver, but also of wood and clay, some for honor and some for dishonor. Therefore if anyone cleanses himself from the latter, he will be a vessel for honor, sanctified and useful for the Master (God) prepared for every good work.

You see, what I discovered in my search for the truth is that when a person is truly born again, they become vessels of gold and silver. When God places his seal upon those who truly believe in his Son, Jesus Christ, that person is seen as a vessel (person) of gold and silver in the eyes of God; and God begins to prepare that person (vessel) for every good work that the Holy Spirit will guide that person to do. In other words, when God's seal is placed upon those who name Jesus Christ as their Lord and Savior and truly repents of their crimes toward God, they can then begin their journey on the narrow path that leads to life eternal (heaven). But wait! Paul tells about the good vessels, which are defined as gold and silver, but he also speaks of another kind of vessel. What is that vessel, you ask? It is the one found in verse 20 where it says that in a great house, there are not only vessels of gold and silver but there are also vessels made of wood and clay. What do those vessels made of wood and clay represent, you ask? Well, for the answer to that question, you'll have to move on to the next chapter.

However, before you move on, I will tell you this much. So far in our search for the truth, we've touched on some pretty heavy stuff, especially if you're not a true Christian. I say that because the fact is if you've never been born again, you're not really a follower of Jesus Christ, and you are still living a life that is apart from God. You are living your life on the wide path (Matthew 7:13) that will lead to your ultimate destruction; and unless you find the narrow path (Matthew 7:14) that leads to life eternal, you will spend eternity apart from God. If your name is not found in the Book of Life (Revelation 20:15), you will be cast into what the Bible calls the Lake of Fire (same verse). It is a place described by Jesus Christ himself as a place of outer darkness (Matthew 8:12). It is also described as a place of torment (Revelation 14:11). If you recall, it is kind of like what Marley was going through when he came to warn Ebenezer Scrooge of his pending doom if he didn't change his ways. Marley was being tormented by the choices he had made when he was alive, and one of the biggest torments he was dealing with was the fact that he rejected the Son of God who is Jesus Christ. You see, I can very much relate to the message that Marley was bringing to Scrooge. In what way, you ask? I can relate to Marley's plea to Scrooge because the same plea (warning) that Marley gave to his friend Ebenezer Scrooge is the same warning I'm giving to you, my friend. And what is that warning, you ask? It is the same one that Marley had missed when he was still alive. It is the one that tormented him the most. Remember Marley's words from a previous chapter (chapter 7) where he said, "Why did I walk through crowds of fellow-beings with my eyes turned down, and never raise them to that blessed Star which led the Wise Men to a poor abode!" As we discovered previously, the star Marley was speaking of was the one that led the Wise Men to the manger and birthplace of Jesus Christ. Marley had rejected God's only begotten Son and was in a place of torment and suffering, and his fate was sealed for eternity. Marley never found the narrow path that leads to life, but you don't have to meet that same fate, my friend. That is one of the reasons I truly believe God has called me to write this book. I say that because God doesn't want to see anyone perish, but he desires that all should come to repentance (2 Peter 3:9 and 10) and give their hearts and lives to him by and through his Son, Jesus Christ. That is God's desire for you, and it is also his warning as well. Will you listen to that warning, my friend? Will you raise your eyes and heart to that blessed Star that leads to life (Jesus Christ), or will you be like Marley and be tormented forever at life's end because you traveled your life on the wide path of this life (world)? It is a simple question, my friend, but as it is a simple question, it is the most important question of this (your) life. Are you listening to me, my friend? Marley understood it, but for him it was too late. Now the story of Marley and Scrooge is really what many would consider as a secular story. What I mean by a secular story is that a secular story would be a story that the world (wide path) might relate to. It is a story that more than likely doesn't have any religious implications or appearance in the story. I mention that fact because what I have discovered in my search for the truth is that nearly everything I (we/you) do in life really does have a religious implication attached to/with it. You may not think so, but please believe me, it does. How so, you ask? I say that because of what I have learned in God's word (Bible) where it says, "So then each of us shall give account of himself to God" (Romans 14:12). Likewise in 1 Peter 4:5, we read, "They [every person] will give an account to Him [God] who is ready to judge the living and the dead." And then this one which has huge implications from the Son of God (Jesus) which says, "But I say to you that for every idle word men may speak, they will give account of it in the day of judgment" (Matthew 12:36). Question: What did Jesus mean when he said that every idle word men may speak they will give account of it? What was Jesus speaking of? Well, first of all, you must know that Jesus was speaking to those who thought they were the most religious people of that day. He was speaking to a group of so-called religious people known as the Pharisees. It is also important for you to know that the Son of God (Jesus) spoke some of his most severe words to this group of people. He called them such things as hypocrites, blind guides, liars, fools, and extortionists (abuse of authority). He said that they were like whitewashed tombs on the outside, but inside, they were full of dead men's bones and all uncleanness (Matthew 23). In other words, they appeared to be pure and clean and very religious in their outer appearance, but on the inside (in their hearts), they were full of hypocrisy and lawlessness (without regard for the law). Whose law, you ask? The law of God's standard (holiness) that can only be achieved by and through the renewing of one's mind through the process of being born again of God's Spirit. You see, the Pharisees were deceived. They were being used by the great deceiver, the devil, and they didn't even know that they were. The devil had them right in his snare and as Jesus said, "They were indeed full of dead men's bones and the snare of hypocrisy and lies were embedded deep within their hearts." They were supposed to be the representatives of the one true God of the universe, but instead they were representatives of the god of this world, the devil himself. How do you know that, you ask? Once again, I know it because of what the Son of God (Jesus) told them in the New Testament book of John 8:44, "You are of your father the devil, and the desires of your father you want to do." But then again, please keep in mind, I'm just a forklift operator. After all, what do I know?

CHAPTER 10

The Mystery of God's Kingdom

> And Jesus said to them, "To you it has been given to know the
> mystery of the kingdom of God; but to those who are outside,
> all things come in parables, so that "Seeing they may see and not
> perceive, And hearing they may hear and not understand; Lest they
> should turn, And their sins be forgiven them."
> —Mark 4:11 and 12

AS I STATED in the last chapter, so far we've touched on some pretty heavy stuff in our search for the truth of this life, when I said that I followed that statement by saying; especially if you're not a true Christian. Now when I say that, I mean if you've never truly been born again of God's Spirit as we discovered in our last chapter, the new birth that must accompany those who wish to see the kingdom of God (John 3:3). I say that because if you've never been born again of God's Spirit, then you won't be able to understand the wisdom of God and the mysteries that surround his kingdom. Did you say mysteries? Yes, I said mysteries! Why would God use a mystery for people to find his kingdom? And that's a very good question. In fact, it's one of the questions I asked myself back when I first started my search for the truth. Well, for the complete answer to that question, it would take a lot more time than we have here; but for now I'll try and unmask the best and simplest way I can.

First of all, if you take a good look at the scripture verse from Mark 4:11, you will see that Jesus used the words, "To you it has been given." Now the first thing we have to understand who is Jesus speaking to and what is the context of his teaching? Who is the "to you" Jesus is speaking of in this scripture verse? I say that because when Jesus was speaking these words, he was speaking before multitudes of people including the disciples. Even though there were multitudes of people there that day to hear Jesus' words, the words he was speaking could and would only be understood by those who were deemed as being on the inside of God's kingdom. How so, you ask? I say that because of what Jesus said. He said, "To you it has been given to know the mystery of the kingdom of God," and then he uses the word "but," "but to those who are outside." All things come in parables. Jesus was speaking about those who were on the outside of God's kingdom or on the wide path if you will. What is a parable, you ask? A parable as defined in the dictionary is a short story designed to convey a truth or moral lesson. In other words, Jesus used parables to speak to those whose hearts had truly turned away from their wicked ways and truly repented of their sins against God's standards (laws). They believed that Jesus truly was the Son of God, and that by truly believing that they could be saved from the destruction, they were facing by having their sins forgiven because of Jesus' ultimate death on a/the cross. How do you know that, you ask? I know it because of what the Bible says regarding the heart to the saints, to those who have true faith (belief) in Jesus Christ. Those who truly follow Jesus Christ and have been born again of God's Spirit will begin to have the mysteries of God revealed to them. The parables Jesus told were designed to express the truths of God's kingdom to those whose hearts had been truly changed. To those who have truly found the narrow path of God's kingdom become true saints and the mysteries that surround Christ and his true church begin to be revealed. How do you know that, you ask? I know it because God has revealed those mysteries to me by faith and also by/through his word (Bible). In the New Testament book of the Apostle Paul's letter to the saints (a person deemed as being holy and acceptable in God's eyes) in the city of Ephesus we read these words; how that by revelation (something that is/was revealed that was not known before) he (God) made known to me the mystery (as I have briefly written already, by which, when you read, you may understand my knowledge in the mystery of Christ), which in other ages was not made known to the sons of men, as it has now been revealed by the Spirit (i.e., God's Spirit/comforter from our truth search in chapter 9) to his holy apostles (followers/messengers) and prophets that the Gentiles (people who are not Jewish—such as this forklift operator) should be fellow heirs, of the same body, and partakers of his promise in Christ through the gospel, of which I became a minister according to the gift of the grace of God given to me by the effective working of his power (Ephesians 3:3-7). Notice the last two words that Paul uses—his power! Do those words sound familiar? They should because I spoke about that in an earlier chapter (chapter 6) regarding that power. What power, you ask? Whose power, you ask? The power of God! The effective working of his power comes into play in a person's life when a person truly believes and receives Jesus Christ into their heart as their personal Lord and Savior (John 1:12 and 13). They (you) become a new creation in Christ (God). Their (your) old life is gone and a new life dedicated to God's Son, Jesus Christ, becomes the very center of their being. They (You) become an ambassador (representative) of God's Son, Jesus Christ, by and through the power given to them when they truly receive and believe that Jesus Christ bore our sins by dying on that Roman cross for us. When we truly believe this in our hearts, we become reconciled (acceptable) back to God because of our belief and imputes upon us the ministry of reconciliation (God's will to be reconciled with sinners), or if you will, those who are traveling on the wide path of this life. The Apostle Paul knew this, and he knew it because he experienced it personally in his own life. He wrote about it in the New Testament book of 2 Corinthians 5:16-18, "Therefore, from now on, we regard no one according to the flesh." Even though we have known Christ according to the flesh, yet now we know him thus no longer. Here, Paul was teaching that once a person is born again they take on the new nature of God/Jesus Christ, which is spiritual. He speaks of the flesh of Christ here because at that time, the ones Paul was speaking to had seen the physical Jesus before he was crucified on the Roman cross. He then goes on to say, "Therefore, if anyone [that's anyone folks] is in Christ, he is a new creation; old things [he wide path] have passed away; behold [look/see] all things have become new." Now all things are of God, who has reconciled us to himself through Jesus Christ and has given us the ministry of reconciliation (Paul is referring to the power he received from God when he was reconciled [born again] with God); another word for this would be salvation or deliverance or rescue or escape. In other words God made a way for us to escape the destruction we are all facing by sending his Son Jesus Christ to earth to pay the price we as human beings could not pay. We could not reconcile our way back to God because we are not holy and perfect in God's sight until we are truly born again (we studied that in chapter 7). As Paul puts it, "a new creation; our old life is gone [wide path] and a new life has begun [narrow path]." You see at one time the Apostle Paul was also traveling on the wide path of destruction, and he was an enemy of God. In the New Testament book of James chapter 4, it reads that friendship with the world (wide path) is enmity with God. Paul was an enemy of God (Christ) at one time. He was an enemy of God (Christ), and he didn't even know it. In fact, not only was he an enemy of God (Christ), but he was a follower of the devil (John 8:44). How do you know that, you ask? I know it because before he became a follower (born again) of Jesus Christ; he was a member of the most religious sect in all of Israel, the Pharisees. And if you remember from our previous chapter (chapter 9), you will remember that God's Son, Jesus Christ, unleashed his most severe words on the Pharisees. In fact, in his own words, the Apostle Paul said in Acts 26 when appearing before a king named Agrippa that he himself had lived his life as a Pharisee from his youth (v. 5). He goes on further to tell that he thought that he must do many things contrary to the name of Jesus of Nazareth (v. 9). He goes on to tell that it was he who cast his vote against the saints (born-again believers in Christ) to have them put in prison and yes, even have them put to death (v. 10). He was so enraged with them that he severely persecuted them and forced them to commit blaspheme by renouncing their faith in Jesus Christ (v. 11). If you read further on in the twenty-sixth chapter of Acts, you will discover how this persecutor of God's people (saints) was visited by the Lord Jesus Christ from heaven after he died on the Roman cross. Jesus confronted Paul (whose name at that time was Saul) and told him that by persecuting the saints, he was persecuting him (Jesus) (v. 15). Now there is much, much more to this story, and it is one you will have to search for yourself; but before we leave this part of our journey, I would like to take a look at one more thing regarding the mystery of God's kingdom. I say that because it is the issue, and/or mystery of the new birth (born again), that is really where the journey on the narrow path to heaven begins. In other words, as we discovered earlier in this chapter, the mysteries and/or knowledge with regard to Jesus Christ cannot begin to be revealed to someone until and unless they are truly born again of God's Spirit.

Question: Who was this Paul I've been speaking about since we began this book in our search for the truths of this life? Why do I say that Paul was an enemy of God? And notice I said, was. Well, that's a good question. And it is one that we're going to spend some time looking at. I say we're going to spend some time looking at because as we continue on the narrow path of our search for the truth, Paul the Apostle is probably the one person in all of God's word (Bible) who was allowed to see and understand the mysteries of God's kingdom the most. Why was that? Why did God allow Paul to see the mysteries of his kingdom the most? Answer: I happen to believe it's because of God's grace. Yes, I said grace. You see, the word "grace" in the dictionary is defined as elegance or beauty of form, manner, or motion; a pleasing or attractive quality; favor or goodwill; mercy or clemency; favor shown in granting a delay; the freely given, unmerited favor and love of God; the condition of being in God's favor; to favor or honor. Notice that one of the definitions used is the freely given, unmerited favor and love of

God. Did you catch what it says? The freely given, unmerited favor and love of God. But wait! Didn't I say that Paul persecuted and even put to death the saints (followers) of Jesus Christ? Didn't I say that Paul even got them to renounce their faith in Jesus Christ? Didn't I say that the Apostle Paul was an enemy of God? Answer: Yes, I did. But the questions we have asked here are the ones that I truly believe are the main reason I (and possibly you) would want to follow a God like this. Why, you ask? You see, we look at a person such as Paul and ask why would God use someone like this to be one of his representatives? Why would God use a man like this to be an ambassador to represent his kingdom? Why would God place his grace on someone like that? After all, he certainly didn't deserve it (in our eyes). If God is God then he should have destroyed Paul, but instead he (God) poured out his grace and ultimately his blessings on to Paul. Why did he do that? Answer: Because the God of the Holy Bible is a God of love. In fact, one of the most well-known verses in all of scripture (Christendom) is found in the New Testament book of John 3:16 where it says, "For God so loved the world that He gave His only begotten Son, that whoever believes in Him should not perish but have everlasting life." Now you say, well, that's a pretty straightforward teaching. In fact, maybe you've reached this far in this book and possibly the God of the Bible has begun to open your eyes to some of his truths. Maybe he's begun to open your eyes and your heart and you're saying, "Hey, this Christian thing is pretty easy. According to this verse here, all I have to do is believe in Jesus and I won't perish [go to hell], but I'll have everlasting life in heaven." In other words, "I'm going to heaven if I only believe that Jesus was God's only begotten Son." However, what I have discovered in my personal search for the truth is that the world of Christendom loves to refer to this verse because the words really put in to proper perspective the ultimate love of God, but there are very few who claim these words that even know who these words were directed to. In other words, though this is the most well-known verse in all of Christianity, multitudes, and I mean multitudes, of those who claim Jesus Christ as their personal Lord and Savior do not know who these words were directed to in the first fifteen verses. In fact, not only do they not know who the person was that these words were directed to, multitudes don't even know what it means to be born again, and therefore cannot begin to understand the mysteries of God's kingdom. They are stuck on the wide path that leads to destruction and have never encountered the fullness of God's grace because they are like the Apostle Paul once was. They too are enemies of God, and their father is also the devil. How so, you ask? Well, for the answer to that question, you'll have to move on to the next chapter; but before we (you) move on, I will tell you this much. The person Jesus was speaking to in the first fifteen verses that come before this most well-known verse in all Christendom just so happened to be a Pharisee also. In other words, he too was a member of the most religious sect in all of Israel. In fact, not only was he a member of the Pharisees, but he was also a contemporary of the Apostle Paul (Saul). What I mean by contemporary is that both the Apostle Paul and this man were living at the same time as Jesus Christ. They were both Pharisees, and I truly believe not only were they both Pharisees, but that they knew each other. I also believe they were both given the same opportunity to believe that Jesus Christ was indeed the very Son of God. The grace of God was extended to both of them, but did they both become followers and representatives of Jesus Christ? Who was this other man? What was his name? Answer: His name was Nicodemus. In fact, we are first introduced to this man at the beginning of John 3:1 where it says in God's word, "There was a man of the Pharisees named Nicodemus, a ruler of the Jews. This man came to Jesus by night and said to Him, 'Rabbi [meaning teacher] we know that You are a teacher come from God; for no one can do these signs that You do unless God is with him" (v. 2). And then Jesus hits this Pharisee named Nicodemus right between the eyes and gets right to the very point (heart) of Nicodemus's problem when Jesus says, "Most assuredly, I say to you, unless one is born again, he cannot see the kingdom of God." And then Nicodemus and Jesus get into a back-and-forth discussion regarding what really is a mystery, the mystery of the new birth that really is at the center of being able to see into God's kingdom. How do you know that, you ask? I know it because of what Jesus said in his own words. He said, "unless one is born again, he cannot see the kingdom of God." And I will add that the mysteries of the kingdom of God can only be given (revealed) to a person by the effective working of His (God's) power (Ephesians 3:7) that comes through true belief in God's Son, Jesus Christ. You see, what I have discovered in my personal pursuit of the truth of this life is that the words "born again" are probably the most misunderstood mysteries in all of the word of God (Bible). I say that because of what God has revealed to me in my personal walk down the narrow path of this life and the mystery of the new birth. To be born again. In fact, the issue of the new birth is one of the main reasons God called me to be like the Apostle Paul. I was called to be a minister. Minister, you say? Yes, I said minister. But please keep in mind there are two kinds of ministers in this world: ministers called by the one true God of the Bible to reveal the truth (narrow path), and there are ministers of the devil/Satan who are known as deceitful workers. How do you know that, you ask? I know it because it says so in God's word (Bible). But then again, please keep in mind, I'm just a forklift operator. After all, what do I know?

CHAPTER 11

Fruit Inspectors

For such are false apostles, deceitful workers, transforming
themselves into apostles of Christ. For Satan himself transforms
himself into an angel of light. Therefore it is no great thing if his
ministers also transform themselves into ministers of righteousness,
whose end will be according to their works.
—2 Corinthians 11:13-15

I N OUR LAST chapter, we began to uncover some of the mysteries
of God's kingdom. We discovered that to really fully understand
those mysteries, it is essential to be born again. To be born again by and
through the renewing of your mind (Romans 12:2). Now you may be
asking yourself, "Why do I have to have my mind renewed?" Well, whether
you realize it or not, if your mind isn't transformed (changed), you will
never understand what the will of God is. And if you can't understand what
the will of God is, then you will never be able to present your body (your
life) as a living sacrifice that is holy and acceptable to him (Romans 12:1).
Did you say living sacrifice? Yes, I said living sacrifice! You see, to fully
understand the mysteries of God's kingdom, you must be willing to give up
your life to/for him. You must be a sacrificial lamb that is referred to in the
Bible as a lamb without blemish and without spot (1 Peter 1:19). To fully
understand this principle, you must understand that when Christ died on
the cross, he became a sacrificial lamb for all of us. If you do the research,
you will find that before Jesus Christ was born and eventually died on
the cross, the requirement for people's sins (transgression against God's
laws/rules) came by/through the sacrificial blood of an animal, preferably
a lamb (Exodus 12:5 and Leviticus 1:2). All of this came about as God
instructed his servant Moses on how to truly worship God in the tabernacle
(a house of worship). The shedding of the animal's blood represented the
purifying of a person's heart before God. All these offerings were forms of
worship to God, to give expression of a penitent and thankful heart. In
the Old Testament, the tabernacle and the temple were the places where

these sacrifices were offered. In the New Testament, these types of offerings were done away with after Christ's death. Jesus Christ was the ultimate lamb without blemish and spot and if we're (you're) truly born again, the blood that Christ shed on the cross takes away our (your) sin(s); and we (you) are now acceptable in the eyes of God. Christ made the ultimate sacrifice for our (your) sins and when you truly believe that in your heart, God will begin a covenant relationship with you personally. You can read a great deal about this covenant relationship in the New Testament book of Hebrews. But regarding the shedding of blood for the remission (forgiveness) of our (your) sins, this is found in Hebrews 9:22. And according to the law, almost all things are purified with blood; and without shedding of blood, there is no remission (forgiveness).You can also read in the Bible where God's word tells us that Jesus was the Lamb of God who takes away the sin of the world (John 1:29 and 36). Jesus was the Lamb of God who willingly sacrificed his life for all who repent of their sins and have their minds renewed (born again) by the power of God's Spirit (the comforter).

Now if you notice, I said that the tabernacle and the temple were the places where the people would go to offer these sacrifices to get right with God. These sacrifices were offered up by those who were supposed to be God's representatives which are known as priests. Now the dictionary defines a priest as a person who performs the religious rites of a deity. In other words, a/the priest is supposed to be a representative of God, and he was actually supposed to be an intercessor between a person and God. In the Old Testament, the priests were the ones who were set apart to intercede or act as a mediator between an individual and God. The priest presented the person's offering (lamb, sheep, etc.) and sacrificed it on the altar (where sacrifices were made to God) so that they would/could be made acceptable again in God's eyes. Their lives would be made pure and acceptable to God because of the animal sacrifice presented by the priest who interceded for that individual person and their sins. So the tabernacle and/or temple would be the place where a person would go to get right with God. In the modern-day world of Christendom, many would consider it to be a/the church. People believe that a building, such as a church, is where God is; and when people go to that building, they believe that they're honoring and worshipping God, when in fact that type of thinking in many instances is a form of idolatry (blind adoration or devotion). How so, you ask? Well, it's the same thing as I stated earlier. Those who were truly God's by faith gave these offerings with an attitude of worship; for the rest, they were external rituals only (kind of like believing a building is where God is). You see, before Christ, there was a whole different set of scenarios of the way God did things in leading up to Jesus' birth. The Old Testament is a guide leading up to Jesus Christ's physical birth, and the New Testament is a guide after Christ was physically born of a virgin named Mary. Though these physical scenarios on the surface might be different, the spiritual scenarios are not. If you get to the gist of what we're trying to discover in our search for the truth, the bottom line is, God knows our hearts. He knows our hearts, and he wants us to realize that we can't save ourselves from ultimate destruction (wide path) on our own. That is why he sent his son, Jesus Christ, to pay the price that we ourselves cannot pay. Now whether or not you realize that or not, that is true love. To think that there is nothing I (we) can do to save myself from hell. Now that, my fellow truth searcher, is some pretty heavy stuff. But not only is that heavy stuff, but to think that the God of this universe would love me (you) enough to send his son to take my place by shedding his blood for me (us) so that I could now be made right with that same God and have eternal life because of it. Now that's real heavy stuff. But you know what? That's the good news of the Bible. But do you know another thing? As there is the good news, there is also the bad news. Bad news, you say? Yes, I said bad news! You see, most everyone likes to hear the good news, but many don't like to hear the bad news. Now you may be asking yourself at this point: "Who in their right mind(s) wouldn't want me to hear good news, who in their right mind would want to keep me from hearing good news instead of bad news?" And that, my friend, is a great question! But what is the answer? The answer is exactly what this book is all about. It's about combating the wiles of the devil who wants to keep you from hearing and believing the good news (truth) about Jesus Christ. The devil wants to keep you on the wide path that will lead you down the path of destruction.

You see, as we've discovered throughout this book, there is a battle going on between God (narrow path) and Satan (wide path). It started in the Garden of Eden when the serpent (devil/Satan) laid a trap for Adam and Eve, and they fell for it, hook, line and sinker. And that deception continues until this very day throughout the human race. The battle between good (God) and evil (Satan) and as we've learned in earlier chapters—the real battles of life—are being fought within the spiritual realm (Ephesians 6:12), the unseen world that is described in 2 Corinthians 4, the unseen world of the invisible rulers and powers of the darkness of this age. What age, you ask? The age described here is referring to the age that exists from the time of Adam and Eve's fall (deception) in the Garden of Eden (Genesis 3) until the second coming of Jesus Christ which is described in the last book of the Bible, the book of Revelation. The bottom line of this whole scenario in a nutshell (forklift operator term) is the devil wants you to go to hell, and God wants you to go to heaven. So the battles rage on. The struggles that have existed throughout the history of mankind comes down to a power struggle for who or whom you will serve—Satan or God. As we discovered in the opening chapters of this book, the God of this world, Satan, wants to cloud your vision (heart) so you can't see or understand the truth of God's word. Satan will use every weapon in his arsenal against you, so you will never find the narrow path that leads to life (heaven). They are known as the fiery darts of the wicked one in Ephesians 6:16. Satan is God's enemy and so are those who have not been born of God's Spirit. With this in mind, there is a question that a true born-again follower of Christ must take into account and that is, "Who are God's friends, and who are God's enemies?" Or better yet, "Am I a friend of God or am I one of his enemies?" I say that because if you're not born again of his Spirit, you are in fact his enemy. You are an enemy of God. How so you ask? You are his enemy, because without the indwelling of his Spirit (as we discussed in chapter 9), you cannot see the things of God (John 3:3). And if you cannot see the things of God, then you are being deceived. Deceived, you say? Yes, I said deceived. Now you might be reading this book, and you may have the attitude that I'm trying to push religion down your throat. Or you might be reading this book and you claim to believe in God. In fact, you may even claim to be a follower of Jesus Christ and in fact belong to a church. You may even be a leader in a church, possibly an elder or a deacon. You may attend Bible study. You may have been baptized as a child. You may have been confirmed in the church. Maybe you've attended church all your life and attended church school as a child. Possibly you're even a pastor or a minister. But do you know what? You might be deceived! How so, you ask? I say it because just like those people who brought their animals to be sacrificed by the priests in the Old Testament, if your heart isn't right with God, all you're doing is going through the externalities (motions) of what you consider a (your) religion. The scriptures are literally full of examples of people who thought they were right with God when in fact they were deceived. If you go through the whole Bible, you will see that multitudes have been deceived by what they thought was their religion. One thing I have learned in my search for the truth is that religion is just a word. Most everyone claims to be religious. But the question remains, "Who is at the heart of their religion, God or Satan? And if they claim to be a true follower of the one true God of this universe (Jesus Christ), how can one (you) know if their religion is the right one?" I believe the words of Jesus himself answers that question when he said, "Beware of false prophets, who come to you in sheep's clothing, but inwardly they are ravenous wolves. You will know them by their fruits" (Matthew 7:15-20). Question: What did Jesus mean when he said, "You will know them by their fruits?" What fruits? What were or what are the fruits that Jesus was speaking of? Well, first of all, you must know that the you he is speaking about here is referring to anyone who is a true follower of his. They have been born of God's Spirit and therefore they can and will know the qualities that that person shows in their life. In other words, a true believer will know if a person is a true believer by what they do instead of what they say. The reference Jesus is using here refers to a person's heart. A true believer must understand that they are to be fruit inspectors. Jesus calls a true believer to be a fruit inspector. But you ask what are the fruits that a true believer is called to inspect? What is the fruit inspector's guide? Answer: The word of God, which is the holy—Bible. When you do an examination of a true believer's life, do their actions line up with God's words? Far too often in today's world, there are multitudes of people who claim to be a true follower of God (Jesus Christ), but their actions do not line up with the truth of God's word (Bible). In other words, they give God lip service. It reminds me of the words of Jesus when he was speaking to the religious elite of his time (scribes and Pharisees) where he said to them in Matthew 15:7-9, "Hypocrites! Well did Isaiah prophesy about you, saying; These people draw near to Me with their mouth, And honor Me with their lips, But their heart is far from Me, Teaching as doctrines the commandments of men." Jesus also said to those same people, "Hypocrites! For you cleanse the outside of the cup and dish [outer appearance], but inside [in their hearts] they are full of extortion and self-indulgence" (Matthew 23:25). "Hypocrites! For you are like whitewashed tombs which indeed appear beautiful outwardly, but inside [their hearts] are full of dead men's bones and all uncleanness. Even so you also outwardly appear righteous to men, but inside [their hearts] you are full of hypocrisy and lawlessness" (Matthew 23:27 and 28). "Hypocrites! For you travel land and sea to win one proselyte [convert], and when he is won [converted], you make him twice as much a son of hell as yourselves" (Matthew 23:15). And "Hypocrites! Because you build the tombs of prophets of the righteous, and say, 'If we had lived in the days of our fathers, we would not have been partakers with them in the blood of the prophets. Therefore you are witnesses against yourselves that you are sons of those who murdered the prophets." (In other words, they plotted to discredit and kill God's true messengers and tried to say they didn't and wouldn't). They were deceived! Furthermore, Jesus says to them, "Fill up, then, the measure of your father's guilt. Serpents, brood of vipers! How can you escape the condemnation of hell? Therefore, indeed, I send you prophets, wise men, and scribes: some of them you will kill and crucify, and some of them you will scourge [a whip used on human beings to punish or criticize severely] in your synagogues [churches] and persecute from city to city, that on you may come all the righteous blood shed on the earth, from the blood of righteous Abel to the blood of Zechariah, son of Berechiah, whom you murdered between the temple and the altar. Assuredly, I say to you, all these things will come upon this generation" (Matthew 23:29-36).

Now folks, these are not my words; they are the words from the very lips of the son of God himself, Jesus Christ. And they are some pretty cruel and powerful words. But then again, I'm not the least bit surprised. How so, you ask? I say I'm not the least bit surprised because since the time God began to open my eyes to the truth of his kingdom (narrow way), I have learned that the same kind of religious hypocrisy that existed in Jesus' day is also very prevalent in the world today (2011). And please keep one thing in mind as we continue down the path of our search for the truth. These words Jesus spoke were not words spoken to those outside the religious community. They were words that were spoken to those who were in the so-called religious community of that day. They were spoken to those who were supposed to be the representatives of God. They were spoken to those who thought they were serving God. They thought their hearts were right with God. They thought they were traveling on the narrow path to life eternal, but the truth was, they were traveling on the wide path that was leading them to their ultimate destruction. But wait! There is another part to this that is often missed. I say it is missed because in most cases, those who are pondering these words of Jesus don't really consider the totality of what Jesus was saying. How so, you ask? Well, if you do your homework, you will discover that there is a direct connection between what Jesus was saying and what the Apostle Paul's words were teaching us in the scripture we used at the beginning of this chapter. Let's recall what it says. It says that Satan transforms himself into an angel of light. But do you know what? So do his ministers. What is a minister, you ask? In the light of today's religious institutions (church), a minister is primarily a person who is known as the shepherd of a flock. In most religious circles (Christian), the minister is basically the one who teaches people the word of God (Bible). In other words, they are the teachers of God's word, and they are the ones that have usually gone to a seminary (school) to be educated in the ways of God. You can read about this in the fourth chapter of Ephesians where it speaks about the different gifts God (Christ) gives to those in the makeup of the church. What church, you ask? Jesus Christ's church. The church is an extension of what the tabernacle and temple represented before Christ's death. It was a place where the people of God gather together to join in the true sanctuary of God. A sanctuary is a place of refuge, a place of safety, a place to worship God. You see, after Jesus Christ's death on the cross, the physical sanctuary of the temple was replaced by the sanctuary of the heart. In other words, after Christ's death and atonement (punishment) for our (people's) sins, the physical sanctuary (building) was replaced by the sanctuary of the heart. It is a combination, or a gathering if you will, of those who truly follow Jesus Christ and have had their hearts truly sanctified (born again) by God's Spirit. But wait! There is much more to the story. And what is that, you ask? Well, for the answer to that question, you'll have to move on to the next chapter; but before you do, I will tell you this much. The Bible teaches about a spirit that opposes God. It is known as a/the spirit of Antichrist. Antichrist spirit, you say? Yes, I said Antichrist spirit. You see, the spirit of Antichrist is really all about deception. It's about changing the truth of God's word into a lie. In many cases, the deception that comes into people's lives (hearts) are so deceptive that if they (you) don't have God's Spirit living within them, they (you) will not be able to discern or detect what is and what is not an Antichrist spirit. They (you) will be vulnerable just like Adam and Eve in the Garden of Eden, and they too will fall prey to the fiery darts of deception that the wicked one (devil) will throw their (your) way. They too will fall for the devil's snare of deception and swallow it hook, line, and sinker as well. But you say, "Okay Joe, that's well and fine, but what does this whole scenario have to do with our search for the truth?" After all, a church is a church, isn't it? Don't all churches believe in Jesus Christ and follow the Bible? Good question. And do you know what I have discovered in my personal search for the truth? Are you ready for this? Even the devil and his demons believe in Jesus Christ. But you know what? That's why it's so absolutely imperative to be an excellent fruit inspector, especially within a church setting. How so, you ask? I say so because if you do your homework, you will find that from the time of Adam and Eve's fall, the Antichrist spirit has been prevalent throughout the world you and I live in. Satan's seductive spirit has attempted to penetrate and corrupt everything that is of the one true biblical God. And that includes his penetration into Christ's church. But then again, please keep in mind that I'm just a forklift operator. After all, what do I know?

CHAPTER 12

Sincerity

Hypocrite! First remove the plank from your own eye, and then you
will see clearly to remove the speck from your brother's eye.
—Matthew 7:5

I N THE LAST chapter of our search for the truth, we began to take
a look at what it means to be a fruit inspector. In other words, how
can we (you) know what is good fruit and what is bad fruit according to the
word of God? Well, for the answer to that question, I think we have to start
with the words of Jesus that are found in the fifteenth chapter of the New
Testament book of John. Now if you remember from an earlier chapter
(chapter 3), we established that God's son, Jesus Christ, told one of his
disciples (followers), known as Doubting Thomas, that he was the way, the
truth, and the life, and that no one could get to God unless they first came
through him (John 14:5 and 6). In the 15th chapter of John, we read what
I believe is a parallel verse in which Jesus uses a metaphor (figure of speech)
comparing Himself to being a vine. Jesus said, "I am the true vine, and My
Father is the vinedresser. Every branch in Me that does not bear fruit He
takes away; and every branch that bears fruit He prunes, that it may bear
more fruit. You are already clean because of the word which I have spoken
to you. Abide in Me, and I in you. As the branch cannot bear fruit of itself,
unless it abides in the vine, neither can you, unless you abide in Me."

Question: What was Jesus speaking about? What did he mean in this
metaphor regarding him (Jesus) being the vine and his Father (God) being
the vinedresser? Well, for the complete answer to that question, it would
probably take me another book to write; but in a nutshell, a vine has two
types of branches: (1) branches that bear fruit, and (2) branches that do not.
In this teaching, Jesus is referring to the branches that bear fruit being those
who are genuine believers. The branches that do not bear fruit are those
who profess to believe, but their lack of fruit indicates genuine salvation
has never taken place and they have no life in/from the vine (Jesus). If this
is true, and it is, then the Father (God), being the vinedresser, cultivates,

prunes, and cares for the truth of his word, by and through the Holy Spirit (comforter) which dwells within the heart of the true genuine believer. This in turn fits right in with an earlier teaching in the last chapter where Jesus said, "By their fruits you will know them" (Matthew 7:16 and 20). So obviously the fruit Jesus is speaking about is something within a person's life that will help distinguish a true believer from a false believer. Or another way of looking at it is, if you're a true believer and your life has been truly regenerated by God, and the comforter (Holy Spirit) truly lives within you, then the fruits of God will be evident in your life, and you will be able to determine what is a good fruit and what is a bad fruit. But not only will you be able to determine what is a good fruit and what is a bad fruit within your own life, but you will be able to determine what is and what is not a good or bad fruit within the life of others as well. This is true especially within the sanctuary of those hearts who claim to be followers of Jesus Christ (Christians).

Well, by now you may be asking yourself, "This is all well and fine Joe, but what the heck does this mean to me? Why are you spending so much time on the subject of fruit inspecting? Good fruit, bad fruit; what difference does it make?" Answer: It makes a great deal of difference. It makes a great deal of difference because the whole issue of fruit inspecting is at the very core of the Christian faith and the Christian battle. Battle, you say? Yes, I said battle. If you recall, throughout this book, we have been speaking about the battle that is taking place between God and Satan. If you also remember, we learned that everyone that is born begins their lives traveling on the wide path that leads to destruction (Matthew 7:13). In our search for the truth, we have been uncovering ways of how a person can find their way from traveling on the wide path of life that leads to destruction (hell) onto the narrow path that leads to life (heaven). We've also discovered that traveling on the narrow path will be difficult (Matthew 7:14), while traveling on the wide path will not be as difficult. In other words, you won't find as much resistance when traveling on the wide path, but you will face much resistance when you travel on the narrow path. You see, there's a significant message about fruit bearing that goes to the very core of a true relationship with the true vine, Jesus Christ. If you notice the scripture we just looked at in the fifteenth chapter of John, you will notice another key teaching when Jesus says in verse 7, "If you abide in Me, and My words abide in you, you will ask what you desire, and it shall be done for you." Why? Why did Jesus say, "Ask what you desire and it shall be done for you?" He said it because if your motives are in direct connection to the truth of God's word, then you will have the desires of your heart fulfilled. But you must remember one thing. The desires you seek must be directly connected to glorifying Jesus' Father, who is Almighty God. How do you know that, you ask? Well, look in verse 8 of chapter 15 where it says, "By this My Father is glorified, that you bear much fruit; so you will be My disciples. Most of the time people expect God to fulfill their desires but their desires are based on their own personal selfishness and prideful desires instead of the desire to glorify God first and foremost." But you say, "You know Joe, this sort of makes sense to me, but how can I reach the point in my life to where I know I am pleasing God and I can know for sure that I'm bringing nothing but glory and honor to his name?" And that, my fellow truth seeker, is a very good question. But you know what? Before we can get to the answer to that question, I believe the first question we have to search for is, "What is a good fruit and what is a bad fruit, at least according to the truth of God's word?" What is the blueprint for knowing whether a person is producing a fruitful life that is glorifying God and not trying to glorify themselves or others? Well, if you've been reading this book up to now, I truly believe we have uncovered many things that must take place in a person's life if they ever want to find the narrow path that leads to life. But please keep in mind, the first thing that must take place in a person's life is, a person must be born again to even begin their journey on the narrow path, born of God's Spirit (comforter), which we've learned about in earlier chapters.

As we continue on the path of our search for the truth, I think it's extremely important at this point that we discuss three words, three words that are so synonymous with each other, that if you don't have the three working together in unison, it will be literally impossible to be not only a good fruit inspector but to be a good fruit bearer as well. The three words I'm speaking about are the words "manifest," "humility," and "grace." I say that because of some verses from the Bible that have to do with connecting these words together so that they fit into our search for the truth.

First, I use the word "manifest" because there is a direct connection to Jesus revealing his truth to those who are truly his disciples. How do you know that, you ask? I know it because of the words Jesus shared in John chapters 14 and 15 regarding loving him (Jesus) when he said, "He who has My commandments and keeps them, it is he who loves Me. And he who loves Me will be loved by My Father, and I will love him and manifest Myself to him." The dictionary describes the word "manifest" as such: readily perceived by the eye or the understanding; to show plainly;

to put beyond doubt. In other words, Jesus is saying, if you obey God's commandments then you truly love Jesus, and he will reveal himself to you, plainly and without doubt. Question: Who does Jesus qualify as being loved by him and because he knows they love him, he will manifest (reveal) himself to them? Answer: He manifests himself to those who keep his commandments. Another thing for us to consider is the words Jesus uses in verse 3 of John chapter 15 where he says, "You are already clean because of the word which I have spoken to you." The connection here is to the fact that true believers are cleansed by the word of God. In other words, if you've been regenerated (born again) by God's Spirit (comforter) you are seen as being clean and acceptable to God because of Jesus' sacrificial death on the cross. We learned about this in earlier chapters. This truth spoken by Jesus is an extension of the true believer being cleansed when he declared in the previous verse that his Father (God) prunes true believers. Pruning here means refining—or fine tuning if you will—a believer's heart and life so they can be used by God to produce the kinds of spiritual good fruits that glorify him and he can use for the furthering of his kingdom. This pruning or cleansing of God's children (true believers) will produce the kinds of fruit that the Spirit can and will only produce which are goodness, righteousness, and truth (Ephesians 5:9). This cleansing and pruning in a person's life is also known as sanctification (to free and purify from sin), and it is through the process of sanctification that God also cleanses his church as well. The key to sanctification is the word of God. Ephesians 5:25-27 reads, "Husbands, love your wives, just as Christ also loved the church and gave Himself for her with the washing of water by the word, that He might present her to Himself a glorious church, not having spot or wrinkle or any such thing, but that she [Christ's church] should be holy and without blemish. As God prunes and cleanses the lives of those who are true believers, he also does the same thing to the church by and through his holy word.

Second, I use the word "humility" because God's word says in Proverbs 22:3 and 4 that "a prudent man [someone who uses good judgment] foresees evil and hides himself, But the simple [lacking in intelligence] pass on and are punished. By humility and the fear of the Lord are riches and honor and life. Question: Who is a prudent man? Well, according to this word from God, it is someone who foresees and makes a judgment about what is evil and then when they've judged what is evil, they hide themselves from that evil. In other words, they stay away from it, which then begs another question: how does someone determine what is good and what is evil?

Answer: Without God's Spirit (the comforter) living within them (you), it is literally impossible. Why is that, you ask? Well, if you remember what we have discovered in some earlier chapters of our search for the truth, there is a battle going on in life: the battle between good and evil. The battle that rages on between those on the wide path that lead to destruction and those on the narrow path that leads to life. This scripture reading is just another piece of the puzzle in finding the narrow way that leads to life. How so, you ask? Well, again take a look at what it says. It says a prudent man foresees evil and stays away from it, but the simple pass on and is punished. But you say, who are the simple this scripture is referring to and how are they punished? The simple person this scripture is referring to is anyone who turns their back on the truth of Jesus Christ and the word of God. Why does this happen? Why do people turn their backs on the truth about Jesus Christ and the word of God? Well, I'm sure if you were to take a survey regarding the answer to this question, you would get a myriad of answers. However, I truly believe the answer to this question can be found within the bounds of humility. I say that because I truly believe God does not extend his total grace upon anyone who does not first humble themselves before him. What do I mean by this? I mean that if you truly want to have and enjoy the complete benefits (fruits) of God's grace, then I truly believe it will be extended to you if you first humble yourself before him. What do I mean by this? I mean that by humility and a humble heart, you realize that you are lost and actually dead without God's Spirit living within you (I spoke about this in chapter 5). This brings us to the third word I mentioned earlier, which is grace. What is grace? When you think about the word "grace," you probably associate it with something you do before you eat a meal. You thank God for the food you are about to receive (eat). But there is far more to this word than just table grace. In fact, the word "grace" in the dictionary is defined as such: elegance or beauty of form, manner, or motion; a pleasing or attractive quality; favor shown in granting a delay; the freely given, unmerited favor and love of God; the condition of being in God's favor; to favor or honor. In the New Testament book of Ephesians 6:24, there lies yet another clue that I have found to be a direct connection to those who say they love Jesus Christ and also to those who are deceived. The Apostle Paul speaks to us and says, "Grace be with all those who love our Lord Jesus Christ in sincerity." Amen. So what is the key to receiving God's grace in a person's (your) life, to love Jesus Christ in sincerity? In the dictionary, the word "sincerity" is defined as such: free from pretense or falseness; real or genuine; candid (truthful), earnest, frank, and honest. So according to these words from God, there must be a direct connection with the fact that grace and sincerity go hand in hand to those who truly love Jesus Christ. In fact, those three words—manifest, humility, and grace—are so intertwined with the word "sincerity" that unless you first sincerely humble yourself before Almighty God and admit that you can do nothing without him, he (God) cannot completely manifest himself to you, and therefore you cannot receive the fullness of his complete grace and/or blessings in your life. There are multitudes of people today who say they love Jesus Christ, but they are not sincere; just like the definition of the word "sincerity" said, free from pretense or falseness; real or genuine, candid (truthful), earnest, frank, honest. God wants to extend the fullness of his grace by manifesting himself to everyone who calls upon him. But the truth is, he cannot and will not fully manifest himself to a person (you) unless they (you) first humble themselves before him by submitting and obeying his words (commandments). Now this does not mean that a person can win God's favor by doing certain works. There are some religious sects that believe and teach that the way you get to heaven is by doing certain (good) works. It is a works salvation mentality. This kind of salvation focuses on what a person does, instead of what Jesus Christ did. The only requirement for salvation is to sincerely believe in your heart that God sent his only begotten Son Jesus Christ as a sacrifice to atone for a person's sins (transgression of God's laws). The Bible says in the New Testament book of the Apostle Paul's letter to the Romans that "whoever [that's anyone folks] calls on the name of the Lord shall be saved" (We covered this in an earlier chapter). Now my fellow truth seeker is the ultimate grace that God has extended to anyone who wants to go to heaven. However, even though a person can be saved by and through belief in Jesus Christ, there is a work mentality that a true believer in Jesus Christ must do. What is that, you ask? Well, for the answer to that question, we'll have to move on to the next chapter; but I will tell you this much before we (you) do. The answer to that question comes from the very lips of a man who was once an enemy of God. He came from a religious sect that had a works mentality. In fact, not only did he believe that doing good works would get him favor with God, he—along with many others—believed that he was doing the work of God when he took part in the very killing of one of God's true believers (saint) whose name was Stephen, and he was the first man martyred in the church of Jesus Christ. He was stoned to death (Acts 7:59). He was stoned to death by a mob that was encouraged by a man named Saul of Taurus. Who was this Saul of Taurus, you ask? Saul of Taurus was a Hellenistic Jew (a non-Greek, especially a Jew of the Hellenistic period (from 323 BC to the advent of Christianity), who adopted the Greek language, customs, etc. He was not only a devout Jew, but he was also a Pharisee (separated ones—Acts 23:6, 26:5, Phil. 3:5) who was transformed by God's Spirit, from being an enemy of God, into one of the most significant and influential pillars of all time to the Christian faith. Saul of Taurus's name was changed to Paul the Apostle. There is so much to learn about the Apostle Paul's life, but for now, it's important to know that the Apostle Paul is responsible for authoring at least thirteen of the twenty-seven books in the New Testament. In fact, some believe that he may have authored as many as fourteen out of the twenty-seven books. Now I wanted to bring the Apostle Paul into our search for the truth because if you noticed throughout this book, I have been using many of the scriptures he authored. This was made possible by and through the guidance of God's Spirit (comforter).

One of the major questions I personally had when I first started my own search for the truth was this, "Why would God take a man like Saul of Tarsus, who he knew was his enemy, and allow him to become not only his friend, but to elevate him to become one of the most well-known pillars of all time of the Christian faith?" But you know what? It was through this question that I first learned a good lesson about the grace of God. It was also by and through this lesson that I learned a great deal about myself and the God of the Holy Bible. Why do I say that, you ask? I say it because it taught me about the fact that I was a hypocrite (fraud) in the eyes of God. And so was Saul of Tarsus. The only difference was at that time, I wasn't a representative of God and Saul of Tarsus was. So in reality, now I can understand why Jesus had such harsh words for the Pharisees and Sadducees of his day. Now I understand why he said what he said to them as we learned in the last chapter (chapter 11). They were the ultimate hypocrites (frauds), and they needed to repent and change the course of their lives. But you know what? That's true for all of us, especially if you're not a true Christian. Grace begins with humility, and humility begins within the heart. In the scripture verse I used at the beginning of this chapter, the plank Jesus is referring to is the sin in one's own life. Before you can be a faithful servant and follower of Jesus Christ, you must first do a self-examination of your own life (2 Cor. 13:5). There are many today who claim to be sincere followers of Jesus Christ but in reality they are sincerely wrong in their thinking. They are the modern-day Pharisees and Sadducees of our day. But then again, please keep in mind, I'm just a forklift operator. After all, what do I know?

CHAPTER 13

Self-examination

(Blind Faith)

> Test yourselves to see if you are in the faith; examine yourselves! Or
> do you not recognize this about yourselves that Jesus Christ is in
> you—unless indeed you fail the test?
> —2 Corinthians 13:5

IN THE LAST few chapters in our search for the truth, we've been looking at the subject of fruit inspecting as it relates to the word of God. I wanted to draw to your attention the importance of being a good fruit inspector because whether you realize it or not, when you become a follower of Jesus Christ (Christian), you will have to determine what is a good fruit (of God) and what is a bad fruit (of the devil). Another way of looking at this truth is found within the framework of God's word that says, "Beloved, do not believe every spirit, but test the spirits to see whether they are from God, because many false prophets have gone out into the world" (1 John 4:1). Question: What is a prophet? Well, in the dictionary, the word "prophet" is defined as such: a person who speaks with divine inspiration; a person who foretells future events. I'm telling you this because throughout the Bible, you will find the word "prophet(s)." In fact, the word "prophet" (singular) is used 227 times, and the word "prophets" (plural) is also used 227 times. In the Old Testament, the word "prophet" is used 159 times; and in the New Testament, it is used 68 times. In the Old Testament, the word "prophets" is used 139 times; and in the New Testament, it is used 88 times.

Probably by now you're asking yourself, "This is well and fine, Joe, but what does this have to do with being a good fruit inspector?" Why is this so important and what the heck does this have to do with our search for the truth? And that's a very good question. For you see, the key to the whole issue of fruit inspecting really boils down to the reality of what is true and what is false. I say that because as we've learned throughout this book, truth can only be found within the pages of the Bible. Furthermore, as we've also learned, if you want to truly worship God you must worship him in Spirit and in truth (John 4:24). Why? Again, because God is Spirit and those who worship him must worship in spirit and truth (John 4:24). This begs the question of the scripture we used earlier in 1 John 4:1. How can one know whether a spirit is from God or a spirit is from a false prophet? Well, for the answer to that question, I believe you have to first determine what a spirit of God is, and what is a spirit of a false prophet? According to the dictionary, a prophet is someone who speaks with divine (godly) inspiration. So obviously, if a prophet is someone who speaks with divine (godly) inspiration, then a false prophet would be someone who speaks without divine inspiration. In other words, they aren't speaking truth so they must be speaking that which is not the truth, which brings us to another question. How can we know who or what is of God and who or what is not of God, which leads us, in part, to take a look at the next part of 1 John chapter 4 which will give us a glimpse into how we can determine what is of God and what is not of God. God's word teaches us through the Apostle John these words, "By this you know the Spirit of God: every spirit that confesses that Jesus Christ has come in the flesh is from God; and every spirit that does not confess Jesus is not from God; this is the spirit of the antichrist, of which you have heard that it is coming, and now it is already in the world. You are from God, because greater is He who is in you than he who is in the world. They are from the world [wide path]; therefore they speak as from the world, and the world listens to them. We are from God [narrow path]; he who knows God listens to us; he who is not from God does not listen to us." By this, we know the spirit of truth and the spirit of error. So as we look at this teaching, it appears that all someone has to do in determining whether or not a spirit is from God or not is whether someone or some spirit confesses that Jesus Christ has come in the flesh. Someone or some spirit, you ask? Yes, I said someone or some spirit. I say that because in the modern-day church today there are multitudes of so-called leaders (pastors, clergy, layman, etc.) who deny this very fact. They deny that Jesus Christ has come in the flesh. They are false teachers, or if you will, false prophets. Of such people, you should be aware. I spoke about that in an earlier chapter when Jesus Christ himself spoke and said, "Beware of false prophets, who come to you in sheep's clothing, but inwardly they are ravenous wolves" (Matthew 7:15). And then this is where Jesus makes the point that true believers will know them (unbelievers, false prophets, ravenous wolves, deceivers, etc.) by their fruits (Matthew 7:16). But wait!

JOSEPH TRAVER

Is that all that is involved in determining whether or not someone has the Spirit of God versus the spirit of Antichrist? I don't think so, because on the surface, it looks like that's all that's required; but I believe in our search for the truth, there's much, much, more to the story than just this simple test. Why do I say that, you ask? I say it because if you'll recall the scripture we used in 1 John 4:1, it stated that true believers, who in this case are referred to as beloved (those who are greatly loved) are instructed not to believe every spirit. But they are instructed to test the spirits! Why? Why are they instructed to test the spirits? They are told to test the spirits to see whether or not those spirits are from God or from the false prophets (Antichrist). Question: What does it mean when it says Antichrist spirit? Well, the word "Antichrist" means any opponent of Christ; a false Christ (i.e., a false prophet, an Antichrist spirit, a ravenous wolf, a non-truth or a false truth, a lie or a deception). Another way of looking at this would be a deceiving spirit or a deceptive spirit and who is the author of lies and deception? Answer: The devil. If you recall throughout this book, we have been uncovering the fact that there's a battle going on between God and Satan/devil. We've been spending time in the area of testing the spirits because fruit inspecting and testing the spirits really go hand in hand. Once again, remember what we learned in an earlier chapter regarding the struggle that is being fought in the spiritual (unseen) realm in the heavenly places by spiritual beings (2 Corinthians 4:18). The battle that is being fought is for the very souls of people. Thus, the reason for spending so much time with fruit inspecting and testing the spirits.

What is a soul, you ask? In the dictionary, a "soul" is described as such: the principle of life, feeling, and thought, in humans, regarded as a distinct spiritual entity (existence) separate from the body; the emotional part of human nature; a human being; the inspirer of some action. So in essence, the devil wants to deceive you and the true God by and through Jesus Christ who wants to open your eyes to the truth. As there is a battle raging on between God and the devil, that same battle is being fought within the hearts of people, and that includes your heart as well as mine. God is the ultimate truth teller, and the devil is the ultimate liar and deceiver. Which brings us to the question about who do you personally want to serve, God or the devil, which happens to be the question for everyone, not only today, but throughout the history of mankind. The one question that we've been attempting to uncover throughout this book, in our search for the truth, is all about finding the narrow path that leads to life eternal (Matthew 7:14).

Well, up to now in this book, I've been sharing quite a few of the truths that God's Spirit (the comforter) has revealed to me in my personal walk of faith down the narrow path of my life. But now I'd like to shift gears into another aspect down the path of our search for the truth. And what is that, you ask? It is one that I truly believe is eluding multitudes of people within the world of Christendom today. I say that because I truly believe that the modern-day church today is under severe attack by the adversary, old Satan himself. But then again this is nothing new; ever since Adam and Eve's rebellion in the Garden of Eden, the human race has been being deceived by the (our) adversary, the devil. And that includes the modern-day church of today. Why did I mention the modern-day church of today? Well, for the complete answer to that question, it would again take another book; but for now, all you have to know is that one of the reasons God called me out of the darkness of this life (wide path) and into the light of his grace (narrow path) was so that I could sound the alarm. What alarm, you ask? The alarm of God's pending judgment. You see, there are many signs that time is running out. Running out for what, you ask, running out for people (you) to find the narrow path that leads to life eternal through/by God's Son, Jesus Christ.

Throughout this book, God has been using this/our search for the truth to open your eyes to the truth of his grace and his love for you. He loves you so much that he used me to share with you what his Spirit (the comforter) has taught me. But before I end our time together in our search of finding the narrow way to life, I'd like to begin to finish this book by taking a look at the lives of two people. Both people have been mentioned within the pages of this book before. One of them I spoke about in the last chapter, and the other one I mentioned a few chapters back. The two I'd like to end this book with are the two that God has greatly used in my life, as he has renewed my heart and my mind as one of his servants (Romans 12:2 and Titus 3:5). I'm speaking about two people who were both walking on the wide path to destruction, but they truly believed in their hearts that they were walking on the narrow path; and for sure their entrance into heaven was a slam dunk (sure thing). In other words, they truly believed that God would be waiting at the pearly gates of heaven to welcome them into his presence. They thought they would hear the words that most people want to hear. "Enter into the joy of your God/Lord [paradise] thou good and faithful servant" (Matthew 25:21). The problem was at this specific time of our search for the truth, these two men were both God's enemies. They were God's enemies because they didn't have God's Spirit living within them. And you know something else? As I've said throughout this book, if you're not born again of God's Spirit, you are his enemy as well. They were both deceived. Both of them were of their father the devil and so was their sect or denomination, if you will. They were both full of hypocrisy and lawlessness (lack of control). They were both described as having hearts that were full of dead men's bones and all uncleanness. They devoured widows' houses. They were both blind (meaning they couldn't see the truth). They offered long prayers for appearance sake (in other words, they offered their prayers to show off). They wore leather boxes called phylacteries which made them appear more spiritual to people. They more than likely were both students of the most prominent and celebrated rabbi (teacher) of that time, whose name was Gamaliel. As students of Gamaliel, they would have received the most extensive training, both in the Old Testament law and rabbinic traditions. They were both Pharisees and members of the Sanhedrin (rulers of the Jews). They tithed (an amount of their personal material resources, usually 10 percent) to God to support things like the temple, synagogue, etc.; but they neglected the weightier matters of the law, which are justice and mercy and faithfulness. Not that tithing was a bad thing, but they were so focused on the incidentals (minor issues) and externals, but they willfully resisted the spiritual meaning of the law. And lastly, and I believe one of the most sorrowful of all. Jesus told them about how they traveled all over both sea and land to find those they could proselyte (convert—change to one's philosophy or way of life). And now watch this! Jesus said when they change to your way of thinking (religion), you make him (them) twice as much a son of hell as yourselves. Whoa! Did you hear that, my fellow truth seekers? Did you hear what the very Son of God says to those who thought they were representing the God of this universe? He said (and I'm paraphrasing), once you've converted that person to your religion, you make them twice as much a son of hell as yourselves. Now that, my fellow truth seekers, is some heavy, heavy stuff! But you know what? The same thing is happening today. And you know something else. The hypocrisy that the Pharisees and Sadducees displayed was bad enough, but the hypocrisy of modern-day Christendom is even worse. How so, you ask? I say it is even worse because at least the Pharisees and Sadducees of Jesus' day didn't claim to be his (Jesus') followers. They didn't claim to be his followers, but there are multitudes of people in the world of Christendom today who claim to be followers of Jesus Christ, but they only give God lip service. They are like the people that Jesus spoke about at the end of his Sermon on the Mount found in Matthew chapter

7. Those people were the ultimate in hypocrisy and giving lip service to God. And what does Jesus say to them? Well, after they tried to make their case for being faithful servants in serving him, Jesus says to them, "I never knew you; depart from Me, you who practice lawlessness" (v. 23). Now you ask, "What did Jesus mean by this?" Well, if you look up the word "lawless" or "lawlessness" in the dictionary, you will find that it means without regard for the law; uncontrolled by a law; illegal. In other words, they talked the talk about being a follower of Jesus Christ, but they never really walked the walk with regard to the truth of God's word. They gave God lip service by claiming to have faith in Jesus Christ. They claimed they believed in Jesus Christ, but they didn't obey the word of God. They had built their house (lives) on what Jesus says in Matthew 7:26 is sand. They built their lives on the sinking sand of this world (wide path). Jesus said they were foolish and because they didn't obey God's word (law), they had a great fall. Like the Pharisees and Sadducees, they were traveling on the wide path to destruction, but they truly believed they were on the narrow path to life eternal.

By now, you're probably asking yourself, "This is all well and fine Joe, but what the heck does all of this have to do with our search for the truth?" After all, we've talked about good fruit and bad fruit. We've talked about testing the spirits. We've talked about fruit inspecting. We've talked about prophets and false prophets and ravenous wolves and Antichrist spirits and deceivers and Pharisees and Sadducees and scribes and Satan/devil and judgment and souls and on and on and on. Question: What's so important about all of these things? Why are all these things so important in our search for the truth? Answer: These are important because in the final analysis of our search for the truth, it really boils down to one conclusion and one conclusion alone. Are we (you) truly following the one true God of this universe, or are we (you) following the one true god of this world, the devil? Are we (you) on the narrow path that leads to life eternal, or are we (you) on the wide path that leads to destruction (hell)? As we've discovered in previous chapters, as well as throughout this book, if you're not truly born again of God's Spirit, you will not be able to answer that question. You will not be able to answer that question because you will be like the two people that we're going to be looking at as we begin to move toward the conclusion of this book. Now the two people we're going to be looking at as we begin to close out our time in searching for the truth are the two we've mentioned previously, the Pharisees named Nicodemus and Saul of Tarsus (who became the Apostle Paul). Now the reason I want to take a look at these two men is because at the time Jesus spoke to both of them, they weren't born again. They were traveling on the wide path of destruction instead of the narrow path of life. They were traveling on the wide path, but they thought they were on the narrow path. They both were building their lives on the sinking sand of this world and didn't even realize it. They were supposedly God's ambassadors and representatives, but in fact, as we've learned previously, they were ambassadors and representatives of the devil and not of the one true God of the Bible. They were doing the devil's work and were deeply rooted in the wiles (snares) of the devil's deception. In fact, not only were they deceived themselves, but the ones they were bringing into their religious circles as converts were twice as bad as them. Question: How did that happen? How could they have been so deceived that they ended up following the devil instead of the one true God? Well, for the answer to that question, you'll have to move on to the next chapter; but before we (you) do, I will tell you this much. One of the reasons they were so deceived was because they didn't examine their own lives. They were so caught up in the sect and/or denomination if you will, that they didn't do a deep-down examination of their own personal lives nor did they do a deep-down examination of their own sect and/or denomination. They had blind faith. They had a form of godliness, but their hearts were far from the one true God. Why was that? Well, I happen to believe that they got so caught up in the religious traditions they had created within their sect, that those traditions had clouded their hearts and minds to the truth of God's word. They had created a sense of religiosity, but in fact they were far from the truth of God's word. It's like in the Bible where it speaks of the traditions of men and having an appearance of being godly when actually one's life (religion—denomination) is really far from God. They had a form of godliness, but their hearts were far from God. Jesus said in Matthew chapter 15, "Why do you transgress [disobey] the commandments of God because of your tradition?" Thus, you have made the commandments of God of no effect by your traditions. Hypocrites! Well, Isaiah (a prophet) did prophesy about you saying, "These people draw near to Me with their mouth, And honor Me with their lips, But their heart is far from Me. And in vain [without real value or worth] they worship Me, Teaching as doctrines the commandments of men."

But then again, that's why Jesus rebuked and criticized the so-called religious establishment (leaders) of his time. They were phonies. They were not genuine or real. They were misleading and deceiving people into becoming twice as evil as them. They had a character flaw, and their hearts were far from God. They were deceived and because of their own inner self-deception, they were being used as agents for the devil instead of God. Now did the Pharisees and Sadducees ever realize this? I don't believe so. In fact, as we begin to uncover this question, it is extremely important to understand that the two people we're looking at were sought by God in different ways. In other words, God pursued both of them but he pursued them in different ways. Kind of like what happened to me as I explained in chapter 1 of this book. If you recall the scripture verse we used in the New Testament book of Luke 19:10 which says, "For the Son of Man has come to seek and save that which was lost." Just as I was lost, so were the Pharisees named Nicodemus and Saul of Tarsus. They were both lost in the muck and mire of religion, and God was extending his grace to both of them. I say grace because that's exactly what kind of god the true God is. He is a God of grace and love, and he extends that grace to all who call upon him. He knows the hearts of all people, and he will extend his grace to those who willfully and faithfully humble themselves before him. He doesn't want anyone to perish but that all will come and repent. God's word tells us in 2 Peter 3:9, "The Lord [God] is not willing that any should perish but that all [that's anyone, folks] should come to repentance. And what is repentance? The dictionary defines "repentance" as to feel sorry for a past action, attitude, etc.; to feel such remorse for sin or fault as to change one's ways. And that's exactly how anyone who wishes to experience the grace of God must come. They must come to God with a humble and repentant heart and be willing to change their ways. And that's exactly where Nicodemus and Saul of Tarsus were at. They needed to change their ways and their hearts. But you know what? So do you and I, which takes us back to the scripture verse we used at the beginning of this chapter in which God's word asks us (you) a question. Test yourselves to see if you are in the faith; examine yourselves! Or do you not recognize this about yourselves that Jesus Christ is in you—unless indeed you fail the test? Question: What faith is God speaking about? He's speaking about the genuine saving faith that only Jesus Christ can provide to/for you. Is your faith in Jesus Christ genuine, or is it not? I ask you this question because true faith begins with true self-examination. I say that because both Nicodemus and Saul of Tarsus were blinded by their faith, and at that point, they both failed the test. They were among the most religious of their time, but they failed the test because Jesus Christ was not in them. They were blinded by what they thought was true faith. How about you?

Have you encountered Jesus Christ yet? Do you have genuine and real faith in him, or do you have a blind faith? Do you have any faith at all? It is an important question. But then again, please keep in mind, I'm just a forklift operator. After all, what do I know?

CHAPTER 14

The Childlikeness of a Believer

Jesus said; "Assuredly, I say to you, unless you are converted
and become as little children, you will by no means enter
the kingdom of heaven.
—Matthew 18:3

AS I HAVE spent literally thousands of hours studying and seeking the heart of the biblical God (Jeremiah 29:13), there is one statistic that I found pretty incredible to comprehend. As I look back upon this statistic, I wish I had written down who and/or where this statistic came from. But as sometimes often happens in life, at least for me, when I hear something like this, it oftentimes doesn't click until I'm searching or experiencing something else in another area of my life. I would compare the situation I'm trying to explain by what oftentimes happens when I'm reading the word of God (Bible). I can read a specific word or verse of scripture one day and nothing clicks, but then I can come back to that same specific word or verse at another time, and that same word or verse hits me right between the eyes and the meaning fits perfectly into my mind and then I get it. I understand what God is saying to me, and then I apply his word to my life. Now the statistic I'm talking about was a statistic that said that once a person reaches the age of eighteen, there's an 80 percent chance that that person will never have a personal relationship with Jesus Christ. Now whether that statistic is true or not, I have no way of knowing. But I can tell you one thing. In many ways, that statistic really lines up with what the word of God says. How so, you ask? Well, if you remember the words of God's Son, Jesus Christ, when he spoke in Matthew 7:14 that "narrow is the gate and difficult is the way which leads to life, and there are few who find it." Which if you really think about it, that lines up with what the 80 percent statistic implies. Now I don't know about you, my fellow truth seeker; but for me, that statistic really bothers me quite a bit. In fact, that very statistic bothers me so much that it is one of the reasons why I ultimately decided to write this book. I say that because throughout this book, I've been sharing things with you that really boils down to deception, or being deceived if you will. I say that because if you're not truly born again of God's Spirit, then there is one thing for sure. You are being deceived in some area of your life, and you probably don't even know it. That was the case before I came to a personal relationship with Jesus Christ, and it was also the case in the lives of the Pharisees named Nicodemus and Saul of Tarsus. In fact, it was also the case in the life of someone we spoke about in earlier chapters (chapters 7 and 8), and that was the man named Ebenezer Scrooge. Did you say Ebenezer Scrooge? Yes, I did. I said Ebenezer Scrooge!

Now you may be asking yourself the question, "What does Ebenezer Scrooge and the Pharisees named Nicodemus and Saul of Tarsus have to do with our search for the truth?" Answer: I believe they have a lot to do with each other. How so, you ask? I say they have a lot to do with each other because with regard to our search for the truth, it was this specific truth that God used in helping me put yet another piece of the puzzle together regarding the conversion (born again) experience that must take place in a person's life in finding the narrow path of life. Now without going back and doing a whole study with regard to the Ebenezer Scrooge (i.e., the Christmas Carol story), you must simply consider this. After Ebenezer Scrooge had his heart changed and humbled by the visit from the three ghosts and his former business partner Jacob Marley, there came a place in the story where Scrooge found himself acting like a baby. Did I say a baby? Yes, I said, a baby. How so, you ask? Well, if you read the story, you will find that Mr. Scrooge was so happy that he wasn't dead after what the Ghost of Christmas Future had showed him, that he was literally beside himself. In fact, he was so beside himself with happiness that the story says he was as light as a feather, as happy as an angel, as merry as a schoolboy, and as giddy (lightheaded/dizzy) as a drunken man. He didn't know what day of the month it was. He didn't know how long he had been with the three spirits that had visited him the night before. In fact, he said he didn't know anything at all, but he didn't care! Why, because he was like a baby. But what did he mean, and what does this mean for you and me in our search for the truth in finding the narrow way to life eternal?

Well, to help understand this whole scenario, we have to take a look at the scripture I used at the beginning of this chapter. I say we have to take a look at this specific scripture verse because the attributes or traits that Scrooge was displaying in his character was the same kind of attributes and traits that the Son of God said must take place in a person's life if they ever expect to enter the kingdom of heaven (God). How so, you ask? Well, take another look at what the Son of God (Jesus) said to his disciples.

After He had called a little child to Himself and set the child in the midst [middle] of them, He said; "Assuredly, I say to you, unless you are converted [born again] and become as little children you will by no means enter the kingdom of heaven."

Question: What did Jesus mean by this? What was he speaking about? What did he mean when he told the disciples that they must be converted and become as little children as a condition for getting to heaven? Well, for the answer to that question, I believe we must first explore what is the condition of a child at least within the parameters or limits of what Jesus was referring to. And another question we must take into our consideration is the one regarding the 80 percent statistic, which implies that there is only a 20 percent chance of a person over the age of eighteen ever finding Jesus Christ and therefore will not ever find the narrow way to eternal life (heaven). Now why is that? Why is that so important and what does that have to do with us in our search for the truth? What does Ebenezer Scrooge, and the Pharisees named Nicodemus and Saul of Tarsus, have to do with us? Answer: It has a great deal to do with us (you), especially if you've never been truly converted and truly born again.

You see, the one thing that Ebenezer Scrooge, Nicodemus, and Saul of Tarsus had in common was that they were all over the age of eighteen. In fact, not only were they over the age of eighteen but all of them were a great deal older than eighteen years of age. All of them were way beyond the age of eighteen. And do you know something else? So was I when I began to have my eyes opened to the truth of God's amazing grace. But you say, "This is all well and fine, Joe, but what does all of this have to do with the scripture verse Jesus spoke about in becoming as a little child to enter heaven?" You see, the one thing that I truly believe is a great stumbling block that keeps a person from finding the narrow way to life is exactly what the 80 percent statistic is referring to. Please let me explain. If you take a good look at the 80 percent statistic, what is the one thing that stands out about that statistic? It is the age of a person. And what is there about the age of eighteen that should stand out in our search for the truth? Answer: It is the age that most people really start leaving their childhood behind and begins their own journey out into the real world beyond the protection and the security of their parents and the family environment that has molded and shaped them throughout their childhood. Now I know there are exceptions to this observation, but as a whole, this is the rule. In many ways, it really is

JOSEPH TRAVER

the age of accountability for one's life. By the age of eighteen, a person's life and character has been pretty much molded and established, and it usually is a good indicator of which way (road) they will travel in their journey through life. Are they headed down the right path in life? Is the compass of their lives pointing them in the right direction? Are they traveling on the narrow path to life, or are they traveling on the wide path to destruction? You see, those are important questions. Why are they important questions, you ask? They are important questions because if you've never been exposed to or taught the truth of God's way's (word) from the time you were born, you are more than likely headed in the wrong direction. In fact, in many cases, even though people are exposed to or taught the truth of God's ways, they still have a hard time finding the narrow path to life eternal. How so, you ask? I say that because of three important things that all of us as human beings fight against in our lives. And it is these three important things that we must understand if we're ever going to begin to see the kingdom of God. What are those three things, you ask? Well, they can be found in the word of God (Bible) in the New Testament book of 1 John 2:15-17 which says, "Do not love the world or the things in the world. If anyone [that means anyone, folks] loves the world, the love of the Father is not in him." Now pay close attention, my fellow truth seekers, because here it comes from the word (mind) of God. For all that is in the world—the lust of the flesh, the lust of the eyes, and the pride of life—is not of the Father (God) but is of the world. And the world is passing away, and the lust of it; but he who does the will of God abides forever.

Question: What is God talking about? What does he mean by the world, and what does he mean by the lust of the flesh, the lust of the eyes, and the pride of life? Well, the first thing we must understand is that the world God is speaking about here is not the physical, material world but the invisible spiritual system of evil that is dominated by Satan. Now I'm not going to get into a long discussion in this area of the devil and Satan. I say that because we've already explored a great deal about the power and influence of the devil throughout this book. We've also established that there is a spiritual battle (war) going on between the devil and God. You see, if you're in the world, then the things God is speaking about—the lust of the flesh, the lust of the eyes, and the pride of life—are all qualities that go against the true attributes and traits of the one true God. In other words, being in or of the world, your mind and body are set on the things of this world and not on the things of God. But you say, "Joe, of course our [my] minds and bodies are set on the things of this world because after all, we live in this world, we work, and live, and have our [my] being in this world. And you know what, you're absolutely correct; but when we (you) are truly converted and born again of God's Spirit, then we begin to take on the likeness of God's Son, Jesus Christ, and God begins to renew our minds into the likeness of his Son, Jesus Christ. The renewing of our minds begins the process of becoming like Christ, and then we can begin to walk in the Spirit of God instead of the spirit of the Antichrist (devil/Satan) that travels around seeking who he may devour/consume. Please remember what we spoke about in earlier chapters regarding the spiritual battles which are being fought in the unseen world by the rulers of darkness and the spiritual hosts of wickedness (Ephesians 6:12). Those spiritual battles are being fought within the hearts and lives of people who in most cases have no idea there is a battle going on at all. There is a parallel teaching in the New Testament book of 1 Peter chapter 5 that I discovered that I truly helps put into perspective what Jesus was/is referring to with regard to becoming as little children. And please keep in mind what we spoke about earlier regarding the age of eighteen and younger being the childhood years. I say that because there is a direct connection to having the childlike trait of being humble and being devoured by the devil. How so, you ask? Well, let's take a good look at what one of Jesus' apostles teaches us in chapter 5 of 1 Peter where he says, "Likewise you younger people, submit yourselves to your elders. Yes, all of you be submissive to one another, and be clothed with humility, for—God resists the proud, But gives grace to the humble." Therefore humble yourselves under the mighty hand of God, that he may exalt you in due time, casting all your care upon him, for he cares for you. And then pay close attention to what the word of God says to us (you) next. Be sober (clearheaded), be vigilant (alert, on guard); because your adversary, the devil, walks about like a roaring lion, seeking whom he may devour. Resist him, steadfast in the faith, knowing that the same sufferings are experienced by your brotherhood in the world.

Question: What is Peter telling us? First, he's teaching younger people to submit to those elders who are older and wiser, and do it by and through the trait and character of humility. He's speaking of the humility that if you're in Christ, you are not in control of your life. You turn everything over to the mighty hand of God; and your life, your will, and your heart now belong to him. But you see, that's why conversion and becoming as a little child go hand in hand with the circumcision of the heart. The regeneration of a person's life must begin with becoming as a little child. It must begin with becoming as a little child, because depending on where you are at in your life's journey, if you've never truly been born again of God's Spirit (the comforter), the Antichrist spirit of the world system may have a grip on you. In other words, you may think everything is okay with you, as far as God goes; but the worldly Antichrist system may have its hold on you, and you may not even know it. You may be one of those who are being devoured by the devil; and unless you are converted and born again of God's Spirit, he will destroy you. That was the case with Ebenezer Scrooge that was the case, with Nicodemus, that was the case with Saul of Tarsus, that was the case with Jacob Marley, and it was also the case with me; as I've discussed throughout this book.

Now when we think of this teaching from the Son of God, we must take into consideration what it means to become as a little child and to do that we must consider the context of why Jesus spoke these words, as well as what Jesus was trying to teach his followers. Well, if we think about what the characteristics of a child are, we should be able to begin to understand what Jesus was referring to. In other words, what has the characteristics of a child have to do with a person finding the narrow path to life (heaven)? The first thing I think we have to consider is how dependent a baby or child is on their parents or on those who are taking care of them. Another thing I think we should consider is how innocent and blameless a little child is. Even though they were conceived in sin, because of their fallen human nature (Psalm 51:5), they first start out at the lowest point of a sinful nature. That sinful nature will begin to manifest itself as the child gets older; but at the point of being a child, they are at the closest point of being as pure in God's sight as they can get without being converted by God's Spirit (born again). And if you think for one moment that a child doesn't have a sinful nature, just let them grow without discipline, and you will begin to see just how rebellious and disobedient that child will become. Another thing I think we have to consider when thinking about a child is how a child must be fed milk because they cannot ingest or digest meat into their system. Depending on the influences and structure a child has been subjected to in their developing years really determines in which direction they will go in their lives. In other words, it's like a verse of God's word that says, "Train up a child in the way he should go, And when he is old he will not depart from it" (Proverbs 22:6). And that's exactly what Jesus is trying to teach us (you). No matter what your age, if you want to come under his care and his guidance, you must first be converted (born again) by and through a humble heart. No matter what age you are, at some point in your life, you must simply empty yourself of the things that are in opposition to the ways of God and His Holy word. Which takes us back to Ebenezer Scrooge, and the Pharisees Nicodemus and Saul of Tarsus; and if you've never been converted and become as a little child, it also brings us to your life as well. Remember well the words spoken by the Son of God, Jesus Christ, "Unless you are converted and become as a little child you will by no means [that means no way, folks] enter the kingdom of heaven."

There is another thing I think we have to consider as we take a look at the lessons we learn from Ebenezer Scrooge, Nicodemus, and Saul of Tarsus. First, the Christmas Carol story with Ebenezer Scrooge is more of a secular or worldly type story than a religious or biblical type story, while the stories of Nicodemus and Saul of Tarsus are right from the very word of God (Bible) itself. So you say, what's your point? You see, the point is in many ways the lessons I learned from these stories fall right into the category of what we have been uncovering throughout this book: the need for salvation, the need for redemption, the need for our lives to be transformed and delivered from our own fleshly desires that put ourselves first and God second. We as human beings actually need to be saved from ourselves. All three of these people were traveling down the wide path to their ultimate destruction, and they didn't even know it. The things they desired were actually keeping them from finding the narrow path to eternal life. And the one thing that is at the forefront of keeping people from finding the narrow path is the word "pride." You see, the older a person gets away from their childhood years, the harder it gets for them to find the narrow path to life, especially if they've never been exposed to the truth of God's words. Why is this? It's because the further you get away from your childhood years, the harder your heart gets toward the things of God. Once you're traveling on the wide path, it is extremely difficult to get yourself on the narrow path. That's why Jesus said that unless you are converted (changed) and start over as a little child, you will never be able to find the narrow path to eternal life. A little child hasn't been exposed to the deception of the world. The devil hasn't been able to infiltrate a child's life by his skillful art of deception. And unless that child is surrounded and engulfed by people and parents who are true born-again believers and committed to the true teachings of the biblical God, there is a good chance that child/person will never find the narrow path to life (heaven). There is a good chance because unless you are exposed to the truth of God's words, your chances of humbling yourself as a little child becomes harder and harder as you are molded and shaped by the things of the world. But then again, please keep in mind, I'm just a forklift operator. After all, what do I know?

CHAPTER 15

A Hardened Heart

Beware, brethren, lest there be in any of you an evil heart of unbelief
in departing from the loving God; but exhort one another daily,
while it is called "Today" lest any of you be hardened through the
deceitfulness of sin.
—Hebrews 3: 12 and 13

ONE OF THE biggest issues we've been discussing in our search
for the truth is all about the word "pride." In our last chapter,
we discovered that the Son of God, Jesus Christ, taught that if a person
ever expects to see the kingdom of God (heaven), they must be converted
and become as a little child. We also took a look at the 80 to 20 percent
statistics with regard to a person ever finding the narrow path to life after
the age of eighteen, especially if a child (person) doesn't receive a proper
upbringing and proper atmosphere in the ways and teachings of God's
word. And one of the key reasons I have discovered why it is so important
for that to take place in a person's life is because of the term known in the
Bible as a "hardened heart." You see, what I've discovered in my own faith
journey as a follower of Jesus Christ is that there is a direct connection to
the word "pride" and the term used in the Bible is called a hardened heart.
And what I've also discovered is that the further a person gets from being
a child, the more pride gets established within that individual's heart. But
then again, that's exactly what God's word is telling us in the scripture
we used at the beginning of this chapter. In this chapter of Hebrews, the
author is speaking about salvation and having a hardened heart toward
the things of God. There is a direct connection to the word "wilderness"
found in verse 8 of chapter 3 as a place of unfaithfulness. Though God had
personally directed the Israelites out of the control of the wicked Pharaoh
in Egypt, the people rebelled and still didn't believe nor commit their lives
to him. Their hearts were so hardened toward the things of God that God
had to punish them because of their hardened hearts. And that is pretty
much the same thing that can happen in our lives as well. But you say, "Joe,

I thought God was a loving God, and if God is a loving God then surely God would not punish anyone, would he?" Well, let's take a look at what the word of God says with regard to that question. And as we take a look at what God's word says about this, let's keep in mind what happened to Ebenezer Scrooge and Saul of Tarsus. Did you say Ebenezer Scrooge and Saul of Tarsus? Yes, I did. And you say, what has Ebenezer Scrooge and Saul of Tarsus have to do with our search for the truth? Answer: It has a great deal to do with our search for the truth because of what happened in both their lives. First, Ebenezer Scrooge was taunted by three ghosts, and Saul of Tarsus was blinded by Jesus. And just as a side note: For me, the three ghosts that visited Ebenezer Scrooge on Christmas Eve reminds me of what God represents in the world today. But not only does it represent God in the world today, but I truly believe it represents God since the very beginning of time. What were the names of those three ghosts that visited Ebenezer Scrooge? They were called the Ghost of Christmas Past, the Ghost of Christmas Present, and the Ghost of Christmas Future; the three in one, God the Father, God the Son, and God the Holy Spirit, the triune God of the Bible. For many a/the triune God is a very hard reality to understand. There are references to the triune God in the Bible, but the word "triune" itself is not found in the Bible. I believe the best reference to it is found in the New Testament book of 1 Peter 1:2 where it says, "Elect according to the foreknowledge of God the Father, in sanctification of the Spirit, for obedience and sprinkling of the blood of Jesus Christ."

The word "elect" is used in scripture to show a specific group of people who have been converted and born again by the sanctifying work of the Holy Spirit (comforter) which we discovered in earlier chapters and specifically chapter 9. In forklift operator terms, this means that God the Father set in place a plan for people to get themselves back in the good graces with Himself. By Jesus' death on the cross, he paid the price for anyone who will believe in/on him. Once we truly believe that Jesus was the Son of God and that he did pay the price for our transgressions against God, then the Holy Spirit (comforter) begins the process of sanctifying our spirit in the true worship of Almighty God. Remember what we've learned throughout this book in our search for the truth that God is Spirit, and those who worship him must worship in spirit and truth (John 4:24). Question: What does it mean to have and see the process of sanctification begin to take hold of one's life? Well, for the answer to that question, I'd like us to take a look back at something I mentioned a couple of chapters back, and that is regarding an error that I truly believe many in the world of Christendom today are making. Many who teach the whole reality in the belief in Jesus Christ I think put a stumbling block before people because they don't teach about this issue.

They teach that a person is not saved by the works they do, which is correct, but they don't teach that there is a works mentality that must accompany a true believer because it is an important essential to receiving the richest blessing of/from God. In the New Testament book of Galatians 5:1, it reads that once a person is in Christ (born again/converted), they are set free and no longer have to live in bondage. What do I mean by living in bondage, you ask? Well, if you take a look further in Galatians chapter 5, you will get a glimpse of what it means to be set free by God's Spirit. I say that because once a person is truly set free by the Spirit of God, they will receive the power to overcome something that is in direct opposition to God's Spirit. What is that, you ask? It is the lust of the flesh. As human beings, our fleshly desires are in opposition to the works of God's Spirit. God's word teaches in Galatians 5:17 that "the flesh lusts against the Spirit, and the Spirit against the flesh; and these are contrary to one another, so that you do not do the things you wish." Question: What are the works of the flesh? They are listed in verses 19 to 21 of Galatians chapter 5: adultery, fornication, uncleanness, lewdness, idolatry, sorcery, hatred, contentions, jealousies, outbursts of wrath, selfish ambitions, dissensions, heresies, envy, murders, drunkenness, revelries, and the like. Now in contrast, the fruit of the Spirit is listed in the same chapter verses 22 and 23: love, joy, peace, long-suffering, kindness, goodness, faithfulness, gentleness, self-control. Against such, there is no law. And then the word of God teaches in verses 24 and 25 that "and those who are Christ's have crucified the flesh with its passions and desires." If we (true born-again followers of Jesus) live in the Spirit, let us also walk in the Spirit.

Now you may be asking yourself: "What the heck does all that mean? What is God speaking about?" Well, for the complete answer to all of that, it would take a lot longer than I have in this book, but I will tell you this much. If you take a look at the three people we've been looking at, you will discover that in each one of their lives, there was an evidence of the flesh working in each of their lives that was in opposition to the fruits of the Spirit. How so, you ask? Well, if you take a good look at Ebenezer Scrooge's life, you will discover that a few of the works of the flesh stand out, which in particular would be idolatry, outbursts of wrath, hatred, and self-ambitions. Now I say this because if you read or watch the Christmas Carol story, you will discover that these qualities are quite evident in the life of Ebenezer Scrooge. And you know what? If you remember the words of Jesus, you will find that many of these fleshly qualities on this list were evident in the lives of the Pharisees named Nicodemus and Saul of Tarsus as well. Oh yes, in some ways they were different, but yet their qualities were still in the category of the works of the flesh. And according to the Bible, if they (you) were practicing those things, they were disqualifying themselves from the inheritance of God's kingdom (Galatians 5:21). But you say, "Come on Joe, everyone is a sinner." In fact, according to the very word of God, we all fall short of God's glory, for all have sinned and fall short of the glory of God (Romans 3:23). But wait! What does the next verse say? It says, "Being justified freely by His grace through the redemption that is in Christ Jesus." You see, at the time, redemption hadn't taken place in the life of Ebenezer Scrooge, the Ghost of Christmas Past, the Ghost of Christmas Present, nor the Ghost of Christmas Future hadn't come into Scrooge's life yet. Redemption, or if you will, the release from the works of the flesh, had not taken place in Scrooge's life. And you know something else? It may not have taken place in your life as well. And you know another thing? If your heart is hardened to the things of God, you may just need a wake-up call as well. You see, Ebenezer Scrooge had to endure some hard times in his life, and sometimes we have to endure some hard times as well. Sometimes God has to get our attention; and just like Ebenezer Scrooge, sometimes we have to endure our own pain as well. But you say, "Come on Joe, pain?" Yes, I said pain. You see, many times our hearts can become so hardened to the things of God that we can't enjoy the fullness of his grace because we are so caught up in the things of this world. Even though his amazing grace is available to all people (2 Peter 3:9), if a person does not glorify God as they should, there comes a point when God turns people over to what the Bible describes as a debased mind (Romans 1:28). Now when this happens, the sowing and reaping effect usually takes place in a person's life. But you say, "What do you mean by the sowing and reaping effect?" Well, if you recall our earlier discussion in chapter 5, you will recall what we discovered about the sowing and reaping effect. In the Old Testament book of Proverbs chapter 1, we discovered that God's word speaks about the Call of Wisdom; and in verse 31 of chapter 1, we read these words, "Therefore they shall eat the fruit of their own way, And be filled to the full with their own fancies." Question: What does this mean? What does it mean to eat the fruit of their own way? Well, to fit all this into what we're uncovering in our search for the truth, let us take a look at what God is speaking about. And to do that, we must take another look at what are the works, or fruits of the flesh, which in this case is a direct clue to what Proverbs 1:31 is speaking about. I say that because the fruit of their own way that this verse is referring to is a direct connection to who God considers as a fool. In a nutshell, those who travel through life fulfilling their own desires of the flesh produce nothing but destruction for and to themselves. They are fools because they think they can do whatever they want, and that there will not be any consequences for their willful disobedience of that which God's word declares as foolishness. They think they are wise, when in fact, they are fools. The reference to this is described in Romans 1:22 where it says, "Professing to be wise, they became fools."

Now there are many in the world of Christendom today who believe that the first chapter of Romans is only speaking about immoral lifestyles, such as sodomy (homosexuality—men with men, women with women) etc. They tend to zero in on a specific part of this chapter, which does indeed address the homosexual mind-set as being one that fits into the category of a debased mind; but there is much, much more to those who fit into the category of debased minds as well. How so, you ask? Well, if you take a good look at the list from which God gives people up to do the things that are not fitting in his sight, you will see the list includes being filled with all unrighteousness, sexual immorality, wickedness, covetousness, maliciousness, full of envy, murder, strife, deceit, evil-mindedness; they are whisperers, backbiters, haters of God, violent, proud, boasters, inventors of evil things, disobedient to parents, undiscerning, untrustworthy, unloving, unforgiving, unmerciful.

Question: Would you say that this list is restricted to only those who are leading immoral lifestyles such as homosexuals? Another question: Does a great deal of what's on this list line up with what God's word says is a works or fruit of the flesh that we read from Galatians 5:19-21? I think they do, which tells me that there's a whole lot more people on God's list of those with debased minds than only those who are practicing an immoral lifestyle such as homosexuality. Now you say, but what's your point? You see, the point is, if you take a good look at this list of who God considers as having a debased mind, you and I are probably on that list. You see, it's easy to throw stones at others. It's easy to point out a flaw or an imperfection in someone else's life, but it's extremely difficult to see the flaws or imperfections in our own lives. We (You) might just be in the same category as those having a debased mind and might just be practicing one of the works or fruits of the flesh that are listed in these truths of God's word. But you say, "How will I know if I am practicing something that is a works [fruit] of the flesh?" And if I am, how can I change that which is not fitting in God's sight? Answer: We can't on our own. But then again, that's what we've been discovering throughout this book in our search for the truth, which takes us back to the scripture from the beginning of this chapter found in Hebrews 3:12 and 13, which also takes us back to the lives of the three characters we've been taking a look at, Ebenezer Scrooge, Nicodemus, and Saul of Tarsus. Which also takes us back to a previous chapter (chapter 13) in which we started to uncover a necessary part of belief, which is self-examination.

You see in this particular scripture lesson, there are some hidden truths that without the illuminating light of the Holy Spirit, it is literally impossible to understand what it is saying. I say that because within these truths of God's word, it is speaking about a hardened heart as it relates to believers. So obviously if these words are meant for believers, then it must be that God is warning those who claim to be Christians to guard themselves against having a hardened heart. And what is a condition that can lead to a hardened heart? Well, according to this word from God, it is the deceitfulness of sin. But wait! If our search for the truth is going to be complete, I truly believe we must apply these teachings from God's word to ourselves first. We must ask the question by beginning with self-examination. I say that because if you read what God's word says, we might just be caught up in the deception of a hardened heart, a hardened heart that is a by-product of sin. And who is the author of deception and sin? You guessed it: the devil. But you say, "What does all of this have to do with the lives of the three people we've been looking at?" And that, my fellow truth seeker, is a very good question. I say that is a good question because in reality, there are two elements to self-examination. First, there is self-examination as it relates to a personal relationship in/with God/Jesus Christ/Holy Spirit. And second, there is self-examination as it relates to whether or not we are free from the bondage of the sins of the flesh, such as those listed within what we've discovered earlier in this chapter from Galatians chapter 5 and Romans chapter 1. Whether we realize it or not, this is a major truth that we must discover if we're ever going to be in a right relationship with the one triune God of the Bible. But also, by and through an honest and truthful self-examination of ourselves, we can enjoy the bountiful fruits of what the Spirit will manifest in a life that is within the truths of God's word. Everyone and anyone who wishes to be a follower of Jesus Christ must begin with self-examination. But not only is self-examination a one-time thing, it must be an ongoing part of the

Christian walk on the narrow path to life eternal. Another very important aspect to this is not only our self-examination, but we are to examine those who claim the name of Christ as well. How so, you ask? Well, take a good look at what it says in verse 13 of Hebrews chapter 3 with regard to exhorting one another daily. It says, "But exhort one another daily while it is called 'Today.'" Why? For fear that our hearts would become hardened to the truth of God's word by and through sins' deceptive power. But this brings to light another question. And what is that, you ask? Well, I happen to believe that the answer to that question is one of the most important questions of the present-day age in which we live. For me, this is such an important question of our time that I truly believe it has led to many of the deceptions we are seeing in the modern-day world of Christendom today. The devil has so penetrated the hearts and minds of those who claim the name of Christ today that the modern-day churches in America (as well as the world) have fallen prey to the wiles and the snares of the devil. Much of what we see in the modern-day churches of today can be found within the pages of God's word and especially within the first three chapters of the book of the Revelation. But before we start examining some of the problems within the modern-day churches of today, let's take a look at some of the problems within the hearts of Ebenezer Scrooge, Nicodemus, and Saul of Tarsus. I say that because I truly believe that self-examination and exhortation has a lot to do with each other. I have found that to be true in my own life and it was evident in the lives of Scrooge, Nicodemus, and Saul of Tarsus. In God's word, there lies a golden nugget of truth that I truly believe is a direct connection to God's love and God's grace in a person's life. It says in Revelation 3:19 these words, "As many as I love, I rebuke and chasten. Therefore be zealous and repent." Question: What does this mean? And what can we learn from this golden nugget of truth from God's word in our search for the truth?

First, we talked about pain and the fact that sometimes God has to get our attention. He has to get our attention because if he didn't rebuke and chasten us, it would go against his very nature. Remember what we learned earlier in this book that God doesn't wish that anyone should perish, but that all should come to repentance. And what did Scrooge, Nicodemus, and Saul of Tarsus need in their lives? They all needed to repent. Their hearts were hardened to the things of God because they all loved the works (fruits) of the flesh more than they did the fruits of the Spirit. And talking about the fruits of the Spirit, what was the one thing Old Scrooge said after his heart-wrenching encounter with the three spirits that one Christmas

Eve. He said, "I will live in the Past, the Present, and the Future! The Spirits of all Three shall strive within me. Oh Jacob Marley! Heaven, and the Christmas Time be praised for this. I say it on my knees, old Jacob, on my knees!" Question: Did you catch what Scrooge said? He said, "The Spirits of all Three shall strive within me." And what did we discover earlier in this chapter the three spirits represented? You guessed it: the triune God; the three in one; God the Father, God the Son (Jesus), and God the Holy Spirit (comforter). Scrooge had made a decision to alter his life, and he was now going to strive to live within the boundaries and limits of the spirits. Question: What does it mean to strive to live within the boundaries and limits of the Spirit (s)? Well, according to Scrooge, the connection to striving and living in the Spirit has something to do with heaven and Christmas. How so, you ask? Well, take a good look at what Scrooge said. He said, "Heaven, and the Christmas Time be praised for this." And who is associated with heaven and Christmas, God and Jesus Christ. Heaven is where God is, and Jesus Christ is the reason why people celebrate Christmas. Christmas is associated with the birth of God's Son, Jesus Christ. Scrooge was making a confession that he had not lived within the boundaries and limits of the God of the Bible. In his own way, the author of A Christmas Carol, Charles Dickens, had wonderfully set in place what the Christmas story represents. It represents redemption and salvation to those who wish to alter their lives by putting their trust in the one triune God of the universe, the God of the past, the present, and the future. Scrooge had to endure the eye-opening power of God's Spirit to soften his heart so he could see what the deceiving power of sin had done in his life. A hardened heart had destroyed his business partner, Jacob Marley. But within the genius writings of Charles Dickens, he used Marley to warn his friend and business partner, Scrooge, of his pending judgment if he didn't alter his life.

Second, the word "strive" in the dictionary is defined as such: to make a strong effort; to struggle vigorously (energetically). But you say, "So what's your point, Joe?" And that's a good question. You see, the point is, once you make a willful commitment to allow God's Spirit to come into your heart, there is a striving or a strong effort to live within the boundaries or limits of what the word or Spirit of God teaches. There is a striving that takes place in a truly repentant heart. Once your heart is truly opened to God's Spirit, a true affirmation of a redeemed heart is to please Almighty God, no matter what! One thing you must keep in mind is that you can't fool God. There are literally multitudes of people who claim to be a true follower of the one triune God of the Bible, but their hearts are actually hardened to the things of God. Their hearts remain hardened to the things of God because of the pride that has manifested within those hearts and oftentimes, God has to intervene to get their attention. Such was the case in Ebenezer Scrooge's life. Such was the case in the lives of the Pharisees named Nicodemus and Saul of Tarsus as well. Like Scrooge, they were arrogant. They were conceited. They were smug (full of themselves). They were self-satisfied. They were self-righteous and just like Scrooge, they truly needed a visit from the one triune God of the universe; the three in one; the ghosts of Christmas Past, Present, and Future. How about you, my fellow truth seeker? Are the ghosts of Christmas Past, Present, and Future visiting the very depths of your heart at this time? Is God's Spirit beginning to soften a heart that has become hardened to his ways (truths)? It is an important question, my friend. It is an important question because it is a question that will begin to determine whether or not you will ever find the narrow path that leads to heaven. Scrooge finally realized that he was headed down a path that was leading him to his ultimate destruction. He finally realized it because of God's intervention in his life. He had to endure some pain before he could enjoy the gain. What gain, you ask, the gain that comes within a truly repentant heart. The gain that comes into a truly repentant heart and life is the gain of the fruits of the Spirit, which are, as we discovered earlier in this chapter: love, joy, peace, long-suffering, kindness, goodness, faithfulness, gentleness, and self-control. And according to the word of God, those who are in Christ (born again) have crucified the flesh with its passions and desires. In other words, the fruits of the flesh are put to death because the Spirit of God that now lives within the heart of a truly repentant sinner will give you the power to help you overcome the fleshly and worldly passions and desires (wide path) that can control a life that is hardened to the things of God. You see, Scrooge had truly been born again of God's Spirit and was now going to be a recipient of the fruits that lie within the realms of God's kingdom. How do you know that, you ask? I know it because of what happened to Scrooge after he spoke those words to Jacob Marley. He got down on his knees and praised and thanked God for what he endured by and through the visit of those three ghosts. His heart had been changed and he was, in his own words, "not the man I was." And because of that, Scrooge could now begin to receive the fruits that come to a heart that has truly and genuinely repented a changed life, a changed man, a changed heart, a heart that is focused on the things of God instead of the things of its own personal passions and desires. But then again, please keep in mind, I'm just a forklift operator. After all, what do I know?

CHAPTER 16

A Jealous God

God is jealous, and the Lord avenges; The Lord avenges and is furious. The Lord will take vengeance on His adversaries, And He reserves wrath for His enemies; The Lord is slow to anger and great in power, And will not at all acquit the wicked.
—Nahum 1:2 and 3a

BY NOW YOU may be getting a little tired of hearing about Ebenezer Scrooge and the Christmas Carol story, but as we continue our search for the truth, I'd like to take a look at what I truly believe was a very important part of Scrooge's redemption story. In fact, not only was it a major part of Scrooge's redemption story, it is a major part of everyone's redemption story as well. I say that because if you read the Christmas Carol story, you will find that in the final analysis of the story, everything turns out okay. What I mean by that is that on the surface, the story ends with a happy outcome. Scrooge sees the light of his transgressions, and his heart and life are changed forever. Scrooge's employee, Bob Cratchit, gets a well-deserved raise, and he gets to put an ample amount of coal in the fireplace from which Scrooge had previously kept him from doing so. Scrooge makes amends with his nephew Fred, whom he had insulted the day before and said that Christmas was a humbug. Scrooge apologized for his behavior and offered a very generous monetary donation to help the poor to the two gentlemen that he had rudely insulted the day before. Scrooge helped his employee, Bob Cratchit's son, Tiny Tim, get the medical attention he needed that saved his life. All in all, it was said of Scrooge that he was even better than his word with regard to how he kept Christmas. In the final analysis, Scrooge was seen by nearly everyone as good a friend, as good a master, and as good a man as the good old city knew. In fact, it was said of Scrooge that he became the best in the world at living out these qualities in his life. But then after these words were offered about Scrooge, we learn an important message for anyone seeking redemption. These words should be so entrenched within the very walls of your memory that you should never forget them. I say that because these words have become such a major component of my personal redemption story that words cannot express my thankfulness to Mr. Dickens for putting them into the Christmas Carol story. What are they, you ask? Well, they come from the very words of Scrooge himself when he says, "Some people laughed to see the alteration in him, but he let them laugh, and little heeded them; for he was wise enough to know that nothing ever happened on this globe, for good, at which some people did not have their fill of laughter in the outset; And knowing that such as these would be blind anyway, he thought it quite as well that they should wrinkle up their eyes in grins, as have the malady (any undesirable or disordered condition) in less attractive forms. His own heart laughed: and that was quite enough for him" (The words of Ebenezer Scrooge).

Now I'm sure by now you're probably asking yourself, "What the heck does this mean, and what the heck is he talking about?" Well, as we explore this very valuable part of our search for the truth, I think it's important that we (you) understand what these words mean in the light of a truly redeemed, born-again life (heart). You see, what Scrooge was talking about here is the fact that people had seen a change in Scrooge because of his actions. They knew the way he acted before his transformation. They knew the way he had led his life before the three ghosts of Christmas got his attention. They knew all of that, and they thought his transformation was funny. They were witnessing Scrooge's repentant heart by and through his actions, but they thought what he was doing was funny. Why? First, I think they probably thought Scrooge was a little crazy. They probably thought that Scrooge had gone or was on his way to being crazy. They were probably a little cynical and suspicious of Scrooge, because they couldn't or didn't understand that Scrooge had truly repented. In fact, I believe even if they had wanted to believe that Scrooge had been transformed, they couldn't fully understand what true repentance is all about. How so, you ask? Well, take a look at what Scrooge said. He was saying that the transformation that had taken place in his life was a good thing, but that there are always those who will make fun of someone because that person has a changed heart (repented/been converted). Those who laugh and make fun of a person for changing their life can't understand repentance because they are blind and can't understand what true repentance is all about. So they laugh and make fun of those who truly have a changed heart and have truly repented of their evil ways. But the key words to this whole transformation of Scrooge were the words "for good." I say that because if you take another look at what Scrooge said, you will see that Scrooge himself understood this truth.

What truth, you ask? The truth that nothing ever happened (takes place) in this world for good, at which some who are blinded to what good is laugh and make fun of those who are trying to do good. But the key to knowing who the blind are Scrooge is talking about goes back to those who have not been changed or transformed by the Holy Spirit. I say that because according to Scrooge, they are blind because they can't completely understand what good is and what the word of God says with regard to the word "good." In the New Testament book of Romans chapter 3, God's word speaks about this with regard to those whom he considers to be good. And what does he say,

There is none righteous, no, not one; There is none who understands; There is none who seeks after God. They have turned aside; They have together become unprofitable; There is none who does good, no not one.""Their throat is an open tomb; With their tongues they have practiced deceit"; "The poison of asps is under their lips"; "Whose mouth is full of cursing and bitterness. "Their feet are swift to shed blood; Destruction and misery are in their ways; And the way of peace they have not known.""There is no fear of God before their eyes."

Question: What does all this mean? What is God referring to? How do we know that Scrooge was referencing goodness with regard to the God of the Bible? Answer: Well again, if you recall what we discovered in our last chapter (chapter 15), after Scrooge had realized that he was still alive after the three ghosts had visited him the night before, you will recall that he got down on his knees and thanked and prayed to the God of heaven for sending his former friend and business partner Jacob Marley to help open his eyes. He had been blinded by the foolishness of this life. He was one of those who had been traveling on the wide path to his ultimate destruction and had now seen the truth of his error and truly repented. But you say, "How do you know that his eyes were open to the things of the God of the Bible (Christianity)?" After all, there are multitudes of gods that people refer to and worship in the world today. How do you know Scrooge wasn't referring to one of those gods? Well, if you do your homework, you will discover that throughout history, people have been worshipping other gods. In fact, if you do your homework properly, you will discover that the worshipping of these gods is what ultimately keeps many people from finding the one true God of the universe, the God of the Holy Bible, which can only be found by and through a truly repentant and truly humble heart and true belief in the Son of God, who is Jesus Christ (a great deal of this truth we have already uncovered).

Now when we think of worshipping after other gods, I (we) think of the word "idol." The dictionary defines the word "idol" as such: an image, as a statue, worshipped as a deity (God or holy being); any person or thing devotedly admired. Now when people think about this, they think in the terms of some statue or some image, perhaps such things as a cow, or the sun, or the moon, or possibly things made of stone or wood. Things like the molded (golden) calf that was worshipped in violation of God's commandments in the Old Testament book of Exodus chapter 32. It says that by worshipping this idol, the people Moses had led out of Egypt had corrupted themselves (v. 7); it also says that because the people had violated God's laws, his anger was hot against them and he wanted to consume them with his wrath. In fact, the exact name the God of the Bible used to describe these people is stiff-necked. And the Lord said to Moses, "I have seen this people, and indeed it is a stiff necked people (v. 9). It means they were stubborn and arrogant. God could have consumed all the people and started over again with Moses. But do you know what? He didn't! Why? Because Moses pleaded with God and reminded God of his covenant with his servants Abraham, Isaac, and Israel (Jacob) with regard to the promised inheritance (vv. 12, 13). Can you believe that? Moses was actually responsible for changing the God of the universe's mind. God's intention was to literally wipe the people out because they had violated his commandments. But do you know something else? If you check out the rest of the story for yourself, you will find that the same people that had violated God's law by worshipping the idol made of gold were ultimately put to death. Not all of them. But about three thousand of them fell that day (v. 28). Why did they die? They died because they didn't repent of their transgressions toward God. They died because they choose to stand on the side of idol worship instead of on the side of the Lord (God). How do you know that, you ask? Well, if you take a look at what happened, you will see that after Moses came down from his meeting with God on the mountain, you will find that Moses was very angry because the people had violated God's commandments by worshipping a false idol. In fact, if you do your homework, you will discover that the summation of all that was happening to these people that God has chosen as his own was because God was and still is a jealous god. I say that because of what we learn about God's character. In chapter 34 verse 14 of the Old Testament book of Exodus, we read these words, "For you shall worship no other god, for the Lord, whose name is Jealous, is a jealous God." Did you catch that? The God of the universe, the God of all creation, and the God of the Holy Bible is a jealous god! In fact, it says that his very name is called jealous! And what does the word "jealous" mean? The dictionary defines the word "jealous" as such:

intolerant of unfaithfulness or bitter in rivalry: intolerant of disloyalty or infidelity; (lack of religious faith). In other words, the God who created each one of us is jealous and does not tolerate disloyalty and unfaithfulness. When someone misrepresents the one true God of this universe, they must understand that there may be consequences for that misrepresentation. And what is the consequence for unfaithfulness and disloyalty? The word is called judgment. Now at the time of the writing of this book, that word is not a very popular word. In fact, since the time I've been a follower of Jesus Christ, I have found that most people in the world of Christendom don't like to discuss or even hear about the word "judgment." It's kind of like a taboo or forbidden word in and around the realm of most of Christianity today. In most Christian circles, it's very appropriate and acceptable to speak about the God of love and how God loves us all. But don't even think about discussing or even mentioning the word "judgment" to most people. They don't want to talk about judgment, only about love. Even though the word "judgment" is used 285 times in the Bible, most people don't want to talk about it. In fact, do you know something else? The word "judgment" appears more often in the Bible than the word "love." That's right! The word "judgment" appears 211 times in the Old Testament, and it appears 74 times in the New Testament. The word "love" appears 280 times in the Bible. It appears 124 times in the Old Testament and 156 times in the New Testament. Did you get that? The word "judgment" is used more often in the Bible than the word "love." But in most Christian circles today, the word "judgment" is a taboo or a forbidden word. Question: Why is that? Why is the word "judgment" such a taboo and a forbidden word? Well, for the complete answer to that question, it would take a lot more time than we have in this book. But I will remind you once again what I have discovered in my own personal search for the truth on the narrow path of my own faith journey and that is this. When serving God, you must always remember that there is always going to be an/the adversary (devil/Satan). The devil is the great deceiver and with that kind of thinking in mind, who do you think would want to get people more focused on the word "love" than the word "judgment"? I say it's the devil, and especially within the hearts of those who claim to be his followers. But then again, it doesn't surprise me at all. Because as we've discovered throughout this book that's who people are up against, the wiles and the schemes of the devil. And that's why it's so important to understand that the devil is going to try everything in his arsenal to mislead anyone who chooses to have a relationship with God.

You see, idols or false gods in a person's life can come in many forms. With the people in the Exodus story the false god came in the form of a golden calf. How about you, my fellow truth seeker? Are there any idols in your life? If there is, then possibly the devil is using that idol to keep you from the one true God of the universe. In return, that idol may just be a deterrent from allowing that same god from opening your heart to the truths that we have discovered throughout this book. Make no mistake about it; the God of the Holy Bible is a God of love, but he is also a God of wrath and judgment to/for those who reject a personal relationship with his Son, Jesus Christ. Both Scrooge and Marley had the/an idol of the almighty dollar (money). Could that be the idol that is separating you from God? Could it be the idol of pride? Could it be the idol of a sport and/or a specific sports team, possibly skiing or basketball or bowling or softball? Could it be the idol of a person? What I mean by that is there a person in your life who you are trying to please, and you're putting that person ahead of Almighty God. Maybe by trying to please that person and/or yourself, you are caught up in the idol of illicit sexual activity that is in direct violation of God's word, possibly fornication (sex before marriage) or adultery (having sex with someone you're not married to). Maybe it's the idol of pleasure, meaning you want to please yourself and your inner feelings instead of God. Maybe you're addicted to the idol of pornography, and you have to continually feed that pleasure idol. Maybe you're caught up in the idol of power and prestige that fuels your own ego and self-ambitions at the cost of hurting others, including your family and those who are the closest to you. And maybe, just maybe, you may be caught in the idol of the television set. In fact, I happen to believe that the idol of the television set may just be the biggest idol of the modern-day world that we live in today. Now please don't get me wrong. I'm not saying that the television set is necessarily evil. But please believe me when I tell you that there is no doubt in my mind whatsoever that unless your well prepared and under the protection and guidance of the Holy Spirit (comforter), the television set is a huge weapon that is being used in the devil's arsenal of keeping people on the wide path of/to destruction.

Well, by now you may be saying to yourself, "You've got to be kidding." What does all of this have to do with me and our search for the truth? Answer: It has everything to do with us (you)! Why, you ask? Well, take a good look at our scripture reading at the beginning of this chapter, and then take a good look at what we read from the story of those who were caught in the act of worshipping the idol in their lives, the golden calf.

As we discovered earlier, those who had worshipped the golden calf were responsible for the one true God's anger toward them. But then there's a specific climax to this incident that really challenges anyone who truly wants to serve the one true God. In fact, this is really where the rubber meets the road with regard to a person's relationship with God (Jesus Christ). Now here's the scene. God was mad and so was Moses (God's representative). But even though the people were doing wrong in their idol worship, they were given an out and a chance to repent and redeem themselves. How? Well, look at what it says in verses 26 and 27 of Exodus chapter 32, "Now when Moses saw that the people were unrestrained for Aaron [a priest] had not restrained them, to their shame among their enemies, then Moses stood in the entrance of the camp, and said, 'Whoever is on the Lord's side—come to me!'" And do you know what? That same question is being asked today. In fact, that same question is being asked of you right now in this book. Whose side are you on today? Are you on the God of the Holy Bible's side? Or are you on the God of this world's system's side? The devil himself! If you're not on the God of the Holy Bible's side, then believe me when I tell you that you are in serious jeopardy of God's (Jesus Christ) wrath and judgment. But you say, "I'm not sure of whose side I'm on." And if you're even contemplating that question, my fellow truth seeker, then there's a pretty good chance that you're not on the one true God of the Holy Bible's side. But do you want to know another thing? Within the world of Christendom today, there are literally multitudes of people who believe that they're on the proper side of the one true God of the Holy Bible, when in reality, they are not. They are like those who had to choose which side they were on, but they have never really been on the right side. How so, you ask? Well, take another look at what it says in verse 25, "For Aaron [a priest] had not restrained them to their shame among their enemies." Question: Who are the priests of the modern-day age we (you) are living in today? Answer: Anyone who is truly born again of God's Spirit (the comforter). Anyone who has found the narrow path to life eternal is a royal priest, and therefore they are a member of the royal priesthood. God's word says just that in the New Testament book of 1 Peter 2:9 when it says, "But you are a chosen generation, a royal priesthood, a holy nation." Which takes us back to the question God's representative, Moses, placed before the people who were worshipping the false idol (the golden calf)? Who's on the Lord's (God) side? You see, the people were given a choice to choose. Another place in God's word that helps solidify this right to choose whose side you're on is found in the Old Testament book of Joshua 24:15.

The man Joshua became the leader of Israel when Moses passed the baton on to him before he died. Without getting into great detail about this part of God's word, the summation of this section of scripture is laid out in the fact that the people were given the choice of who they wanted to serve. The false gods of the Amorites (people who welcomed and celebrated evil, i.e., idol worship, etc.) that their ancestors had worshipped, or the one true Lord (God) of the Holy Bible. Joshua, in like manner as Moses before him, asks the question, "Choose for yourselves this day whom you will serve." Now in this particular situation, the people made the right decision. They choose the right path. How do you know that, you ask? Well, take a look at what it says in verses 19 to 21 of Joshua chapter 24, "But Joshua said to the people, 'You cannot serve the Lord, for He is a holy God. He is a jealous God; He will not forgive your transgressions nor your sins.'" And then comes the climax and the ultimate word(s) you and I must pay close attention to. It is the word "if." Here, the word "if" is significant because it declares a condition. It stipulates and specifies a condition in which God will harm and consume (devour) someone who forsakes (abandons) him. How so, you ask? Well, take a look at what it says in verse 20 where it says, "If you forsake the Lord [God] and serve foreign gods, then He will turn and do you harm and consume you, after He has done you good." What? He will do you harm and consume you, after he has done you good. What's that about, you ask? Well, for the complete answer to that question, you'll have to move on to the next chapter. But I will tell you one thing before you do. There is a direct connection to the royal priesthood spoken about in the New Testament and the one spoken of in the Old Testament. How so, you ask? Well, take another look at what it says with regard to the priest named Aaron. What does it say? It says, "Now when Moses saw that the people were unrestrained [for Aaron had not restrained them, to their shame among their enemies]." Question: Who was Aaron with regard to God, and what was his role in restraining the people? Answer: Aaron was a priest. He was God's representative and in the modern-day era in which we live today, he is/would be known as a pastor, a minister, and/or someone who is a member of the clergy. Another question: Who were the people's enemies? Answer: They were supposed to be those who were on the outside of the camp of the chosen people of God (Israelites). But as we learn from this teaching, God's enemies aren't always on the outside of the camp, but they are on the inside as well. There are multitudes of Aarons within the camp (church) of God's chosen people today. But then again, please keep in mind, I'm just a forklift operator. After all, what do I know?

CHAPTER 17

Counting the Cost

Jesus said; "So likewise, whoever of you does not forsake all that he
has cannot be My disciple. For which of you, intending to build
a tower does not sit down first and count the cost, whether he has
enough to finish it—"
—Luke 14:27 and 28

AT THE BEGINNING of the last chapter, I said that by now you
may be getting a little tired of hearing about Ebenezer Scrooge
and the Christmas Carol story. However, as we continue our search for
the truth, there is one more thing that I'd like us to take a good look at
in Scrooge's story. I say that because as we move into the last phase of our
(your) search for the truth in finding the narrow path to life (eternal), there
is one more subject that must be brought out if our search is going to be
complete. And what is that, you ask? Well, for the answer to that question,
we must once again take a look into Ebenezer Scrooge's redemption story.
I say that because within Scrooge's redemption story there lies yet another
key piece to the puzzle of Scrooge's story. But more importantly for you
and me, it is a key piece to our redemption story as well. That is, if you have
a redemption story. How so, you ask? Well, take a good look at what we've
discovered already. I say that because, if you recall in an earlier chapter,
we discovered that after Scrooge realized that he was not dead, he realized
that the time before him was his own. In other words, Scrooge had such a
repentant heart and was so full of regret that he wanted to make up for lost
time. But the question is "Why did he want to make up for lost time?" And
if he indeed wanted to make up for lost time, who was he trying to make
up for lost time to, himself or his family? Those who he came in contact
with in his professional or business life? Who was he trying to make up
time to? Well, I think that question can be asked of you and me as well,
but only if you've been redeemed (converted/born again). Who are you
trying to impress in your life, my fellow truth seeker: yourself, your family,
those whom you work with? Or is there another aspect to making up for

lost time and impressing those around us (you)? And for the answer to that question, let's take a look at what we learn from Old Scrooge himself. I say that because as we learned previously, after Scrooge had seen the errors of his ways, he gave thanks and praise to his friend Jacob Marley, God, and Jesus Christ for opening his eyes to the truth of those errors. But then there's one more thing that Scrooge did that was the key element and key piece in the puzzle of Scrooge's redemption story. In fact, it was such a key piece of the puzzle in Scrooge's redemption story that that same piece of the puzzle must be in our (your) personal redemption story as well. And what is that key piece, you ask? Well, it lies within one of the first things Old Scrooge did after he had his eyes opened to the truth about the errors in his life. And what is that key piece of the puzzle, you ask? Answer: He went to church! He got himself dressed in his finest clothes, and he went to church. Church, you say! Yes, I said church. In fact, if I didn't mention this fact in our search for the truth, most people who read the Christmas Carol story wouldn't even consider this as much of a factor at all. In other words, for most people, it's not a big deal. So Scrooge went to church. So what? And to those who might say or even think that one of the first things Scrooge did after he saw the error of his ways was to visit a church was not a big deal, I would say to them in the words of Ebenezer Scrooge, a hearty "Bah, humbug!" Why would I say that, you ask? I would say that because redemption and the church go hand in hand with each other. In other words, you can't have one without the other. You can't be truly redeemed without being a part of the church. How so, you ask? Well, please let me explain. You see, once a person is truly redeemed (converted/born again), they become a new creation in God's realm, which is the spiritual realm. Oh yes, we are still living in the physical realm of our existence in the present world of being human, but within the spiritual realm of God's kingdom, we are transformed into a holy temple. In other words, once a person is truly born again of God's Spirit that person's body becomes a temple to and for God. And what does a temple of God represent? It represents a place where God is worshipped. It represents a place of holiness. It represents a sanctuary and/or a place of refuge. But there is something else that a person must consider with regard to a temple of God. You see, there are literally thousands and thousands of people in the world today who do not have the slightest understanding about the whole temple scenario. I say that because of my own personal experience while traveling on the narrow path in my pursuit of the truth. How so, you ask? Well, take a good look at what it says in the word of God in the New Testament book of 1 Corinthians

6:19 and 20. It says "Do you not know that your body is the temple of the Holy Spirit who is in you, whom you have from God, and you are not your own? For you were bought at a price; therefore glorify God in your body and in your spirit, which are God's." Did you catch that? It says that you are not your own, and that you were bought at a price. And what is that price? Well, the summation of the answer to that question can be found in the New Testament book of 1 Peter 1:13-21. In a nutshell, this teaching speaks about how God's Son, Jesus Christ, paid the price that was required by God to atone for our sins or transgressions against him (We've uncovered this fact throughout this book). However, the question with regard to the temple of God is something that must be considered in our pursuit for the truth, because it is at the heart of a true believer's journey into finding the narrow path of eternal life. How so, you ask? Well, it begins with the words "you are not your own." In other words, once a person truly comes to believe the fact that Jesus was indeed the very Son of God, then there is a consummation that takes place within that person's heart, the consummation of the Holy Spirit that is given to you by God when you truly believe. The best way to understand this is like when a baby is conceived in a/the women's womb. The seed from the father meets up with a seed from the mother, and a new life is formed. Likewise, the same thing happens in the life of a true believer. The Father (Almighty God the Creator) plants his seed (the comforter) within the body of a true believer, and the Holy Spirit is released into that person's life (body) and then they become an/the actual temple of God; no, not a building but a body. A body that now has God's Spirit living within them. This takes us back to what I stated earlier with regard to the multitudes of people not having an/the understanding of the whole "temple of God" truth.

You see, what I have discovered in my own personal faith journey is that there are literally multitudes of people in the world of Christendom today who have actually embraced a false idol into their lives, and the saddest part about it is they don't even realize that they have. And what is that false idol, you ask? It is the church itself! Oh, I'm not talking about what the true church actually is. I'm talking about what many in the world of Christendom today have actually embraced as an idol and because of it, they are deeply and seriously deceived. Many have embraced the worship of a false idol of a/the church building, rather than the fact that the true church is where the Holy Spirit dwells. And where is that? It is within the bodies (hearts) of those who have truly received the consummation of God's Spirit. Remember what we have learned previously in this book that

"God is Spirit, and those who worship Him MUST WORSHIP IN spirit and truth" (John 4:24).

Now there is much, much more to the whole temple of God teaching and the effects it has had and is having in the world of Christendom today. However, there are two particular thoughts I have in mind that I would like to share in our search for the truth, and these are the following. First, the words; you are not your own and second, counting the cost. By now, you're probably asking yourself the question, "What do these words have to do with our search for the truth? What does Ebenezer Scrooge and him going into a/the church after his redemption have to do with our pursuit in finding the narrow path to eternal life?" And that, my fellow truth seeker, is a great question. In fact, I happen to believe it is at the heart of one's pursuit of God himself. I say that because at the heart of belief in Jesus Christ itself, these two thoughts must play a part in a person's personal pursuit of God. How so, you ask? Well, remember the words we learned back in chapter 3 of this book with regard to finding the narrow path to life (heaven) being a difficult one (Matthew 7:14). It's difficult because as human beings, we don't want to give up control of our lives. Our fleshly desires want to control us and as human beings, we don't have the capacity to fight off our personal fleshly desires on our own. And that's why it's so important to realize that if we (you) truly want to pursue the God of the Bible, it must come by and through the shed blood of God's son, Jesus Christ's death on the cross at Calvary. Now why is that so important? It's important because once you become a true follower of Jesus Christ, you must realize that your life is no longer your own. Your body becomes a/the temple of God, and what was the temple known for? It was known for worshipping God, but it was also known for sacrifice. We learned about this in an earlier chapter (chapter 11). You see, once you make a/the decision to follow Jesus Christ, you must realize two things. Your life is not your own anymore. Meaning, you now live to please God and not yourself (flesh). It belongs to God. It belongs to God, and we must realize that finding the narrow path to life eternal comes by and through a life of sacrifice. In other words, we sacrifice our lives to and for God. We become a sacrifice so that others may live. Just as Jesus Christ sacrificed his life for others, so too does anyone who wants to follow him. And that's why it's so very important to understand that there is a cost involved with being a true follower of Jesus Christ. A cost, you say? Yes, I said a cost, the cost of sacrifice and the cost of being hated by the world. Now what do I mean by the world? The world represents the philosophies of those who are traveling on the wide path of destruction

(Matthew 7:13). Their personal attitudes, their personal viewpoints, their personal ideas, their personal thinking, their personal way of life, their personal values, and their personal beliefs are all in opposition to the one true God of the Bible. They've never really embraced Jesus Christ as their personal Lord and Savior. They've never really had a personal relationship with God by and through Jesus Christ. Oh, they say they believe in Jesus Christ, but they are like the scribes and Pharisees of Jesus' day. And what did Jesus have to say to them? Well, if you recall what we discovered again in chapter 11, you will remember that Jesus had this to say to them, "Woe to you, scribes and Pharisees, hypocrites! For you cleanse the outside of the cup and dish, but inside you are full of extortion and self-indulgence." In other words, they had an outward appearance of being godly people, but deep inside where it really counts to God, they were full of themselves. Their hearts were empty and so were the words they spoke. You see, they were self-deceived. They thought they were on the right path to heaven, but they were actually traveling down the road to their ultimate destruction in hell. But you say, "Okay Joe, I think I understand what you're saying, but what does all of this have to do with me and our search for the truth?" After all, what you're speaking about happened back in Jesus' day. It took place nearly two thousand years ago. So what does this have to do with me (us)? And that, my fellow truth seeker, is yet another great question. And do you know what? For the answer to that question, let's take a look back at what we discovered earlier in this chapter with regard to the first thing Ebenezer Scrooge did after his eyes were opened to the truth. He went to church! However, there lies a question that just so happens to be a greater question within the act of what Scrooge did by going to a church. I say that because the question that lies within the act of what Scrooge did is a question that lies at the very foundation of our (your) redemption story as well. And what is that question, my fellow truth seeker? It is the one that lies at the very heart of God's light (truth) in this world. It is the church itself. But the question for us in our pursuit for the truth is not that Scrooge went to a church, but, the question for you and me is "What kind of a church did Scrooge go to?"

In other words, what was going on in that church? Or better yet, "What did God think of the church Scrooge went to?" Now you're probably asking yourself: "What is he talking about?" A church is a church. A church is where God is. A church is a church is a church is a church. Oh yeah! A church is a church. Well, let's take a good look at what God says about a church. I say that because one of the key elements and key pieces to the puzzle of true redemption lies within the cost of representing the truth of God that was established by Jesus Christ after his death. The church is known as the bride of Christ. Jesus is known as the bridegroom. In the New Testament book of John chapter 3, there is a reference to this analogy or likeness where it says in verse 29 and 30 that "he who has the bride is the bridegroom; but the friend of the bridegroom, who stands and hears him, rejoices greatly because of the bridegroom's voice." Therefore, this joy of mine is fulfilled. And then comes the clincher when it says, "He [God/ Jesus Christ] must increase, but I must decrease."

In other words, going back to what I stated earlier in this chapter, if you want to be a true follower of Jesus Christ and therefore be a representative of God in this evil and wicked world, then you're going to have to count the cost. Why? Well, take a good look at what it says. He who has the bride is the bridegroom. He who has the bride (Jesus Christ—the Holy Spirit, i.e., comforter) is God's Temple in the body (church) and is the true sanctuary (safe haven, shelter, refuge) for God. In other words, the true church of God lies within the hearts of those who hear his words (voice) and obeys them. The true church is not a building, but it is a collection of people whose bodies are now being indwelled by the driving force of the Holy Spirit. But take another look at what it says. I say that because here is a key element to finding true joy in your life, to having your life fulfilled with joy. I know about this joy because I personally live with that joy each and every day of my own life. And what is that joy, you ask? It is the joy of exalting Jesus Christ (God) instead of me (ourselves); in other words, whatever I (we) do, it is imperative (cannot be avoided) that Jesus (God) comes first. Therefore, if a person (you) truly wishes to have a personal relationship with Jesus Christ, they must first put Jesus' (God's) integrity and honor ahead of themselves. Their ambitions, their goals, their objections, their aspirations, their dreams, their hopes, their desires must take second place to Jesus Christ (God).

Now you may be asking yourself, "But what does all of this have to do with me?" Well, if you're not a true Christian and you are still traveling on the wide path to destruction, it probably doesn't mean anything. I say that it doesn't mean anything because if you've never been born again of God's Spirit, your destiny is being sealed for destruction as you're reading this book. But you see, I hope that's not the case for you, my fellow truth seeker. It is my hope and prayer that by now, God has opened your eyes to his truth, and that you have made a decision to follow Jesus Christ as your personal Lord and Savior. However, before we move on to the next chapter in our search for the truth, there is yet one more piece to the puzzle I'd like to uncover. And what is that, you ask? Well, it is the one that goes along with what we learned about hearing God's (Jesus's) voice. It also goes along with what was said in God's word that we just uncovered with regard to the word "stand." You see, I use the word "stand" because the word "stand" is at the very core and heart of the Christian faith. In fact, if you do your homework, you will discover that the word "stand" is used some 267 times in God's word (Bible). It is without a doubt one of the key elements to a true believer's arsenal as they stand in the gap for the truth of God's word. In the scripture I used at the beginning of this chapter, the writer (Jesus) places a question of you and me. And what is that question? The question is "For which of you intending to build a tower does not sit down first and count the cost, whether he has enough to finish it?" Here, Jesus was teaching on discipleship, and the multitudes of people who were following him were positive that they wanted to follow him. However, they had a problem. And the problem was that they weren't committed. Oh, they were ready to follow Jesus if it wasn't going to cost them anything. But when Jesus laid out some of the conditions for following him, the multitudes walked away. But we shouldn't be surprised. I know I'm not. For I see the very same thing happening in today's world (so-called church). You see, in this teaching from Jesus, he is speaking about the tower as being someone's (your) life. And what he is saying is that if you want to be his disciple (follower), it won't be an easy road. So you had better count the cost of what is required to follow him. There will be consequences involved for being one of his followers. Jesus speaks about bearing a cross. And as we learned in an earlier chapter, the cross represents an instrument of death. So in other words, if you're going to follow Jesus, you had better be prepared for the worst-case scenario. It might possibly cost you your very life. And that is what it means to stand. No one likes to be hated. But if you're going to follow Jesus, you had better be prepared for that very thing happening in your life. But then again, remember what we have learned about the narrow path to life (Matthew 7:14). There are few who find it. How about you, my fellow truth seeker? Will you be one of the few who find the narrow path to life? There is one thing that we can know for sure. If you're going to find the narrow way to life, there will be a cost to following Jesus? But then again, please keep in mind, I'm just a forklift operator. After all, what do I know?

CHAPTER 18

A Peculiar People

But you are a chosen generation, a royal priesthood, a holy nation, a
peculiar people; that you should show forth the praises of Him who
has called you out of darkness into His marvelous light.
1 Peter 2:9

IN THE LAST chapter, we discovered that a church is not a building,
but a church is a collection of redeemed (born again) people whose
physical bodies have had their hearts changed by the power of God's
Spirit. The physical church building represents the place where people
gather to share in the attributes and characteristics of the Christian faith.
Those attributes and characteristics that are carried out in the physical
world we live in are supposed to be in line with the spiritual side of God's
characteristics as well. Those characteristics are placed within the physical
bodies of true believers when they are born again of/in God's Spirit. There
is a distinct comparison between the nation of Israel in the Old Testament
and the church in the New Testament. The nation of Israel was God's
chosen people as we have discovered earlier in our search for the truth. The
covenant (promise) that God made with Israel goes all the way back to the
Old Testament book of Genesis chapter 11 where we first read about a man
by the name of Abram, whose name was later changed by God to the name
of Abraham. Abraham means father of many nations. Now without getting
into great detail with regard to the study of this comparison, I will simply
offer this. When God first made his covenant with Abraham, God gave
Abraham a specific command that he was to adhere to. And what was that
command? It was the command that God placed before Abraham that he
was to circumcise (cutting away the male foreskin) every male child born
on the eighth day. He was to adhere to it because it was to be a sign of the
covenant between God and his chosen people (Genesis 17:11). Now as I
said, the cutting of the foreskin and the command God gave to Abraham
in the circumcision ritual was to be a symbol or a sign of the covenant
between God and his people. But the ritual or ceremony of circumcision

has a great deal more to say to us than just a ritual or a ceremony, that is, if you're one of God's chosen people. You see, the gist of all of what I'm trying to tell you lies within what the symbol of the circumcision ritual represents. And what is that, you ask? The symbol or sign of circumcision has to do with the need to cut away sin and be cleansed. You see, it was the male organ which most clearly demonstrated the depth of depravity (wickedness and evil) because it carried the seed that produced depraved sinners. Thus, circumcision symbolized the need for a profoundly deep cleansing to reverse the effects of that depravity. But do you know something else? As it turns out, the whole ritual of circumcision had a far greater meaning than just the physical act of being circumcised. Yes, it represented a sign of the covenant between God and Abraham. Yes, it placed a physical distinction between the chosen people of God and Abraham's descendants. Yes, it put in place a/the distinctive trait and quality that was a sign of God's covenant relationship to the chosen people of that time. But the far greater meaning I'm speaking of is the one that included what God said with regard to the circumcision of those in the generations to come. I say that because the generations that were to come has brought us all the way from that time, down through the centuries of time until this present age. The present age we live in today is included as one of those generations that were to come. God was speaking about you and me, my fellow truth seeker. That is, if you've been circumcised. Circumcised, you say. Yes, I said circumcised.

You see, the physical act of being circumcised was meant to distinguish those who were God's chosen people versus those who were not God's chosen people. But the circumcision itself was not the most important piece to the puzzle of what God intended for the circumcision to represent. The most important piece of the puzzle is the piece that represents the covenant, the covenant between us (you) and God. And what is that covenant? Well, to fully understand the whole covenant relationship between God and his chosen people, we must first understand what the word "covenant" means. Now according to the dictionary, the word "covenant" means an agreement, usually formal, between two or more persons; the conditional promises made to humanity by God, as revealed in the scripture (Bible); to enter into a covenant (agreement); to promise by covenant. In other words, God says that if you are one of mine then I will have, or be in or extend a covenant with/to you. Now there is much more to the whole scenario of a covenant with God and how it relates to the physical circumcision. There is also a more important side of the circumcision covenant with God that is seen within the spiritual dimension as well. And what is that, you ask? Well, for the answer to that question, it's important for us to understand that through the generations, there have always been a special people that God has chosen as his own. And that is where the covenant started. It began with Abraham and has moved down the generational lines of people, all the way down to us to the generation that you and I are currently living in today. But you say, "Wait a minute! I'm not Jewish." I'm not of the line of Judah, which is a whole other subject in itself; but if you do your homework and allow the Holy Spirit to direct your path, you will discover that a distinct qualification between who is a Jew and who is not a Jew really boils down to one determining factor. And what is that, you ask? Well, let's take a look at what God's word says with regard to this determining factor and why it is so very important. I say it's important because this part of God's word ties into the scripture I used at the beginning of this chapter. It ties into the scripture I used at the beginning of this chapter because it clearly defines the covenant relationship between God and mankind. Both before the birth of God's Son, Jesus Christ, as well as after Jesus Christ died on the cross some two thousand years ago. I say that because once again, in our search for the truth, it is imperative that we (you) must keep in mind that there are two realms which we're dealing with in our lives: the physical realm as well as the spiritual realm. Remember what we've learned throughout this book, "God is Spirit, and those who worship Him must worship in spirit and truth" (John 4:24). So this reminds us (you) that when we're dealing with the issues of this life, it is extremely vital that we (you) always keep in mind that we are dealing with those two sides: the physical side and the spiritual side. The things that are seen in the physical world and the things that are unseen in the spiritual world, the visible vs. the invisible. A good place to see this in God's word is found in 2 Corinthians 4:16-18 where it says,

> Therefore we do not lose heart. Even though our outward [physical] man is perishing, yet the inward [spiritual] man is being renewed day by day. For our light affliction, which is but for a moment, is working for us afar more exceeding and eternal weight of glory, while we do not look at the things which are seen [physical], but at the things which are not seen. [spiritual] For the things which are seen (physical) are temporary, but the things which are not seen [spiritual] are eternal.

This leads us to the next step in our search for the truth: the physical circumcision of God's people vs. the spiritual circumcision of God's people. I say that because with regard to the physical realm of God's covenant, the physical act of circumcision was a physical sign that clearly distinguished that the Jewish (Israel) people were set aside by God as a special people. Why was that? Why were the Jewish people set aside as a special people? Well, for the complete answer to that question, you must understand that God is sovereign. It means he is the supreme ruler of all things. He is all powerful and because he is the creator of all things, he can do whatever he wants to do. However, with regard to the whole issue of the covenant of the physical circumcision versus the covenant of the spiritual circumcision, it all really boils down to one determining factor. And what is that, you ask? It is all about faith, faith in the one true God of the Holy Bible. Faith with regard to the fact that God is sovereign, and he can do whatever he wants. Faith in the fact that the God of the Holy Bible is a God of love, and because he is a God of love, he formulated a plan in which those who truly love him and put their complete faith in him might be saved from their ultimate destruction of living on the wide path (Much of this we've already uncovered in earlier chapters).

You see, within the physical realm of God's plan for humanity, God used a physical means to unleash his plan of salvation and deliverance to those he chooses as his own. But as we consider that God used the nation (people) of Israel as a physical means to fulfill his plan of restoring mankind back to himself, we must also take into account the spiritual side as well. And what is that spiritual side? It is found within the spiritual act of circumcision. Notice I said within the spiritual act of circumcision. It is found within the spiritual act of circumcision, because it is the spiritual act of circumcision that separates those who are truly God's chosen people from those who are not. What I mean by that is that the covenant that God has with those who are truly his is first established within the hearts of those who truly belong to him. In other words, God knows our (your) heart, and he knows who truly loves him, and therefore he knows who is truly willing to submit their very lives to him. God established a covenant with his chosen people. Yes, God did use a physical sign for distinguishing those people who were and who were not his in a fleshly way. But more importantly, in the end, it is not the fleshly covenant that matters the most, it is the spiritual one. It is the covenant of the heart, the agreement between you and God. That covenant relationship that can only come by and through true belief in God's Son, Jesus Christ. But remember one thing. Whenever a covenant relationship is established between two people, there are always parts to a covenant that those people agree to live up to. It's like when two people get married. The covenant relationships between the two people getting married are put forward within the vows that those two people promise to each other. Things like to love, to honor, to cherish, and to obey, for how long, for the rest of their lives together. Now when those two people make those wedding vows to each other, they aren't only making those vows to each other, but they are placing into existence a vow before Almighty God as well. How so, you ask? Well, for the complete answer to this question, it would take a lot longer to explore than we have in this book, but I will share this much with you. In the marriage ceremony, the covenant relationship between a husband and a wife are exactly like the covenant relationship a person is supposed to have when that person places into effect a covenant between themselves and Jesus Christ (God). In the spiritual realm, that person is joined together in an intimate love relationship with Jesus Christ (God). That person is, in the reality of the unseen world (spiritual realm), marrying Jesus Christ. Now according to the dictionary, the definition of the word "intimate" is defined as marked by close acquaintance, association, or familiarity; relating to or indicative of one's deepest nature; essential; innermost; very personal; private. So in other words, when we take on a personal relationship with Jesus Christ, it's like being married to Jesus Christ. In the spiritual realm, God knows our hearts and he knows who is and who is not serious about having a wedding ceremony with his Son, Jesus Christ. He knows who is ready and willing to submit themselves to the lordship and will of the Holy Spirit in their lives. But do you know something else. In the spiritual realm, it also places into effect a necessary element to the spiritual sign between God and a true follower of Jesus Christ. Just as Almighty God used the physical sign of circumcision to identify or distinguish his chosen people in antiquity (ancient times) past, he also uses a form of circumcision to identify and distinguish those who are truly his. And what is that sign, you ask? Well, it can be found within the new-covenant relationship. The new covenant that was established when Jesus Christ died on the cross, the new covenant that was established for all those who wish to marry and have a covenant, personal relationship with God's only Son, Jesus Christ. It is found within what God's word calls the circumcision of the heart, the spiritual transformation of a person's heart, a heart that truly seeks after the things of God. If you recall, I spoke earlier about the faith of Abraham and of those in the generations that were to come after him. Yes, there was the physical sign of circumcision, but more importantly, it is the spiritual sign of a circumcised heart that is the most important. In the physical realm, it is the Jewish people who are God's chosen people. But within the spiritual realm, the chosen people of God (i.e., the church, the collective temples of God), lies within anyone who has received the true circumcision of their hearts from God. God's spirit is now living within them and a covenant relationship between God and them now exists. How do I know that, you ask? I know it because of what I discovered within the word of God that says,

> For he is not a Jew who is one outwardly, nor is circumcision that which is outward in the flesh; but he is a Jew who is one inwardly: and circumcision is that of the heart, IN THE SPIRIT, not in the letter; whose praise is not from men but from God. (Romans 2:28 and 29)

Notice it says "and circumcision is that of the heart, IN THE SPIRIT," which establishes the direct connection to John 4:24 in which God's word teaches us once again that "God is SPIRIT, and those who worship Him must worship in spirit and truth." So you see, if a person has truly received the circumcision of the heart, the outward rite (acts) is of value only when it reflects the inner reality of a heart that is separated from sin unto God. True salvation and deliverance from that sin results from the work of God's Spirit living in the heart, not mere external efforts to conform to his law. Thus, the true salvation of one's life is conceived within the heart and because of that spiritual conception, it is reflected or demonstrated within the physical realm of one's physical life. The laws of God will be consummated within a person's (your) heart by God's Spirit, and the covenant relationship between that person (you) and God/Jesus Christ/Holy Spirit may go on forever. It's like in a marriage between a husband and wife. The physical act of having sex usually seals the covenant vows that the husband and wife make with each other at/in the marriage ceremony. The physical act of sex completes the covenant vow of marriage, and the husband and wife are joined together and now are to become one flesh. There are references within the word of God that speaks of this oneness. It can be found in Genesis 2:24, Matthew 19:5 and 6, Mark 10:8, 1 Corinthians 6:16, and Ephesians 5:31.

Therefore shall a man leave his father and his mother, and shall cleave [to hold firmly] unto his wife: and they shall be one flesh (Genesis 2:24).

Likewise, in the spiritual realm, when a person receives the spiritual circumcision of the heart, the marriage relationship between God/Jesus Christ and that person begins to come to fruition. It comes to fruition because there is a desire within that person's heart to conform and be in harmony to and through the spiritual consummation of God's Spirit. The consummation of God's Spirit and that person comes by the way of belief in Jesus Christ. However, there is much more to the story than just belief in Jesus Christ. I say that because even the devil and his demons believe in Jesus Christ. They too know about the very Son of God and they tremble (James 2:19). Even fallen angels affirm the oneness of God and tremble at its implications. Demons are essentially orthodox (conforming to tradition) in their doctrine. But orthodox doctrine by itself is no proof of saving faith. They know the truth about God, Christ, and the Spirit, but they hate it and them.

Now I know that this is some heavy stuff to understand as we continue down the road of our search for the truth. But though it may be some heavy stuff to understand, it is vitally important for you to comprehend this reality. I say it is vitally important for you to understand this truth, because I truly believe that there are literally multitudes of people in the world today who are being deceived by the whole concept of this covenant relationship between them and God. How so, you ask? Well, for the answer to that question, let's take a look at the scripture we used at the beginning of this chapter with regard to being a peculiar people.

First of all, I think it's important for us to explore and discover what the word "peculiar" means and why this is so important to one's faith in Jesus Christ. The dictionary defines the word "peculiar" as such: unusual or eccentric; odd; distinct or separate from all others; belonging distinctively or primarily to one person, group, or kind; special or unique. So what is God teaching us? God is saying that if you want to have a true covenant relationship with him, a person (you) must realize right up front that the world (those on the wide path) is no longer your friend. Once you begin your journey on the narrow path of truth, the world is going to look at you in a whole new way. They will see you as being very odd, very unusual, and yes, in many instances, they will think that you are crazy. Did I say crazy? Yes, I said crazy. Why? Because those who still have their minds set on the things of this world (earth) can't understand the ways or things of God. They are not living for the things that bring praises to God, but they are living to hear the praises of men. They are full of pride. In many cases, they think they are worshipping God by and through the works they do, when in fact, they are only fueling their own egos and self-esteem through the pride of life that we discovered earlier in this book. In fact, the so-called most religious leaders of Jesus's time thought that the very Son of God, Jesus Christ, was a madman. How do I know that, you ask? Well, let's take a good look at what those religious leaders said to Jesus in the tenth chapter of the New Testament book of John.

Now to set the stage for this confrontation between Jesus and the religious leaders (Pharisees) of Jesus's time, we must understand that Jesus was trying to convince them that he was indeed the Messiah (the anticipated savior of the Jewish people) that had been foretold and predicted for centuries and centuries. He was indeed the true shepherd, and that God had sent him to be their savior and their redeemer. For hundreds and hundreds of years, the prophets (God's messengers) had spoken about the Messiah that would come to save God's chosen people, the Jews. But they wouldn't listen. They wouldn't listen because their hearts were so full of pride and selfishness that the God of this world (Satan) had blinded them from the truth. In fact, many of them accused Jesus of being a madman and having a demon in him. They said in John 10:20, "He has a demon and is mad." But then listen to the question they asked next: "Why do you listen to him?" You see, the truth is, Jesus didn't have a demon living in him, they did! They had the demon of unbelief. They were traveling on the wide path to their ultimate destruction, and they didn't even realize it. They didn't realize it because their hearts had never been circumcised by God's Spirit. They bore the physical rite of circumcision but not the spiritual one. They had the chance to be invited to the wedding covenant with Jesus Christ but because of their unbelief, they were left out. In the word of God, there is a reference to the marriage feast that is spelled out in the form of a parable (story) in the New Testament book of Matthew chapter 22. In this parable, Jesus is speaking about those who share the gospel (good news) message with others. Those who have placed their faith and trust in Jesus Christ and are being used by God in this physical world to invite others to the wedding feast (all those whose hearts have been spiritually circumcised). By sharing the good news about the saving grace of God's Son, Jesus Christ, they are given the chance to put on the wedding garment of salvation that accompanies all those who are in a true circumcision of the heart, covenant relationship with Jesus Christ. But there are also those who were invited to the wedding, but the reality is, they were not worthy. Question: Why weren't they worthy? After all, they were invited to the wedding. So if they were invited to the wedding, then why weren't they worthy? Well, for the answer to that question, let's take a look at what God's word says in verses 8 through 14 of Matthew chapter 22: "Then he said to his servants, 'The wedding is ready, but those who were invited were not worthy. Therefore go into the highways, and as many as you find, invite to the wedding.' So those servants went out into the highways and gathered together all whom they found, both bad and good. And the wedding hall was filled with guests. But when the king came in to see the guests, he saw a man there who did not have on a wedding garment. So he said to him, 'Friend, how did you come in here without a wedding garment?' And he was speechless. Then the king said to the servants. 'Bind him hand and foot, take him away, and cast him into outer darkness; there will be weeping and gnashing of teeth.' For many are called, but few are chosen."

This leads us back to the scripture we used at the beginning of this chapter in 1 Peter 2:9. You see, many people hear the good news about Jesus Christ and are invited to a covenant wedding relationship with Jesus Christ (God), but the fact is they strive to enter heaven without a wedding garment. In other words, they were never really married to Jesus Christ because their profession of faith was empty. They heard the call of God to receive his Son Jesus Christ as their personal Lord and Savior, but they were never chosen by God as part of the royal priesthood. Why was that, you ask? It is/was because they didn't want to present themselves as a peculiar people. They don't/didn't want those who have a worldly mind-set to see them as being very strange or odd. It is/was because when a person is truly married to Jesus Christ, their profession of faith is genuine and God knows that that person (you) really means business, and therefore he places within their (your) heart the seed of truth by the circumcision of his (God's) Spirit. When this takes place, that person now becomes a part of the chosen generation of peculiar people that God uses to proclaim the truth of the gospel message. Now when that takes place, when a person (you) is truly chosen by God as a peculiar people, they (you) must understand that they (you) will be rejected by those who have a worldly mind-set and do not truly believe the gospel message. This brings into play another important piece of the puzzle as we continue on our search for the truth in finding the narrow path to eternal life. And what is that piece of the puzzle, you ask? Well, for the answer to that question, we need to look at the question that was asked back in Matthew 22:12. If you recall, the question was asked by the king as to how one of the guests got into the wedding feast. He questioned the guest's presence because he wasn't wearing a wedding garment. Question: Who was the king? Answer: The king is/was Jesus Christ (God) himself. The one who would have known who he was married to and therefore who has on a wedding garment? But then again, please keep in mind, I'm just a forklift operator. After all, what do I know?

CHAPTER 19

What Is Just? What Is Fair?

Bondservants [employees], obey in all things your masters according to the flesh, not with eye service, as men-pleasers, but in sincerity of heart, fearing God. And whatever you do, do it heartily, as to the Lord and not to men, knowing that from the Lord you will receive the reward of the inheritance for you serve the Lord Christ.
—Colossians 3:22-24

And also

Masters [employers], give your bondservants [employees] what is just and fair, knowing that you also have a Master in heaven.
—Colossians 4:1

A FEW CHAPTERS back (chapter 13), I told you that we were going to begin to end this book and our search for the truth by looking at the two Pharisees named Nicodemus and Saul of Tarsus that were alive in Jesus's day. If you recall, the Pharisees were a small sect of the Jews who were known for their rigid adherence to the ceremonial fine points of the law. If you also recall, Jesus's interaction with the Pharisees was usually adversarial in nature. Why? Because Jesus usually rebuked and scolded the Pharisees for using human traditions to nullify the very word of God (scripture). The Pharisees were so full of themselves with pride that Jesus also rebuked and scolded them for their rank (having an offensive strong smell) of hypocrisy. They were two-faced. In fact, if you recall what we discovered in an earlier chapter (chapter 11), you will remember that Jesus said these words to them in Matthew 23:25 and 26.

Woe to you, scribes and Pharisees, hypocrites! For you clean the outside of the cup and of the dish, but inside you are full of robbery and self-indulgence. You blind Pharisee, first clean the inside of the cup and of the dish, so that the outside of it may become clean also.

In other words, in a nutshell, the Pharisees had an outer appearance of being godly, but inside, in their hearts where it really mattered the most, they were dead. Jesus didn't care much for the way the Pharisees conducted themselves. He didn't care much for the way they conducted themselves because they were supposed to be representing God (him). They were supposed to be, as the word of God says in Matthew 5:13-16,

> You are the salt of the earth; but if the salt loses its flavor, how shall it be seasoned? It is then good for nothing but to be thrown out and trampled underfoot by men. "You are the light of the world. A city set on a hill cannot be hidden; nor do they light a lamp and put it under a basket, but on the lamp stand, and it gives light to all who are in the house. Let your light so shine before men in such a way that they may see your good works, and glorify your Father who is in heaven.

The Pharisees were supposed to be representing God and his righteousness. They were supposed to be the salt of the earth. They were supposed to be the seasoned salt. They were supposed to be the salt and light of the world that represented Almighty God. Their lives were supposed to represent the light of God's truth and righteousness that would draw people to the one true God of the universe. But that wasn't the case. It wasn't the case because they were representing the kingdom of darkness (devil), instead of the kingdom of light (God). How do I know that, you ask? Well, remember what we learned earlier in this book where Jesus said to these self-proclaimed representatives of God,

> You are of your father the devil, and the desires of your father you want to do. (John 8:44)

And it's to these very words of Jesus that I'd like to begin to end this book and our search for the truth. I say I'd like to finish this book with these words from Jesus because I truly believe these words Jesus spoke to these supposed representatives of God are some of the most damning words a supposed representative of the one true God could possibly hear. Can you imagine? To think that you are supposedly a representative of Almighty God and then you hear these words from the lips of the very Son of that same God. The Messiah, the redeemer of the world, the one who had been prophesied for centuries and centuries, and then you hear that same Messiah telling you that your father is the devil. Now I don't know about you, my fellow truth seeker, but if I were in the same position as those Pharisees, I think those words would have definitely got my attention. Or would they have? Would they have gotten my attention, or would they have fallen on deaf ears? Well, for the answer to that question, we must begin with the facts that surround the death of Jesus Christ. And the first fact we must uncover is the fact that the Pharisees were one of the main players in having Jesus Christ crucified. But there is yet another fact for us to consider, and that fact is the one that we have been dealing with throughout this book. And what is that fact, you ask? It is the one that determines whether or not you can hear the voice of God/Jesus Christ. It is the one that truly determines whether or not you're serving Jesus Christ or the world system which has the God of this world (devil) at his control. Jesus told the most religious leaders of his time that their father was the devil. And do you know something else? I truly believe that Jesus is saying that very same thing today. He is saying that there are those within the realm of Christianity today that have the same problem as the Pharisees of Jesus' day. They are representatives of the devil and not Jesus Christ. How do you know that, you ask? I know it because of what the word of God says. I know it because it came directly from the lips of the two most well-known figures in all of God's word (Bible). And who are those two people, you ask? They are Jesus Christ himself and Saul of Tarsus, the Pharisee who was converted (born again) and became an apostle and follower of Jesus Christ. He was born again of God's Spirit, and his eyes were opened to the truth that his father was indeed the devil himself. His eyes were opened to that fact, and his life and his eternal future was completely changed forever. His life was so changed that he went from being a persecutor of Jesus Christ into a believer and follower of Jesus Christ. Out of the sixty-six books written in the Bible, Saul of Tarsus is recognized throughout the realm of Christianity to have written at least thirteen of those books. In fact, the words that he wrote within those thirteen books have become the main cement and the main foundation of what the Christian faith is all about.

Well, by now you're probably asking yourself, "That's all well and fine, Joe, but what does all of this have to do with our search for the truth and the probability that there are representatives of the devil within the realm of Christianity today?" And you know what? That's a great question. But to know the complete answer to that question, it would probably take us yet a whole other book to uncover that truth. But for now, let's go back to the beginning in our search for the truth. I say the beginning because to answer that question, we must start at the beginning of the two organizations involved, the realm of the Pharisees and the realm of Christianity. Both entities were (are) suppose to represent God. Both started out with a strong foundation, that foundation being the very words of Almighty God. They were supposed to be God's representatives on this earth. And so they were. But how did that change? How did they go from being a representative of the one true God of the universe, into being the representatives of the kingdom of darkness, a kingdom that represents the worldly system and a system of the devil? How did that happen? Well, let's take a look at how that might have come about. And for that to happen, I'd like to take a look at how God opened my eyes to that very fact. And how did that happen, you ask? Well, as I said, for the complete answer to that question, it would take another book, but I will tell you this much. For me, it came about when I became an elected official in the Teamsters union. The Teamsters union you say! Yes, I said the Teamsters union. If you read the introduction to this book, you would have learned that I was a member of the Teamsters union for thirty years. You would have read that in those thirty years of being a member in the Teamsters union, I served as both a union steward and as an officer on the executive board of that union.

Now before I go any further in our search for the truth, I want to make myself very clear. I say I want to make myself very clear because there is a tendency for many to denounce and criticize and condemn labor unions. And if I had more time, I could name you a number of reasons why people may feel the way they do toward unions, whether in a positive or a negative way. And in many ways, I can understand how and why they might feel the way they do toward unions. However, I happen to believe that labor unions, in many ways, are a good thing. I say that because of my membership and affiliation in a labor union for thirty years. Now if I was going to get into why I say that in many cases labor unions are a good thing, I would have to start with the word of God. I say I would have to start with the word of God because in God's word, I believe there are specific references to how and how not both employers (masters) and employees (servants) are supposed to act. In other words, God's word gives clear guidance and counsel on how employers and employees are supposed to treat each other. Both employers and employees should have mutual respect for each other, and no one should try and take advantage of the other; when labor unions were formed, that was not the case, at least in the case of the Teamsters union. In most cases, employers were clearly taking advantage of their employees, and the employees were forced into a situation where their only choice was to join a labor union. In many cases, the multitude of grievances they had with regard to safety, fair compensation (pay) for their labor, and working conditions were not being addressed by their employers (masters) and their collective voices (servants) were falling on deaf ears. Why was that? It was because they didn't collectively carry out and/or follow the word of God which we saw at the beginning of this chapter. Now if I was going to dissect these words from God, in our search for the truth, I would have to put the emphasis on the words "what is just and fair." Now I say that because those words are words that really encompass just about everything in life. I say that because if you really think about it, just about everything we do in life really boils down to what is just and what is fair. Because if you think about what is just and what is fair in this life, we (you) must take into consideration about how the parameters of what is just and what is fair is determined. I say that because when it comes to what is just and what is fair, there has to be some guidelines to determine what is just and what is fair. That's why I've stated throughout this book that unless you're truly born again of God's Spirit, you won't begin to be able to fully determine what is just and what is not. There is one more thing with regard to labor unions and the word of God I'd like to take a look at, and that is in the New Testament book of James chapter 5.

In this chapter of God's word, we (you) can read about the firm warning that is given to those who oppress others, those who are rich in wealth and use their power of having wealth to oppress those who are less fortunate. Now in this chapter, we read about the warning that is given to those who oppress others, but we also read about what it says with regard to those who cry out to God because of this injustice. How so, you ask? Well, take a look at what it says in verses 4 through 6 of James chapter 5.

Indeed the wages of the laborers who mowed your fields, which you kept back by fraud, cry out; and the cries of the reapers have reached the ears of the Lord of Sabaoth. You have lived on the earth in pleasure and luxury; you have fattened your hearts as in a day of slaughter. You have condemned, you have murdered the just; he does not resist you.

In a nutshell, I believe God hears the cries of those who are being oppressed and oftentimes come to their rescue. How does God come to their rescue? Well, I believe that depends on the situation, and it also depends on how God decides to intervene and answers the prayers of those who are crying out to him (God). In verse 6, we read that the rich have condemned and even murdered the just. In verse 5, we read a very scary scenario where James reminds the readers of God's word that those who practice such atrocities (bad things) are fattening their hearts as in a day of slaughter. Like fattened cattle ready to be slaughtered, the rich that James condemns had indulged themselves to the limit. I believe this is a vivid depiction of divine judgment to/for all those who have been corrupted by the love of power and money. Now when we (you) think of those who might be considered as rich, we oftentimes think of certain people within the world in which we live. People who have more money and more material things than most people in the world will ever have. But the question is "Not that those people have those things, but how did they get them?" Did they get them legitimately or justifiably? Or did they get them by and through the means of what James is describing in God's teaching? Did they get their money and power legitimately, or did they get their power by and through deceptive ways? Now when we think of this scenario, we can get caught in the trap of thinking about someone else, someone else that has millions and millions and sometime billions and billions of dollars. In this scenario, it is very easy to go to the extremes of our world but lose out on what God's word says to each and every one of us. Whether we have millions and millions and/or billions and billions and/or what we consider as chump change by and in worldly standards. The question is the same for each one of us: How did we get what we have with regard to material wealth? How do we look at the material riches of this life? This takes us back to what we learned in chapter 11 with regard to being a fruit inspector. How so, you ask? Well, if you recall in chapter 11, we discovered that in 2 Corinthians chapter 11, we learned about what God's word says with regard to false apostles, deceitful workers, who transform themselves into apostles of Christ. In other words, they are people who are supposed to be representing Jesus Christ (God) and his righteousness, but in reality they are representing the ruler of this world; and in most cases, they don't even realize that they are. They don't realize it because they are caught in the snare of the devil and are still walking in the course (wide path) of this world (Ephesians 2:2). Such was the case of the two Pharisees named Nicodemus and Saul of Tarsus. Even though they were the religious leaders of Israel, they were representatives of the devil and not the one true God of the universe. How could that have happened? How could they have been so blinded to the fact that they were representing the devil, instead of the one true God of Israel? Answer: They were living their lives within the worldly realm of the devil (wide path) instead of the spiritual realm of God's kingdom (narrow path). They were caught in the trap and snare of what God's word says in the New Testament book of 1 John chapter 2.

Do not love the world or the things in the world. If anyone loves the world the love of the Father is not in him. For all that is in the world—the lust of the flesh, the lust of the eyes, and the pride of life—is not of the Father but is of the world.

They loved the world more than they loved God. And because they loved the world more than they loved God, they were caught in the devil's trap, and their minds and hearts were being deceived by the world leader (devil), and they couldn't see it. Jesus called them hypocrites. They were two-faced. They were two-faced because they wanted things both ways. They wanted the rewards that go along with being a true follower of God, but they tried to get those rewards by and through the deception of the worldly traits, the lust of the flesh, the lust of the eyes, and the pride of life. God opened my eyes to this while serving as a representative in the Teamsters union. How so, you ask? Well, it first began with the word of God that I just quoted in 1 John chapter 2 with regard to not loving the things of this world. I say that because if you're going to be a true follower of Jesus Christ (Christian), you're going to have to understand that the word of God will stand forever (Isaiah 40:8), and that no weapon formed against you (God's servant) shall prosper (do well) (Isaiah 54; 17). Now when we think about the words "no weapon formed against you shall prosper," we think about those words in a fleshly manner or material ways, such as a gun or a knife or a club or whatever. But when God speaks of a weapon, he thinks in the spiritual realm. And that's why you must learn how to discern what is just and what is not just by God's word. Why, because God's weapon is his word (Ephesians 6:17). The dictionary defines the word "discern" as such: to perceive or to recognize by the intellect (mind, brain), to distinguish mentally. In other words, you're going to have to have the ability to distinguish what is just and what is unjust; what is truth and what is not the truth; what is of the world (devil) and what is of the one true God of the Holy Bible. And how does/can one determine what is just and what is not? It begins with a pure heart for the things of God. It begins with a new heart, a new beginning, a new way of life. It begins with a heart that understands that this present world we live in is not our final destination. In fact, the word of God literally begs people to abstain from fleshly lusts which war against our (your) soul. Did you say war? Yes, I said war! Well, I didn't say war; the word of God says war. Did you know that the word "war" is used some 220 times in the word of God (Bible)? Now when you think of war, you usually think of soldiers. And what do soldiers do? They fight wars. Did you know that when a person comes to Jesus Christ, they are called to be soldiers? That's right, soldiers. They are commanded to endure hardness as a good soldier of Jesus Christ (2 Timothy 2:3). But then again, please keep in mind, I'm just a forklift operator. After all, what do I know?

CHAPTER 20

A Good Steward

For a bishop must be blameless, as a steward of God, not self-willed,
not violent, not greedy for money, but hospitable, a lover of what
is good, sober-minded, just, holy, self-controlled, holding fast the
faithful word as he has been taught, that he may be able, by sound
doctrine, both to exhort and convict those who contradict.
—Titus 1:7-9

IN THE LAST chapter in our search for the truth, we learned about what God's word (Bible) teaches with regard to followers of Jesus Christ being soldiers. We learned from God's word that we must endure hardship as a good soldier of Jesus Christ. And what does it mean to endure hardship? Well, according to the dictionary, the word "endure" means to sustain (maintain) without yielding (to surrender, as to a superior force); to bear (stand) with patience; to continue in existence (life, survival), to suffer patiently. Also according to the dictionary, the word "hardship" means a condition difficult to endure, as poverty. In other words, if you're going to be a true follower of Jesus Christ, you have to be mentally prepared to take a stand for the truth of God's word, no matter what the circumstances are. Now when I use the word "mentally prepared," I'm referring to it in more than just a mental capacity. In other words, I'm speaking about it in a much broader range than just a/the mental state of mind. I'm speaking about in a range that includes spiritually, emotionally, psychologically, and physically. Why do I say spiritually, emotionally, psychologically, and physically? I say it because when you make a/the conscious decision to truly follow Jesus Christ, every one of these traits (qualities) will come into play in your pursuit of finding the narrow path (way) to life eternal (Matthew 7:14). I say they will come into play not as a casual statement but in a much broader range, because within these traits are where the battles and struggles of this life really exist. What I mean by this is when you make a serious and truthful commitment to follow Jesus Christ, God, by and through the power of the Holy Spirit, begins the process of renewing your mind. (We've discovered this earlier [chapter 18] etc.)

And do not be conformed to this world, but be transformed by the renewing of your mind, that you may prove what is that good and acceptable and perfect will of God (Romans 12:2).

Now when your mind begins to be renewed by the Holy Spirit, you begin to see things in and from a different perspective (point of view). You begin to see things from a spiritual viewpoint instead of a physical viewpoint. Now please don't get me wrong. We (You) will still see things from a/the physical viewpoint, but when God begins the process of renewing your mind, you will begin to see beyond the physical world we (you) live in and become more spiritually tuned in to the things which cannot be seen, the spirit world, the unseen things which are eternal. Second Corinthians 4:18 speaks of this when it says,

While we [true born-again believers] do not look at the things which are seen, but at the things which are not seen. For the things which are seen are temporary, but the things which are not seen are eternal.

A parallel verse of God's word that ties right into this whole spiritual renewing of the mind is found in the New Testament book of Titus 3:5.

Not by works of righteousness which we have done, but according to His mercy, He saved us, through the washing of regeneration and renewing of the Holy Spirit, whom He [God] poured out on us abundantly through Jesus Christ our Savior [rescuer], that having been justified by His grace we should become heirs according to the hope of eternal life [narrow path].

I say it's a parallel verse because when you begin to make the transition (change) from the things which are seen (worldly things) into the things which are not seen (spiritual things), you must always keep one thing in mind. And what is that, you ask? You must always remember that we (you) are not better than anyone else. We (You) must never look down our noses at another human being. In fact, we (Christians) are commanded not to think of ourselves more highly than we ought to. I say that because in the New Testament book of Romans 12:3, we read these words,

For I say, through the grace given to me, to everyone who is among you, not to think of himself more highly than he ought to think, but to think soberly, as God has dealt to each one a measure of faith.

Question: Who wrote these words? Answer: Saul of Tarsus, thee Saul of Tarsus who was a Pharisee, thee Saul of Tarsus who became the Apostle Paul, thee Apostle Paul who was once a Pharisee, but by and through true humility and the grace of Almighty God, became a follower of Jesus Christ. But do you know something else? When he became a follower of Jesus Christ, he also became a soldier in Christ's army. And when he became a soldier in Christ's army, he then became an enemy of/to this world. And who is in charge of this world? That's right, you guessed it: the devil. But do you know something else? That same thing applies to you, my fellow truth seeker. When and if you become a true follower of Jesus Christ, the same thing is going to happen in your life as well. I say that because if you've never been born again of God's Spirit (the comforter), you are living your life within the realm of the devil, and you don't even realize that you are. How can that be, you ask? Well, as I stated in the last chapter (chapter 19), for me personally, the answer began when I first became a representative in the Teamsters union in the year 1983.

Now if you recall the words I shared in the introduction of this book, you would have remembered that the year 1983 was also the year that I became a follower of Jesus Christ. Now why is this a big deal, you may ask? Well, for me it was a big deal for this reason. You see, I accepted Jesus Christ as my personal Lord and Savior in the spring of 1983. And in September of that same year, I was elected unanimously to the office of union steward. Now you may be saying to yourself, "So what?" So what's the big deal about being elected to the office of union steward? And even if you were elected to the office of union steward, what the heck does that have to do with being a follower of Jesus Christ? And that's a good question. And do you know what? It's a good question because it lies at the very heart of what every true follower of Jesus Christ must learn. I say that because of what God's word says with regard to being a steward of God. Now when we (you) take a good look at what the word of God says with regard to the qualifications a person must have to be a good steward, we learn that they must possess the following qualities:

1. Blameless (innocent, spotless, clean, unblemished, guiltless, above suspicion)
2. Not self-willed (stubborn willfulness, as in pursuit of one's own goals)
3. Not quick tempered (not easily angered)
4. Not given to wine (stays away from mind-altering drugs or anything that would cloud the (your) mind, i.e., alcohol, etc.)
5. Not violent (not unkind, not brutal, meaning ruthless or cruel and nasty)
6. Not greedy (having or showing a selfish desire for wealth and possessions)

JOSEPH TRAVER

Now with regard to God's word, a good steward of God must have these qualities. But do you know what? When I was first elected as a union steward, I didn't have all these qualities. I was very much lacking in some of these qualities, and I truly believe God had allowed me to serve in the capacity of union steward for a specific reason. And what was that specific reason, you ask? It was to prepare me for a/the ministry that he was calling me to fulfill. The position I was elected to as a union steward was to help me prepare for the office of overseer in Christ's body, his church.

Now I mentioned that when I was first elected to the office of union steward, I was very much lacking in the qualities that God's word says are required for being a good steward (overseer, i.e., bishop). But you say, "Isn't God's word referring to these/those qualities within the structure of the church?" What does the office of steward possibly have to do with the church? Answer: It has everything to do with the church, that is, if you're truly within the structure of a/the true church, because if you're under the true structure of the church of Jesus Christ, then you carry a/the responsibility of a steward wherever you go. Oh, you may not be elected to any office of authority by an organization or a church. But if you're truly born again of God's Spirit, we (you) have a higher calling which is given to you by God himself. No matter where you go or what you do, you must always remember you are representing God, and therefore, you must strive to achieve the qualities that are spelled out in his word. But there is yet another thing that a true follower of Jesus Christ (God) must be aware of. And what is that, you ask? It is the dilemma of the wide path and the narrow path. It is the catch-22 that once we're (your) born again of God's Spirit, we (you) will have major problems with those who are still in the worldly mind-set and traveling on the wide path to destruction. We (You) will face a hostile crowd, just as Jesus faced a/the hostile crowd, because if you're a true follower and good steward of/for Jesus Christ, then you will have to learn that you're going to be going against the flow of the worldly crowd (mind-set). When your heart and mind begin to be renewed of the things of God (spiritual ways), then you will be encountering people who do not or cannot understand where you're coming from. They can't understand spiritual things because if they (you) have never received God's Spirit, then they are still in the natural man mode and will not understand where you're coming from (1 Corinthians 2:13 and 14). Oh, they may be honorable people as far as the world goes, but they are still not in the mind-set of the God of the Holy Bible. They are still being held captive to the God of this world, who is the devil himself. But you see, that's why discernment is such an important piece of the puzzle of/to being a good steward. I say discernment is an important piece of the puzzle because as we learned in chapter 11 of this book, fruit inspecting plays a major role in knowing the things of God (Jesus Christ). Remember what Jesus said,

"You will know them by their fruits." (Matthew 7:16) and "Therefore by their fruits you will know them." (Matthew 7:20)

In other words, if Jesus Christ (the Holy Spirit) is truly living within us (you), then you have an/the advantage. You have an advantage because you will be able to discern whether or not what's in a person's heart is coming from the world (wide path) or whether it is coming from the truth of God's word (kingdom—i.e., narrow path). You will have the advantage because you will know what is of God (the truth) and what is of the world (the devil). And so it has been in my personal walk with Jesus Christ since 1983. Now you may be saying to yourself, "That's a pretty bold statement to make." In fact, that statement in itself is pretty much bordering on the edge of arrogance and conceit. But you know what? That's exactly the type of thinking that many of the leaders and the people of Jesus's day thought about him. And do you want to know another thing? If you want to be a true follower of Jesus Christ and a good steward (soldier) of God's word (truth), you had better get used to that very fact. You are going to be seen by those who are traveling on the wide path as arrogant and conceited. How do I know that, you ask? I know it because I have lived it! I know it because within the framework (structure) of the unseen world of spiritual warfare, there is a battle going on between truth and error, a war between good and evil, a war between the ways/things of God and the ways/things of the world (devil) (Much of this truth we have already uncovered throughout this book). I know all about the spiritual war that exists within the world I (we) live in, because it was by and through my personal walk of faith with Jesus Christ, as a union steward in the Teamsters union that God first began to open my eyes to the reality of this truth. What truth, you ask? It is the truth to what we discovered at the end of the last chapter (chapter 19). And what was that, you ask? It was the reality that I (as well as all true followers of Jesus Christ) was commanded by Almighty God himself to endure hardness as a good soldier of Jesus Christ. I (We) am commanded by God to endure hardness as a good soldier in Christ's army. And what are the traits of enduring hardness as a good soldier? Well, the first trait that any good soldier must have is probably the most important one of all.

And what is that, you ask? It is the one that every soldier must know and understand. It is knowing who is their (your) enemy. And that's why it's so very, very important to be a truth seeker. To know the truth of God's word. To know what is of God and what is not. Remember what we learned earlier in this book about finding the narrow way (path) to life, the words of God that we discovered with regard to worshipping him. Words like those found in the New Testament book of John 4:24 which says,

> God is Spirit, and those who worship Him must worship in spirit and truth.

You see, worshipping God is much more than just going to a worship service on Sunday mornings (or whatever day you choose to worship him); it's much more than being in a Bible study group; it's much more than singing in a/the church choir, it's much more than putting money in the offering plate; it's much more than offering your time to serve others. It's much more than simply teaching a Bible study, or mentoring a children's youth group, or cooking and/or cleaning the church building. It's much, much more than that. I say it's much, much more than that because even though these things I mentioned are in themselves very important elements of the Christian faith, there is very little enduring hardness that takes place within these elements. Now does that mean that these certain elements of a/the church environment exclude any indication of enduring hardness? Absolutely not; there could be some elements of what I mentioned that could be considered by God as an enduring hardship. I say that because maybe that's where God has opened a person's (your) heart by/with the opportunity to serve him (Jesus Christ) and his church. Maybe that's where that person (you) is being tested and molded and purified by him at this/ that present time. But as a whole, there isn't much enduring hardness as a soldier when it comes to the specific things I mentioned. Why? Because those things I mentioned are really a no-brainer when it comes to the Christian faith. Those are the kinds of things that a supposed follower of Christ should do. But if you think about these/those specific things, they really don't include much hardship, especially in the United States of America. The real enduring hardship comes when you are taking a stand for the truth of God's word with those who are in opposition to the truth of his word(s). When you're taking a stand for the integrity (truth) of God's word, and because of that stand, it may cost you something. It may cost you your friendship with your best friend. It may cost you a relationship between a brother or a sister or a father or a mother. Why, it may even cost you your marriage. But do you know what? According to the very word of God, that's exactly what it might cost you to follow Jesus Christ. I say that because to be a true follower of Jesus Christ and a good steward, soldier, and worker of God's truth, you can't be ashamed to take a stand on God's truth. How do I know that, you ask? I know it because the word of God says so. In fact, the first message (sermon) I ever preached in my personal ministry was regarding this very word from Jesus's own lips found in the New Testament book of Matthew 10:32-39 which says,

> Whoever confesses Me [Jesus Christ] before men, him I will confess before My Father [God] who is in heaven. But whoever denies Me before men, him I [Jesus Christ] will also deny before My Father [God] who is in heaven. Do not think that I came to bring peace but a sword. For I have come to set a man against his father, a daughter against her mother, and a daughter-in-law against her mother-in-law; and a man's enemies will be those of his own household. He who loves father or mother more than Me is not worthy of Me. And he who loves son or daughter more than Me is not worthy of Me. And he who does not take his cross and follow after Me is not worthy of Me. He who finds his life will lose it, and he who loses his life for My sake will find it.

In a nutshell, these scripture verses sum up what every good steward, soldier, and follower of Jesus Christ must know and understand. I say that because of what I have discovered in my own personal walk of faith as a follower of Jesus Christ. What I have discovered is that there are many who really do not fully understand what the cost of following Jesus Christ might/may be. In fact, verse 39 of Matthew chapter 10 really sums up what the core and the foundation of following Jesus Christ may cost them (you). And what is that, you ask? Well, look at what it says, "He who finds his life will lose it, and he who loses his life for My sake will find it." It's about sacrifice. It's about giving up your life for Jesus Christ no matter what the circumstances of this life may be. But then again, please keep in mind, I'm just a forklift operator. After all, what do I know?

CHAPTER 21

Stewards of the Mysteries of God

Let a man so consider us, as servants of Christ and stewards of Christ
and stewards of the mysteries of God. Moreover it is required in
stewards that one be found faithful.
—1 Corinthians 4:1 and 2

IN THE LAST chapter, we started to uncover some truths about
being a good steward and soldier in Christ's army. I shared how
God started to open my eyes to this truth when I first became a union
steward in the Teamsters union. I say God began to open my eyes to the
truth of being a good steward because when I was first elected to the office
of union steward, I had to understand that as a steward, I was taking on a
very deep responsibility. What was that responsibility, you ask? It was the
responsibility of enforcing a/the contract between those who were involved
within the framework of a collective bargaining unit agreement, which
also included me. The terms and conditions were set in place between
the employer and the employees (workers) in that mutually agreed upon
contract. In other words, certain terms and conditions of how the employer
and the employee were to conduct themselves within the boundaries of an
employer and the employee workplace environment were spelled out in the
context for all to understand and to live by. The contract is like a compass
that guides and directs those who are under the blanket or confines of
the terms and conditions of that specific contract. With that being said,
it also placed within my mind that that same scenario is exactly the same
as being within the covenant of God's words, the covenant that we make
within our hearts and lives between Almighty God and ourselves is really
a contract between us (you) and God. When we make a commitment to
follow Jesus Christ, we are actually making a/the commitment to be good
stewards and soldiers in his kingdom. When we (you) truly commit our
lives to Jesus Christ (God), a portion of the renewing of our minds includes
God's commitment of opening the mysteries of his kingdom to those who

truly humble themselves and truly repent of their wicked ways before him (a portion of this [mysteries] we uncovered in chapter 10).

By now you may be asking yourself, "This is all well and fine Joe, but what does all of this have to do with being a good steward and soldier in Christ's army?" And what the heck does all this have to do with you being a union steward in the Teamsters union? Well once again, for the complete answer to those questions, it would take a lot longer to explore that I have in this book, but I will tell you this much. For me, the first thing any good steward must learn is that when you are representing others, you must learn and understand the contract (the agreement) that you are trying to enforce. What are the terms and conditions of the contract that both parties (employer and employees) have to agree on? In other words, within the terms of the contract, there lies specific dos and don'ts that each party within the framework and guidelines of that contract agrees to live by. There are certain things that the employer agrees to, and there are certain things that the employees agree to; and when the terms of that specific contract are violated or broken, there are certain steps and procedures written into a contract that allows either party to address any alleged violations of that contract (agreement). And that's why it is so very, very important for any good steward to know the terms and conditions (i.e., the dos and don'ts) of the contract they are responsible for. But you know what, that same scenario is exactly the same scenario that takes place within the boundaries of God's kingdom as well. How so, you ask? Well, if someone wants to be a true follower and good steward of Jesus Christ, they must know the contract between them and God. What contract, you ask? The contract that takes place within the pages of the Holy Bible, the contract that takes place within the contract and/or covenant relationship between a person (you) and Almighty God, the terms and conditions of how a person is to live their lives if they want to be a good steward and soldier in Jesus Christ's army.

Now knowing the contract is one component of being a good steward. But the biggest component of being a good steward and/or overseer does not only know the contract, but it is living your life within the boundaries of that contract as well. In other words, you don't just give lip service to the terms and conditions of that contract, but you actually live by the terms and conditions of that contract within your own life as well. Another way of putting it is, you don't just talk the talk but you walk the walk. You don't expect everyone else to live by the terms and conditions of the contract without living by the terms and conditions of that contract yourself. In fact, if you really want to be a good steward and overseer of that specific contract, then you must make every effort to set an example for others to follow, and that's exactly what God taught me about being a good steward and overseer as far as his kingdom is concerned. But you say, "Wait a minute Joe, I'm not a union steward and/or an overseer of a contract. I'm just a normal, everyday, regular human being, and I don't want to be an overseer of no one or nothing. I just want to live my life one day at a time, and I don't want to be bothered by such things as stewards, soldiers, bishops, or overseers. I just want to live my life under the radar screen, and I don't want to be bothered by the terms and conditions of any contract." But do you know what I have learned from God by being a union steward and overseer of a collective bargaining unit agreement? If you're going to follow Jesus Christ, that scenario is nearly impossible. I say it is nearly impossible to do because once you make the ultimate commitment of believing in Jesus Christ, not only are you making a commitment to believe in Jesus Christ, but you are also accepting a commission (a charge) from Almighty God to be a steward, a soldier, and an overseer of/in his kingdom. And what is the responsibility of that commission (charge)? It is to live out and live by the very truth of God's word(s). In other words, just as I stated earlier, the commission from God begins with walking the walk and not just talking the talk of being a believer and follower of Jesus Christ. As stewards and soldiers and overseers of God's kingdom, we (you) have the responsibility of not only hearing God's words to us personally; but we (you) also have the responsibility of defending his word(s) no matter what the consequences of this life may/might be, and that's exactly the same kind of responsibility I had as a union steward. My responsibility was to make sure that everyone was living within the framework of the collective bargaining unit agreement which included me as well. And that's where God started to make the scriptures I've used at the beginning of the last two chapters as becoming realities in my life. Things like being blameless, not being self-willed, not being violent, not being greedy for money, being hospitable, loving what was good, being sober-minded, being just, being holy, and being self-controlled are elements of being a faithful steward. God showed me that to be a good steward, soldier, and overseer of his kingdom, I was going to have to strive to make these qualities a priority in/ of my life. But there was yet another element to these qualities that I was going to have to realize as well. And what was that, you ask? I was going to have to realize that when dealing with the people who are within the scope of the life experience (contract of life), there are going to be those who are not going to have these certain qualities especially if they don't have the Holy Spirit (comforter) guiding them along the way. And that's why I've put such an emphasis on being a good fruit inspector just as/like Jesus taught in the New Testament book of Matthew 7:16, "You will know them by their fruits." What kinds of fruit(s) are they producing? Good fruit or bad fruit? And that's exactly where I began to understand the mysteries that surround God's stewards and servants as they retain and preserve the integrity of God's word as they journey down the narrow path to eternal life, which takes us back to what we learned earlier in this book about the spiritual battles that exist within the unseen world that is all around us, the one that we discovered earlier with regard to God's word found in the New Testament book of Ephesians 6:12. The word of God which warns true believers that they (you) are not wrestling against flesh and blood, but they (you) are wrestling (a term used of hand-to-hand combat) against the rulers of the darkness of this age, against spiritual hosts of wickedness in the heavenly places. And where are the heavenly places? They are found within the spirit world, the spirit world which consists of the unseen things, the things of God's Spirit which is based upon one's ability to look beyond the physical to the spiritual, beyond the present to the future, and beyond the visible to the invisible (2 Corinthians 4:18). Therefore, we (true born-again believers) do not lose heart. Even though our outward man (the flesh and/or the physical body) is perishing, yet the inward man (the soul of every true believer in Jesus Christ) is being renewed day by day. Question: How does God make that happen? Well, one way he makes it happen is by and through the afflictions and tribulations that we face in our walk with Jesus Christ each and every day. It is by and through those afflictions and tribulations that God purifies and/or cleanses our (your) heart and our lives so that we can bring glory and honor to/for him/Jesus Christ. It is also by and through those afflictions and tribulations that our faith is perfected so that we can have a better understanding of what true love and grace is all about. For example, in today's society, the word "love" is drastically misunderstood. I say the word "love" is drastically misunderstood because in the world we live in today the word "love" has been replaced by the word "tolerance." What I mean by this is that if we say that we really love someone, then we are supposed to tolerate anything that particular person does or says, or believes even if it is in direct opposition and violation of what the word (Holy Bible) of God teaches. In other words, in using the contract mentality, a person (or society) may be living in opposition to the very word of God; and if they do not repent and turn from that opposition (evil, sin) of God's word, they are in serious trouble of God's wrath and probably don't even realize that they are. And that is where the word "faithful" comes into play. I say it comes into play because as stewards, soldiers, and overseers of God's word a true follower of Jesus Christ has an/ the obligation to reveal (make known) the truth of God's word to those who are living in opposition to that (his) word. And what are some of the ways a good steward can communicate and/or reveal these things? It's by living out these qualities within their (your) own lives so that others may see these qualities and be drawn, so to speak, to the light. What light you ask, the light of God's word. How so you ask ? Well, let's take another look at what God's word says.

In the last chapter (chapter 20) of this book, we took a look at what God's word said with regard to being a good steward of God. And in verse 9 of the New Testament book of Titus chapter 1, we read that a good steward (bishop) must hold fast the faithful word as he has been taught. And why is a good steward supposed to hold fast to the faithful word (sound doctrine) he has been taught? It is so that he (a good steward, soldier, and overseer) may be able to exhort and convict those who contradict. Contradict what, you ask? Contradict the very word of God. So in other words, if you're going to be a good steward and be able to effectively exhort and convict people about their opposition or violation of God's word (contract), then you're going to have to know the contract yourself. And that's what I had to learn in my life as well. I had to learn that if I was going to be an effective union steward, I was going to have to not only learn and understand the terms and conditions of the contract I was working under as an employee of the company, but I was also going to have to live by the terms and conditions of that contract myself. And I learned that that same scenario was exactly the same scenario that must also be in place if I (you) wanted to be a good steward and soldier for God (Jesus Christ) as well. I say that because in most cases, it's not always what you say that makes a difference in drawing people to the light of the gospel message, but in most cases, it's how you conduct your very life in what you claim to believe that makes a difference. In other words, if your actions don't line up with what you claim to believe, then people will figure you out and you will be seen and known as a hypocrite, just as Jesus Christ called the so-called religious leaders of his day (which we discovered earlier in this book).

Now you may be saying to yourself, "That's all well and fine Joe, but what does hypocrisy and drawing people to the light of the gospel message have to do with being a good steward and soldier in Jesus Christ's army?"

And that's a good question. I say it's a good question because that's where the rubber meets the road, sort of speak, when it comes to being a good steward. I say that because of what God's word says is the condition for understanding the mysteries of God. And what is that condition, you ask? Well, look at what it says in verse 2 of 1 Corinthians chapter 4.

Moreover, it is required in stewards that one be found faithful.

Did you catch that? Did you catch what God's word said? It is required that one (a steward, soldier) be found faithful, in other words. If someone (you) wants to know the mysteries of God, that person must be found faithful. Now that, my fellow truth seeker, is not a suggestion. It is a command. It is an imperative. God has said that if you want to know the mysteries that surround his (God's) kingdom, a person must be found faithful. It is essential, and it cannot be avoided. Now the word "required" is defined in the dictionary as such: to call for as necessary or pressing; to demand, as by law. In other words, if someone (you) wants God to reveal the hidden truths (mysteries) that surround his kingdom, that person (you) must be considered by God himself as a faithful steward and overseer of the very truth of his words (Bible). The word "mystery" is used in the New Testament to refer to divine (godly) revelation previously hidden. In other words, when a person (you) is in the natural state of a/the worldly mind-set that exists within those who are traveling on the wide path to destruction (Matthew 7:13), there is no way a person (you) can be considered by God as being faithful. They can't be considered by God as being faithful because as long as a person (you) is in the natural, fleshly mind-set of worldly thinking, a person cannot possibly understand or grasp the mysteries that surround the truth of God's words. They can't grasp the mysteries of God because unless they have been born again of God's Spirit, they can't understand the deep things of God, nor can they have the mind of Christ. And how do I know that, you ask? I know it because of what God's word says with regard to this very subject found in the New Testament book of 1 Corinthians 2:14 where it says, "But the natural man does not receive the things of the Spirit of God, for they are foolishness to him; nor can he know them, because they are spiritually discerned." Why are they spiritually discerned? They are spiritually discerned because they don't have the mind of Christ, and therefore, they can't possibly be good stewards nor can they be considered as being found faithful by Almighty God. This, as we learned earlier, is one of God's requirements for being a good steward. But then again, please keep in mind, I'm just a forklift operator. After all, what do I know?

JOSEPH TRAVER

CHAPTER 22

The Cowardly

He who overcomes shall inherit all things, and I will be his God
and he shall be My son. But the cowardly, unbelieving, abominable,
murderers, sexually immoral, sorcerers, idolaters, and all liars, shall
have their part in the lake which burns with fire and brimstone
[hell], which is the second death.
—Revelation 21:7, 8

IN THE LAST couple of chapters in our search for the truth, I've
been sharing with you how God opened my eyes to some of the
truths of his word when I served as a union steward in the Teamsters union.
Through my experiences as a union steward, I learned how to be a good
fruit inspector. By that I mean I learned a great deal about how to separate
what is true and what is false. As we've learned throughout this book, being
able to separate what is truth and what is not is a key factor in determining
how to find the narrow path to life (Matthew 7:14). In chapter 19, I stated
that I wanted to begin to end this book and our search for the truth with
the words from the lips of Jesus Christ himself when he spoke to the scribes
and Pharisees of his day the words found in the New Testament book of
John 8:44, "You are of your father the devil, and the desires of your father
you want to do."

Now since I stated that I wanted to begin to end this book, I've been
trying to put an emphasis about how imperative it is to be good stewards
and soldiers for Jesus Christ (God). I say that because when you make the
ultimate decision to follow Jesus Christ, your life will change and you will
have conflict with those around you. In other words, when the Spirit of
God (comforter) is released upon you, you will begin to see things from
God's perspective instead of from a worldly, fleshly, human perspective.
Now when this takes place in a person's life, they will begin the journey of
entering by and through the narrow gate that leads to life (much of this
we've already discovered). And you say, "What the heck are you talking
about?" Well, if you remember what we've been discovering since we first

began our journey at the beginning of this book, you will remember that Jesus came to earth to seek and to save those who were lost (Matthew 18:11). He came to redeem all those who would be drawn to him and truly repent of their transgressions (sins) against Almighty God and place their complete trust in him (Jesus Christ) as their personal Lord and Savior. It is the only hope that a human being has in this life and much of this we've also already discovered. But there is one major component to redemption that we haven't fully explored, and it has to do with what I just stated with regard to the word "conflict."

Now I mentioned the word "conflict" because what I've discovered since the time I've been a follower of Jesus Christ is that once a person makes the decision to be a true follower of Jesus Christ, they will have conflict. There is no way around it. Well, maybe I misspoke. In fact, there is a way around it. And do you know what the way around it is? It is to simply ignore that anything is wrong and that the problem you're facing will simply go away on its own. There is an old saying that lines up with this kind of thinking, and it goes like this, "Out of sight, out of mind." Question: Do you know what that is called, my fellow truth seeker? It is called the cowardly way out! And do you know what the word of God says will happen to the cowardly? Well, for the answer to that question, in our continuing search for the truth, let us take a look at what God's word says about cowards found in the last book of the Bible, the book of the Revelation.

Now if you've been reading this book up to now and you've been teetering on the edge of whether or not you want to be a true follower of Jesus Christ, I would strongly caution you to make a decision before you go any farther in this book. Now I say that not to be unkind, but I say it only as a warning to you. What I mean by this is that once you are exposed to the truth of God's word, then you become responsible to his word. What I mean by that is that once you've been exposed to the truth of what God's word says, then you become accountable to that word and to Almighty God himself. But not only are you held accountable to the truth of his word, but there is yet another element that comes into play when a person is exposed to God's words. And what is that, you ask? Well, if you remember what we discovered in our last chapter, you would have recalled what we learned was a requirement for being a good steward and servant for Jesus Christ. And what was that requirement? It was to be found faithful (1 Corinthians 4:2). And why is this such an important piece to the puzzle to understanding the mysteries that God reveals to those who are good stewards and servants for Jesus Christ? Now for those of you who have decided to move forward in our search for the truth, we are going to move on to the answer to that question; and as I said, the answer to that question can be found in the New Testament book of the Revelation 21:7 and 8. Jesus is speaking, and he declares this:

> He who overcomes shall inherit all things, and I will be his God and he shall be My son.

(But then pay close attention to what Jesus says next, because it serves as a warning to those who are traveling on the journey of this life and are carrying these type of characteristics in their lives. In forklift operator terms, I refer to it as their heart DNA.)

> BUT the cowardly, unbelieving, abominable, murderers, sexually immoral, sorcerers, idolaters, and all liars shall have their part in the lake which burns with fire and brimstone [hell], which is the second death.

Woah! Did you hear what the Son of God said, my fellow truth seekers? He said that the cowardly will not inherit all things. Another thing for us to notice is that Jesus listed the word "cowardly" first in the order of those who are going to hell. Question: Do you think Jesus mentioned the word "cowardly" first for a specific reason? I believe he did. Another question: What did he mean by the cowardly? Well, for the answer to that question, I think we first have to know what the word "cowardly" means; and according to the dictionary, a coward is a person who lacks courage in facing danger, pain. And the word "pain" is described in the dictionary as such: bodily suffering or distress, as due to injury or illness; a distressing sensation in a particular part of the body; mental or emotional suffering or torment. Now if you noticed, I put the last part of the definition of the word "pain" in italics. Now I put those words in italics for a specific reason, and the reason I did that was I wanted to make a specific point with regard to what Jesus stated about the cowardly not inheriting all things. This takes us to another point which begs the question, "What does Jesus mean by 'they will not inherit all things'?" Well, without getting into a lengthy search on the subject of inheritance, I will simply tell you this. Now when we think of a coward, we commonly think of someone who stays away from any conflict. I know when I was a child growing up in school, you would be considered as a coward if someone challenged you to a physical fight and you refused to fight that person. I remember going to watch many fights that took place just off the school grounds where I attended school as a child. The reason why I said just off the school grounds was because everyone in the school knew that if you got caught fighting on school grounds; you would automatically be suspended from school. So when a fight did take place, it nearly always took place off the school grounds. And oh, by the way, I hate to admit it, but yes, there were times when I was challenged to a fight and I had to make a decision as to whether I would answer the challenge or turn tail and run from the challenge. I never did run from a fight, and I always answered the challenge.

Well, by now you're probably saying to yourself, "Okay Joe, this is all well and fine, but what the heck does this story have to do with what Jesus said with regard to the cowardly not inheriting all things?" Answer: It has everything to do with what Jesus said because the question really boils down to the ultimate question which is "Who and/or what in God's point of view is considered as being cowardly?" Could it be that God is saying that if you're confronted with defending yourself in a physical confrontation, God considers a person to be cowardly if they don't defend themselves by not fighting back in a physical manner? Could that be what God's word is saying is a qualifier for not inheriting all things? I don't think so. I say that because if you remember what we've learned in our search for the truth, we discovered that God is spirit and those who want to truly worship him must worship him in spirit and truth (John 4:23 and 24). And so what I've discovered in my own personal pursuit of finding the narrow path to life is that God's standards are more in tune with the spiritual aspect of life instead of the physical aspect of life. What do I mean by that? I mean that God sees things more from the spiritual aspect of a person's life rather than from the physical aspect of their life. Now please don't get me wrong. God does look at our outward actions, but the outward actions we live out in the physical are only a direct reaction and/or a direct result of what we place within our hearts in the spiritual realm (kingdom). Please let me explain. If you remember earlier in our search for the truth, we discovered that there is an unseen battle going on between God and the devil. We read about this in the New Testament book of Ephesians chapter 6 where we discovered that there's a war going on in the heavenly places (v. 12). This war is being fought within the spiritual realm, the unseen world that lies within the hearts of people against spiritual hosts of wickedness, against principalities and powers that are wicked. And that's why it's so important to know the Bible and to be a good fruit inspector. Why? Well, take a look at what it says in verse 13 of Ephesians 6, "that you [born-again believer] may be able to withstand in the evil day, and having done all, to stand." Question: When is the evil day? What is the evil day? What is God talking about when he says withstand in the evil day? Answer: Today is the evil day God is speaking about. Yesterday was the evil day. Tomorrow will be the evil day. And how do I know that, you ask? Well, take a look at what the word of God says in Ephesians 5:15 and 16 where it says, "See then that you [born-again believer] walk circumspectly [cautiously], not as fools but as wise, redeeming the time, because the days are evil." So in other words, my fellow truth seeker, when you're a follower of Jesus Christ, you must be extremely cautious in your daily lives because evil is lurking everywhere. And who is the champion of evil? That's right, it's the devil himself. Remember what we learned earlier in our search for the truth where we learned in God's word that a believer is to be sober and vigilant (on guard) because your (our) adversary, the devil, as a roaring lion walks about seeking whom he may devour (1 Peter 5:8). He wants to devour everything and anything in his path. And that's why it's so very important to be a good fruit inspector, my fellow truth seekers, now when I say that someone must be a good fruit inspector (which we discovered in chapter 11), you should know by now that I'm speaking of fruit as a spirit. In other words, what kind of spirit are you dealing with in both the physical and the spiritual aspects of your life? I say that because as I stated earlier, when you make a true commitment to follow Jesus Christ, you will have conflict in your life, conflict on the physical (fleshly) side of life and conflict on the spiritual (heavenly) side of life. But do you know what I have discovered in my personal journey in finding the narrow path to life? The conflicts, or tests if you will, that I have endured since I've been a follower of Jesus Christ have turned out to be my greatest blessings. And do you know something else, my fellow truth seekers? It's by and through those conflicts that I have sealed my inheritance into finding the narrow path of life eternal. What do I mean by that, you ask? I mean that by facing the conflicts that have come into my life straight on, I have not only received the greatest blessings in my life, but I have also sealed my redemption (salvation). I have sealed my salvation and my inheritance by overcoming. How so, you ask? Well, for the answer to that question, let's take a look at what the word of God says. I say let's take a look at what it says because if you're considered to be a coward in God's eyes, then you're in serious trouble. I say that because according to the word of God that we used at the beginning of this chapter, if you're a coward, then you are headed for the Lake of Fire (hell) and the second death. And you say, "Now that's a pretty bold statement to make, Joe!" In fact, that statement is bordering on the edge of being arrogant. And my answer to that is, "You're darn right, it is!" But do you know something else? I didn't say it. God did! And do you know another thing, my fellow truth seeker? If you're going to be a true follower of God (Jesus Christ), then you had better get used to it. I say you had better get used to it because if you're going to be a good steward, a good soldier, and a faithful follower of Jesus Christ, you're going to hear that statement a lot. I say you're going to hear that a lot because when you're taking a stand for the truth of God's word, you must understand that the word of God is like a sword. In fact, the word of God describes his word as a two-edged sword. How so, you ask? Well, take a look at what it says in the New Testament book of Hebrews 4:12 with regard to God's word being a sword when it says,

> For the word of God is living and powerful, and sharper than any two-edged sword, piercing even to the division of soul and spirit, and of joints and marrow, and is a discerner of the thoughts and intents of the heart.

In the spiritual realm, it cuts to the very heart of the matter especially when a person is living their life on the wide path that leads to destruction. God's word is foolish to them, and they can't understand what you mean. God's word is foolish to them, but they take out their hostilities and frustrations on you. Why? Because you're the vehicle and/or the means that God is using to convict their hearts of the truths of their transgressions (sins) against him, just like the scribes and Pharisees did to the Lord Jesus Christ some two thousand years ago. Jesus had uncovered their transgressions against God, but their hearts were so hard and they were so blind that they couldn't understand the truth of what Jesus was trying to tell them. But there, my fellow truth seeker is where the rubber meets the road as to whether you're going to be a good steward, soldier, and a true follower of Jesus Christ. Oh, you may never get into the physical hostilities that come with being a follower of Jesus Christ, especially if you live in the United States of America where I live. But I can assure you of this very fact: you will be persecuted for your faith in Jesus Christ. But you see, that's why I said that this is where the rubber meets the road as to whether or not you're going to be a true follower of Jesus Christ. Are you willing to suffer for the truth and the integrity of the very word of God? And that's one of the reasons that I highlighted the definition of the word "cowardly" earlier in this chapter. You may not ever feel the physical ramifications of taking a stand for the truth of God's word, but I can tell you from personal experience, you will experience the effects of the mental, emotional, and physiological pains that will come in your life when you take a stand for the truth of God's word. But then again, I truly believe that's why Jesus put the word "cowardly" as a qualifier of one of those who would go to hell. It is to serve as a warning to all those who are searching for the inheritance of all things that God promises to those who overcome. In other words, one of the things Jesus is warning us about is the fact that if you want to truly claim the God of the Holy Bible as your God; and if you truly want to be a good steward, soldier, overseer and true Son of God (Revelation 21:7), then you must overcome the trait of cowardliness. But there is yet another aspect to overcoming the trait of being cowardly. And what is that, you ask? It is the one that lies at the very forefront of how a person can truly overcome the trait of being cowardly, and it lies within the very word of God known as the word "fear."

Now the word "fear" is used some 385 times in the Bible. In comparison, the word "love" is used some 280 times in the Bible. Now you may be asking yourself, "So what?" So the word "fear" is used 385 times, and the word "love" is used 280 times. What's the big deal? Well, the big deal, my fellow truth seeker, is this. In case you didn't realize it, we have come pretty much full circle in our search for the truth. How so, you ask? Well, if you remember where we started in our search for the truth at the beginning of this book, you would remember that we pretty much began with the word of God that says in Proverbs 1:7, "The fear of the Lord [God] is the beginning of knowledge. But fools despise wisdom and instruction." This four-letter word "fear" means so much. I say that because I believe that the word "fear" has not only kept multitudes of people from finding the narrow gate (path) that leads to life, but I also believe it may just be the greatest weapon that the devil has in his arsenal in keeping people on the wide path that leads to destruction. Do you know something else? There is yet another side to the story that must be told. And what is that, you ask? Well, for the complete answer to that question, it would take a lot longer to explore than we have in our current search; but before we end our current search for the truth, I will tell you this much. Modern-day Christendom is literally jam-packed with what I refer to as modern-day Pharisees (some of this we uncovered earlier). But there is a big difference between the modern-day Pharisees of today and those Pharisees of Jesus day. And do you know what the big difference is, my fellow truth seeker? The Pharisees of Jesus day didn't claim to be followers of Jesus Christ. The Pharisees of today do. But there is yet another name that the modern-day Pharisees of today are referred to in God's word. And do you know what Jesus called them, my fellow truth seeker? Jesus called them ravenous wolves. But then again, please keep in mind, I'm just a forklift operator. After all, what do I know?

CHAPTER 23

Modern-day Pharisees
(The Good Old Boys Club)

Now I urge you brethren, note those who cause divisions and
offenses, contrary to the doctrine which you learned, and avoid
them. For those who are such do not serve our Lord Jesus Christ,
but their own belly, and by smooth words and flattering speech
deceive the hearts of the simple.
—Romans 16:17 and 18

NOW IN THE last chapter of our search for the truth, we
uncovered the truth that the cowardly will end up in hell. I also
shared with you that I wanted to end this book with what Jesus told the
scribes and Pharisees with regard to their father being the devil and they do
the desires of their father. I also shared a few chapters back that I wanted
to begin to end this book with the story of the two Pharisees whose names
were Nicodemus and Saul of Tarsus (Paul). If you also recall, we discovered
that Saul of Tarsus, once an enemy of God, became one of the greatest
followers of Jesus Christ and was responsible for authoring a great deal of
the New Testament. Now I wanted to end this book and our search for
the truth with the story of the two Pharisees named Nicodemus and Saul
of Tarsus (Paul) for a specific reason. I wanted to end our search for the
truth with this specific story because of what God opened my eyes to by
and through the story of these two (so-called) religious leaders. I say God
opened my eyes to his truth through the stories of Nicodemus and Saul of
Tarsus because of this one specific fact. And what was that specific fact?
It was the fact that neither Nicodemus nor Saul of Tarsus was born again.
Though they were supposed to be the most religious leaders of that time,
they didn't even know what it was or what it even meant. And do you know
what I have discovered since God first opened my eyes to this truth many
years ago? A great deal of modern-day Christendom today is in the same
frame of mind. They don't have a clue about what it means to be born

again. They don't have a clue because they are unaware of what it even means. They lack knowledge because they haven't been properly taught by those who call themselves the leaders (shepherds) in the church today. In fact, if the truth be known, I'm quite confident that a large portion of those who are leading church congregations today have never been born again themselves. They have never been born again of God's Spirit, and they are leading those churches simple because of certain traditions that have crept into a/the church setting. In fact, Saul of Tarsus (Paul) mentions these kinds of people in 2 Timothy chapter 3, where he spoke about the perilous (danger) times and the characteristics of certain men who would creep in among the people of God (church). Those specific characteristics of such men are outlined in verses 2 through 5 where it says, "For men will be lovers of themselves, lovers of money, boasters, proud, blasphemers, disobedient to parents, unthankful, slanderers, without self-control, brutal, despisers of good, traitors, headstrong, haughty, lovers of pleasure rather than lovers of God, having a form of godliness but denying its power." Question: If these are some of the characteristics that will be in place in the end times, are these characteristics meant only to describe those within the framework and structure of the church body, or does it also represent the characteristics of those who are beyond the church as well? Out in the world and/or on the wide path, if you will? Answer: I truly believe it does. How do I know that, you ask? I know it because of what God taught me as a leader and a representative (steward/trustee) in the Teamsters union.

Now to begin to unfold this teaching in our search for the truth, we must go back to Jesus' day and one of the most prominent leaders of the time of Nicodemus and Saul of Tarsus, a man by the name of Gamaliel. Now who was this man by the name of Gamaliel? Well, according to the word of God found in the New Testament book of Acts chapter 5 and Acts chapter 22, he was a Pharisee and a celebrated scholar of the Mosaic Law. He had a reputation for being one of the greatest teachers in the historical records of Judaism. Why, he even had a title after his name. He was a doctor of divinity. He was a man of great prestige and distinction and stature and reputation, and because of those distinguishing qualities, he carried with him a great influence throughout the Jewish people. He was known in the days of Jesus as the Rabbi of Rabbis. In other words, he was the spiritual leader among spiritual leaders. But do you know what? Even though he had all these qualities, prestige, distinction, stature, reputation, influence, and was known as the great rabbi, he didn't have one thing. And do you know what that one thing was, my fellow truth seeker? He lacked discernment. He didn't have good judgment. He was a bad fruit inspector. Oh, please don't get me wrong, I'm not trying to take anything away from the great teacher Gamaliel. All I'm saying is that as good of a teacher and all the other qualities that went along with Gamaliel's standing within the community (society) of his day, he was lacking in the area of discernment and judgment. And you say how do you know that? Well for me the answer is easy. The answer is as easy as this question. If Gamaliel was such a great scholar and was a doctor of divinity, how was it that he didn't know who Jesus was? If he was such a great teacher and he knew so much about the word of God, how was it that he missed the very fact that Jesus was the Messiah that had been spoken of throughout the ages (Old Testament)? If he was such a good teacher and therefore such a so-called good leader within the Jewish community, how was it that he missed the very presence of the promised Messiah? Well, for me, the answer is once again very easy. He missed it because he was a member of the Good Old Boys Club. Now you're probably saying to yourself, "What the heck does he mean by the Good Old Boys Club?" Well, for the complete answer with regard to my personal dealings with the Good Old Boys Club, it would take me yet another book to explain; but in our current search for the truth, let me give you the shortened version of what the Good Old Boys Club is.

You see, I'm a firm believer that most people almost always want to do the right thing. What I mean by that is that when any organization (i.e., group, club, society, institute, union, political party, etc.) get together, they nearly always do so for the betterment of whatever they are trying to achieve. In other words, whenever a group of people form a coalition (alliance), they do so to try and reach an intended goal or objective for their organization. They have a specific intended vision in their minds to what they are trying to achieve by forming that coalition. In other words, there's power in numbers. In the case of the Pharisees of Jesus' day, I truly believe they started off on the right foot. They started off with the right intentions, but somewhere along the line, the Pharisees veered off the road of what they were supposed to be and to whom they were supposed to represent with regard to the vision of their organization, etc. And what was the purpose of their organization? If you remember what we discovered earlier in our search for the truth, you will recall that they were supposed to be God's representatives. They were supposed to be the people that those on the outside of a clear understanding of what God was like could look up to as godly people, and therefore, they were supposed to be representing the one true God of Israel. They were representing the God of the universe that went all the way back to the beginning of the opening verse of the Bible found in Genesis, where it says, "In the beginning God created the heavens and the earth." They were supposed to be what the Bible speaks about in Matthew 5:14-16 where Jesus said, "You are the light of the world. A city that is set on a hill cannot be hidden. Nor do they light a lamp and put it under a basket, but on a lamp stand, and it gives light to all who are in the house. Let your light so shine before men, that they may see your good works and glorify your Father [God] in heaven."

You see, the Pharisees were supposed to be the light in a world full of darkness (sin). Their lives were supposed to be a beacon of light that represented the things (truths) of God, but instead they were representing the things of the darkness and the devil, which gave credibility and glory to the devil, instead of credibility and glory to the one true God of the Bible. So the Pharisees, along with the great rabbi and teacher Gamaliel, believed they were representing God, when in reality they were representing what was truly in their own hearts. And what was that? It was their desires. They were puffed up with their pride and their egos, and Jesus exposed them for what they truly were. Hypocrites and do you know what I have discovered since the time that God first opened my eyes to the truth of his word, my fellow truth seekers? The very same things that Jesus exposed the Pharisees of his day about are going on right in the world of Christendom today, except for one thing. The modern-day Pharisees of today are described by another name and that is the one I mentioned at the end of the last chapter. Jesus referred to them as ravenous wolves, and just like the Pharisees of Jesus' day, they are indeed hypocrites. They are indeed hypocrites, but the modern-day Pharisees of today are even worse than the Pharisees of Jesus' day. Why? Well, just like I also said at the end of the last chapter, the modern-day Pharisees of today claim to be followers of Jesus Christ, but they can't fool God. They claim to be lovers of God, but deep down in the portals (gateway, doorway, entrance) of their hearts, they too are full of dead men's bones and carry within their hearts the words we used at the beginning of this chapter. They serve their own bellies and the desires of their own hearts, and because of that, they are deceivers.

But there is yet another side of this story that goes along with what I spoke about earlier in this book, as well as earlier in this chapter. It also goes along with the Pharisees and what they were doing within their own religious group or the Good Old Boys Club if you will. They had established their own set of rules and regulations. In an attempt to establish how religious they were, they instituted their own rules and regulations (traditions) and used them in an attempt to show how godly they were. Oh, they thought they were very clever. They thought they were very clever because when they were formulating their list of rules and regulations for the Pharisaic organization (the Good Old Boys Club) they created an illusion of how godly they were by establishing over six hundred rules for people to adhere to. But the problem was they didn't adhere to those rules themselves. Jesus spoke about this in Matthew 23:3-5 where he said, "For they [scribes and Pharisees] bind heavy burdens, hard to bear, and lay them on men's shoulders; but they themselves will not move them with one of their fingers. But all their works they do to be seen by men." The illusion that the scribes and Pharisees were trying to portray was exposed by Jesus, and they didn't like being exposed for their hypocrisy. They mixed the word of God into their own self-made rules and regulations, and they called them the canon's (rules) of God's word(s). Do you know what God says about those kinds of people, my fellow truth seeker? He calls them people who cause divisions and offenses contrary to his doctrine (Romans 16:17). He calls that smooth words and flattering speech that are intended to deceive the hearts of the simple. And who are the simple, my fellow truth seekers? They are the unsuspecting. They are the naive. They are those who are so easily led astray (off course) by those who Jesus called ravenous wolves, false prophets (teachers) in sheep's clothing. Jesus uses this expression, ravenous wolves (Matthew 7:15) in sheep's clothing, because he is speaking about this in a religious setting. He is speaking about these types of people who deceive those who lack knowledge and understanding about the truth of God's word. Jesus is speaking about these wolves in sheep's clothing, the so-called leaders in his church (overseers, pastors, elders, etc.) who impersonate being true shepherds but actually promote the wide gate and the wide way that leads to destruction. They are the modern-day Pharisees in the modern-day world of Christendom today.

Now you may be saying to yourself, "This is all well and fine Joe, but what does all of this have to do with the Good Old Boys Club and our search for the truth?" Well, as I stated earlier, God first opened my eyes to the Good Old Boys Club when I first became a union steward and representative in the Teamsters union. Please let me explain.

Now at this point, a lot of things that we've been uncovering in our search for the truth are going to begin to come together. I say these are going to begin to come together because at this point, we're going to shift into the next and last stage of our search for the truth, and that is with regard to what God's word says about being a watchman. And you say,

"What do you mean by watchman?" Well, if you recall what I said with regard to the great teacher and rabbi, Gamaliel, you will remember I stated that he lacked discernment. In other words, he couldn't quite separate the truth from the false. He was a bad fruit inspector. And the reason he was a bad fruit inspector and lacked discernment was because in the words of Jesus himself, his heart was full of dead men's bones and all uncleanness (Matthew 23:27). He had a heart problem and because his heart was focused on himself and his own pride, he was one of the main players in the brood of vipers spoken of by Jesus in Matthew chapter 23. He was one of the main players in the brood of vipers because he was the one who was responsible for teaching those in his organization (Pharisees/Jews) the difference between what was true (of God) and what was false (of the devil). He should have known that Jesus was the anticipated Messiah, but because his heart was set on his own agenda and the desires of his own heart, he missed it. And because he missed it, I truly believe he may also be held primarily responsible for the destruction of many souls that were under his authority as a teacher and leader in Israel. Many souls that were under his authority and guidance, and in my humble opinion, he is one of the key players who are responsible for Jesus Christ being put to death. Now please don't get me wrong. I'm not saying that he was the only one responsible for Jesus' death. All I'm saying is that if his heart had been right with God, I truly believe his judgment wouldn't have been impaired, and he would have known that Jesus was indeed the anticipated Messiah foretold in the Old Testament scriptures (Genesis 3:15, 49:10; Deuteronomy 18:18, 19; 2 Samuel 7:13, 14; Job 19:25, 26; Psalm 2, 110, 132:11; Isaiah 7:14, 8:10, 9:6, 59:20, 61:1, 2; Jeremiah 23:5,6, 31; Daniel 7:13, 14; Micah 5:2; Zechariah 6:12, 12:10, 13, 9:9,10, 11:12, 13; Malachi 3:1, etc.). But you see, that's what goes along with being a good steward, soldier, overseer and watchman for God. If Gamaliel was all that he should have been as a good teacher, he would have also been a good watchman. Now what does all of this have to do with being a watchman? It has a great deal to do with being a watchman.

You see, in the Old Testament book of Ezekiel chapter's 3 and 33, there lays a golden nugget of the word of God. In fact, I happen to believe that it is really the summation of all that we have uncovered in this book in our search for the truth. Now I'm telling you this, my fellow truth seeker, because this golden nugget of God's word really is the summation to finding the narrow path to life. And why is this such an important summation in our search for the truth? Because it has to do with everything that we have uncovered throughout our search for the truth, such things as wisdom, fearing God, perfection, being born again of God's Spirit, sincerity, self-examination, counting the cost, a hardened heart, fruit inspecting, cowards, being a good steward, soldier, and overseer, as well as everything else we have discovered throughout the chapters of this book. The summation of all that we have uncovered throughout this book really boils down to this, my fellow truth seeker. It comes down to glorifying God in all that we do and all that we are. And if we're (you're) really going to glorify God, then a major part of glorifying God really boils down to this fact. It really boils down to what is taught in Ezekiel 3:17 and Ezekiel 33:7. It boils down to two basic themes. And what are those themes, you ask? They are those which include the themes of warning and exposing (Colossians 1:28 and Ephesians 5:11). You see, once you become a follower of Jesus Christ, you are bound to a/ the covenant of what God's word calls warning and exposing. I say that because if you really dissect the whole theme of the Bible, you will discover that God's word is really a warning to all those who reject his word. And what is God's word? It is that which became flesh and dwelt among us (John 1:14). It is the fact that God's only Son, Jesus Christ, came to earth to save us from our rebellion toward the (our) Creator, who is the one true God of the Holy Bible. People (We) are warned to turn from their evil ways (Proverbs 16:17). We (true believers) are also given a command to expose the unfruitful works of darkness (transgressions that opposes God's word) that is being achieved both by and through the wickedness that is found within the hearts of people. But there is a problem. And what is that problem? It is the one found within the wickedness of mankind, which is the problem that Jesus himself was up against, when he exposed the wickedness of the scribes and the Pharisees (the Good Old Boys Club). It is the one found in Romans 1:21; they became futile (useless) in their thoughts, and their foolish hearts were darkened. Jesus exposed the darkness of their hearts, and the Good Old Boys didn't like it at all. But then again, please keep in mind, I'm just a forklift operator. After all, what do I know?

CHAPTER 24

God's Watchman
(Exposing and Warning)

And have no fellowship with the unfruitful works of darkness, but
rather expose them.
—Ephesians 5:11

Him [Jesus Christ] we proclaim, warning every man and teaching
every man in all wisdom, that we may present every man
mature in Christ.
—1 Colossians 1:28

A S OUR SEARCH for the truth continues to come to an end,
there is yet one more truth that we need to uncover before we
end our journey. And what is that truth? It is the one that I spoke about
earlier with regard to what Jesus did to the scribes and Pharisees of his day.
And what did he do? He exposed them for what God's word refers to as
unfruitful works of darkness. In other words, the things they were doing
in their lives were supposedly being done within the framework of the one
true God of the Bible, but in reality they were actually fulfilling the works
of the devil. If you recall what Jesus said to the scribes and Pharisees, you
will recall that Jesus told them that they were of their father, the devil,
and the works (desires) they were doing were being done, not within the
truth of God's word, but they were doing them within the framework of
the wicked one, who is the devil (John 8:44). They were being dishonest
in their actions, and they were actually deceiving others, which actually
sheds greater light on the words we uncovered earlier in this book where
Jesus told the scribes and Pharisees that they were hypocrites. And because
of their hypocrisy, they were actually making those they converted into
their way of thinking twice a son of hell as themselves. Jesus didn't water
down what was going on. He got right to the point of the problem, and
he exposed them for what they were. They were phonies, and Jesus knew

it. They were representing their own personal desires instead of what God desires, the truth! But you see that's where the problem was. They were certain that they were representing the one true God of the universe, but instead they were representing the god of this world, the devil.

You see, the one major truth that God needs to open your heart and mind to before I end this book is a major component with regard to you finding the narrow gate (path) that leads to life. I say that because in the world we (you) live in today, the pathway that leads to eternal life is getting smaller and smaller. I say that because the secular world (wide path) we live in is pushing its agenda of secular humanism more and more down the throats of the lives of those who are caught in its pathway of destruction. Now what do I mean by the term "secular humanism"? Well, there is much to uncover with regard to an in-depth study of rightly defining this term and how it is affecting the world we (you) live in; but if I were to put it in the proper context of a biblical interpretation, I believe the interpretation of what secular humanism represents is exactly what Jesus is exposing and warning the scribes and Pharisees about. How so, you ask? Well, in a nutshell, the term "secular humanism" is an attitude of thought which gives primary importance to human beings. The dictionary defines it as such: any system of thought in which human interests and values are taken to be of primary importance. In many cases, humanists themselves would agree that they adhere to a religious worldview, while in other cases; humanists want to distance themselves from being identified as religious because they understand that religion is (supposedly) not allowed in American education. In other words, the secular humanist holds to a belief that rejects religious values that there is a right way and a wrong way to live. The concept of the modern-day secular humanism movement holds fast to the type of thinking that says that a person can and should be able to do whatever they want as long as they are not hurting others. But then again, that's exactly what Jesus was focusing in on when he exposed what kind of effects the scribes and Pharisees were having on those they were converting to their way of thinking (Judaism).

In Matthew 23:15, we read these words from the very lips of Jesus when he says, "Woe to you scribes and Pharisees, hypocrites! For you travel land and sea to win one proselyte, and when he is won, you make him twice as much a son of hell as yourselves." In other words, one of the goals of the scribes and the Pharisees were obviously to convert others into their way of thinking. They tried to convert them to Judaism, and when those people were converted, those they converted had a serious problem. And what was their problem? They became even worse than those Jesus was speaking to. By allowing them access into the denomination, if you will, they became even worse than the leaders in that Pharisaic system themselves. But then again, that's exactly what's happening in the modern-day church movement of today. In many ways, the modern-day church movement is similar to what Jesus was exposing the religious leaders in his day. Those leaders were living double lives. Their lives were surrounded with the sweet aroma of being very religious (godly) people, when in fact they couldn't hide their extreme hypocrisy from Jesus. Jesus knew that they were two-faced, and Jesus exposed them to that very fact.

Well, by now you may be asking yourself, "This is all well and fine Joe, but what the heck does all of this have to do with me and our search for the truth?" Answer: It has a great deal to do with you, my fellow truth seeker. I say it has a great deal to do with you, my fellow truth seeker, because much of what we've been uncovering as we close out our journey together will prove to be one of the major parts of your faith journey as a follower of Jesus Christ, should you decide to take up your cross and follow Jesus. Now I say that because what I have discovered in my own personal journey as a follower of Jesus Christ is that when you become a follower of Jesus Christ, your life will be surrounded by conflict. Now I know that this statement is not a very popular thing to say, especially in the modern-day world in which we live. I say that because since the time I've been a follower of Jesus Christ, I have learned from experience that the word "conflict" is almost as much a part of a true Christian's journey in the same manner as breathing is to life itself. But we shouldn't be surprised by that because if you understand what's really going on at all in the Bible, you will discover that when you're taking on the ruler of this world (the devil) and those who are under his domain (unbelievers, secular humanists, those on the wide path, etc.), there will be conflict. In fact, we are told about this conflict within the word of God. And who is speaking in this word from God? It is the Apostle Paul (Saul of Tarsus), who was formerly a member of the Pharisees, as we discovered earlier in this book. And that's the reason why I wanted to begin to end our journey with the two Pharisees named Nicodemus and Saul of Tarsus (Paul) in mind. Now I say I wanted to end this book with the account of the Pharisees named Nicodemus and Saul of Tarsus (Paul) because of all the people listed in the Bible, it is my opinion that if anyone understood the command with regard to exposing and warning, it would have been these two people. Now I say that because of all the people who were alive at the time that Jesus Christ walked this earth, there was no other group that received a greater disapproval and condemnation than those of the scribes and the Pharisees. And both Nicodemus and Saul of Tarsus (Paul) were members of that group. And knowing that they were members of this group, there had to come a time when they realized that they were part of the problem instead of part of the solution. They had to realize that the system they were members of was a false system that was actually leading people to their destruction instead of their salvation. Instead of helping people in opening their eyes to deliverance, they were actually leading people off course to their ultimate peril. In other words, they were leading people down the wide path that led to destruction (hell) instead of the narrow path that led to life (heaven). And that's why Jesus said what he said to them in Matthew chapter 23. He disapproved of their actions, and he was condemning them for those actions. But wait! Jesus was actually condemning someone? Could that possibly be? Could it be that Jesus was actually rebuking and admonishing people? I say that because in the world of modern-day Christendom, the command of exposing and warning is under severe attack by those who are under the seducing spirits that exist within the realm of secular humanism. What I mean by that is that with the continuation of the secular humanism movement today, the wide path that leads to destruction has found its way into the (so-called) modern-day church. Kind of like it did within the ranks of the scribes and Pharisees of Jesus' day. But true followers of Jesus Christ shouldn't be surprised. I say they shouldn't be surprised because we've been exposed and warned that this would happen in the final days leading up to the second coming of Jesus Christ. How so, you ask? Well, let's take a look at what God's word exposes us to in the New Testament book of 1 Timothy 4:1 where it says, "Now the Spirit expressly says that in latter times, some will depart from the faith, giving heed to seducing spirits and doctrines of demons, Now in this context, the word "seducing" is used to define the word "deception." In other words, those who are supposedly associated with Jesus Christ and his church will leave their faith by being deceived by and through the seducing spirits that are associated with the devil. How do I know that? I know it because demons are associated with the devil and not God, just as Jesus was exposing and warning that such a thing was happening in the realm of the scribes and Pharisees. The scribes and Pharisees were being seduced and deceived by the devil, and Jesus (God) exposes true believers that the same thing would happen before his (Jesus') return to earth.

Now as we put all of this together, we begin to see why it is so very important to understand that a true believer will have conflict. I say they will have conflict because the forces of evil that are surrounding the modern-day church movement today are so powerful that the devil will not give up his territory very easily. The strong grip he has on Christ's church today has taken quite a while to get established, and he will not let go of his territory without a fight. But then again that's why true believers are called to be soldiers and watchmen. And that's why we (true believers) are commanded to expose what God's word calls "the unfruitful works of darkness." And when we do that, when we expose those who are committing those unfruitful works of darkness, we are actually helping them in their own personal lives. We are actually helping them as they move closer and closer into what Jesus said true believers would be. And what was that? Well, we read about that earlier in this book, and the word is called perfect. In Matthew 5:48, we read these words from Jesus, "You shall be perfect, just as your Father in heaven is perfect." We are told by Jesus that true believers shall be perfect. So when we see things that don't coincide with the truth of God's word, we are commanded to expose those things that are considered by God as works of darkness. We are commanded to expose those things which are the unfruitful works of darkness so that through and by our willingness to expose those things, we might help people see that they need to repent of those unfruitful works. They need to repent so that by our actions in exposing them to their transgression against God's truth, we can help them as they learn to become more mature in Christ, just as 1 Colossians 1:28 teaches. Now please don't misunderstand what I'm saying. I'm not saying that a follower of Jesus Christ (true believer) will ever reach the point of being a completely perfect person. At least as it relates to the perfection that was found in Jesus' life. All I'm saying is that perfection should be the goal that every true follower of Jesus Christ should strive for. And how can a person move more and more toward the kind of perfection that God's word says will be in a true believer's life? It is by understanding that we are to be watchmen over the word of God, which takes us to the lives of Nicodemus and Saul of Tarsus (Paul). I say it takes us to the lives of Nicodemus and Saul of Tarsus because as members of the Pharisees, both Nicodemus and Saul of Tarsus were well established in the unfruitful works of darkness themselves and Jesus exposed them to that very fact. When did Jesus do that, you ask? Well, as a collective group, Jesus did it throughout the time of his earthly ministry, but individually he did it in the New Testament books of John chapter 3 and Acts chapter 9. Now in these accounts of how Jesus exposed the Pharisees named Nicodemus and Saul of Tarsus (Paul) to the truth of God's word, we find that they come to us from completely different directions. What I mean by that is that Nicodemus and Saul of Tarsus (Paul) were exposed to the truth in this manner. First, Nicodemus pursued Jesus, while Saul of Tarsus (Paul) was pursued by Jesus. How so, you ask? Well, if you take a look at John chapter 3, you will find that Nicodemus went to confront Jesus; and in Acts chapter 9, Jesus went to confront Saul of Tarsus (Paul) in what is known as the Damascus road incident. An incident in which Jesus confronted Saul (Paul) and accused him of persecuting him (Acts 9:5) by having his followers put in jail and sometimes even killed for their loyalty as his followers.

Now as I have studied these two different scenarios, through the years, I have come to learn a great deal about the warning and exposing order that a true follower of Jesus Christ must learn to obey. I say they must learn to obey this order from God because it is a major part of a true believer's walk down the narrow path that leads to life. How so, you ask? Well, for the complete answer to that question, we must first take a good look at one of the key words that is in the scripture verse found on the front cover of this book. And what is that word? It is the word "difficult." You see, up to the time that both Nicodemus and Saul of Tarsus were exposed to the reality that they were in serious trouble, they had no idea whatsoever that anything was wrong, kind of like what has taken place within your own heart and mind since you began to read this book. Up until Jesus exposed Nicodemus and Saul to the fact (truth) that they both needed a heart transformation (to be born again), they really didn't understand what was going on in their lives. After all, they were members in the most religious organization of that time. But Jesus exposed them to the fact that they were on the wide road (path) that leads to destruction. But you see, that's where the word "difficult" comes in to play. I say that because just as Nicodemus and Saul of Tarsus were exposed to the truth, so is God opening your heart to that same truth as we begin to end this search for truth. How so, you ask? Well, up until the time Jesus exposed and warned both Nicodemus and Saul of Tarsus that they had a problem, there probably wasn't too much turmoil in their lives. Other than a few skirmishes within their own personal lives they probably didn't have too many difficulties. As members of an elite organization (the Good Old Boys Club—Pharisees), they didn't really have too much difficulty in their lives. That was up until they were exposed to the truth and had to make a decision as to whether or not they were going to follow Jesus. I say that because when a person makes a real commitment to follow Jesus Christ, the difficulties in that person's life will increase. I say that because once you are exposed to the truth of God's word, you will come under attack by those who don't want to hear the truth of God. Saul of Tarsus (Paul) learned this truth. How do I know that, you ask? I know it by his words in 2 Timothy 3:12, "All that live Godly in Christ Jesus shall suffer persecution." Saul learned firsthand that persecution goes along with being a watchman. But then again, please keep in mind, I'm just a forklift operator. After all, what do I know?

CHAPTER 25

A New Lump

Your glorying is not good. Do you not know that a little leaven
leavens the whole lump? Therefore purge out the old leaven, that
you may be a new lump, since you truly are unleavened. For indeed
Christ, our Passover, was sacrificed for us.
—1 Corinthians 5:6 and 7

IN THE LAST chapter in our search for the truth, we started to uncover what God's word says about true followers of Jesus Christ responsibilities with regard to exposing the unfruitful works of darkness that exists all around them. In other words, a follower of Jesus Christ's (Christian) responsibility does not just stop with their own rejection of evil, but they are also responsible for exposing and opposing darkness wherever it is found, especially when it is found within the church setting itself. How do I know that, you ask? Well, for the complete answer to that question, it would take a lot longer than we have in our current search; but to begin to put the pieces of this topic together, we must take a look at some specific areas of God's word. I say we must take a look at these specific areas of God's word because by exploring these specific parts of God's word, we can begin to understand how important it is to learn that God does have a grievance procedure. And why does God have a specific grievance procedure in his word? He has it in his word for the specific reason of purification. Purifying hearts and restoring his church to being in line with the truth of his word. And once again, what is the church? It is the collective bodies of those who are truly born again with the indwelling of God's Spirit (John 3:6; 14:17). But there is a problem. And what is that problem? It is the problem that God's grievance procedure isn't being carried out within the church structure of the modern-day world of Christendom today, at least not on a major scale. Now please don't get me wrong. I'm not saying that there aren't churches that are carrying out this directive from the word of God. But on a major scale, God's grievance procedure is not, and I repeat, is not being carried out within most of Christendom today. Question: Why is that?

Why is it that God's grievance procedure isn't being carried out within the realm of most Christianity today? Well, again for the complete answer to this question, it would take a lot longer than we have in our current search; but if I were to narrow that question down to a basic reason why I believe this directive in God's word is not being carried out, I would have to say that it has to do with the false church movement that is taking place as the world we live in moves toward the final battle that God's word speaks about, the final battle between good and evil, the final battle between God and the devil. That word is primarily laid out within the Bible found in the last book of God's word known as the book of the Revelation.

Now like I said, there's a whole lot to uncover with regard to the time leading up to the final battle between God and the devil, but for now I'd like to take a look into God's grievance procedure. I say I want to look into the framework of God's grievance procedure because of what the implications of this specific part of God's word means to you in your personal pursuit of the narrow path that leads to life. Now I want to look into this specific part of God's word for a specific reason, and the specific reason is this. If you notice the scripture I used at the beginning of this chapter, you will notice two words. The words are leaven and purge. In God's word, the word "leaven" represents sin (transgression against God), and the word "purge" represents washing and/or cleansing; removing, to wipe out, to destroy, etc. Now if you put these two words together in the context of what God's grievance procedure is meant to accomplish, you will begin to understand why this section of God's word is under attack. Did I say under attack? Yes, I did. I said under attack. Why is it under attack? It is under attack because if leaven and purging are taken out of the framework of God's word, then God's adversary, the devil, can further deceive people into thinking they are right with God, when in reality they are not. Just as the Pharisees, including Nicodemus and Saul of Tarsus, thought they were right with God when in fact they were of their father, the devil.

By now, you may be asking the question, but what does all of this have to do with me? Answer: It has a great deal to do with you, my fellow truth seeker. Why? It has a great deal to do with you because if you make a commitment to follow Jesus Christ and God opens up your heart to his truth, you will become a watchman of his word. In other words, just as we uncovered earlier, once you become a follower of Jesus Christ, God will begin to purge (cleanse) the leaven (sin) that exists within your life so that he can begin to use you as a representative of his kingdom here on earth, a representative that will be his eyes and ears to a world that is more in tune with the God of this world (the devil and the wide path) than they are to the one true God, by and through his Son, Jesus Christ (the narrow path). Another way of explaining this is through the word of God found in Matthew 5:13 and 14, "You are the salt of the earth; you are the light of the world." A city that is set on a hill cannot be hidden. In other words, once you truly repent of your transgressions against God and you receive the fact that his Son, Jesus Christ, died on a cross for all those transgressions (sins), then your life becomes a life (light) for truth instead of a life for darkness. But you see, that's where God's grievance procedure comes into play. I say it comes into play because of all the things we've been uncovering in our current search for the truth is the issue of leaven and purging that is such an important piece in the puzzle of being a good watchman (i.e., steward, overseer, ambassador, guardian, etc.) for God. How do I know that, you ask? Well, let me take you to some specific parts of God's word as we discover why this specific section of God's word is so important in our search for the truth in finding the narrow path to life.

Now as I begin to dissect this particular part of our search for the truth, I'd like to go back to my time as union steward in the Teamsters union. I say I'd like to go back to my time as union steward because it was by and through the many trials and tribulations of my time as union steward that God really opened my eyes (heart) to the whole reality of God's grievance procedure being such an important part of my (or anyone's) faith journey. I say it was such an important part of my personal faith journey because what I learned in my time as union steward was that if I wanted to truly live my life by the truth, then I was going to have to learn that much of my personal walk with God would find me going against the flow of the world I lived in. What I learned in my time as union steward was that if I was going to be a good watchman for God and the truth of his word, I was going to be in a battle for the rest of my days in this life. I guess the best way to describe it is like when you see or hear of the fish (salmon) swimming their way upstream to spawn. If you've ever seen a picture of those fish, you will see the urgency, the importance, the determination of those fish in reaching their final destination so that they can release the eggs they have inside them so that others can live. In many ways, those fish are so determined to fight against the powerful current of the water that those fish oftentimes pay a severe price. I say they oftentimes pay a severe price because sometimes the price they pay is their very lives. In other words, they're so willing to take on and fight against the powerful currents they are going against that they are willing to die, if need be, to fulfill their responsibility so that others may live. Now I use that scenario as an illustration in our search for the truth because once I became a follower of Jesus Christ, I understood that my days here on this earth would not be easy. My days on this earth would be filled with going against the flow of the world I lived in. In reality, my life would be like the fish going upstream, taking on the currents of this world. Not always going with the flow, but fighting the good fight of faith just like Saul of Tarsus (Paul) learned to do when we hear in the words he spoke in 1 Timothy 6:12, "Fight the good fight of faith, lay hold on eternal life." The good fight of faith in this instance is the one fought while he was being a good soldier (watchman) for God's word (truth). In 2 Timothy 4:7, Saul of Tarsus (Paul) speaks about the end of his time (life) on earth in which he emphasizes to his fellow brother in Christ, Timothy, that he had fought the good fight of faith. Earlier in this discussion with Timothy (verse 2), Paul gives a charge to Timothy with regard to preaching the word of God in which Paul gives the command to "Preach the word!" He goes on to tell Timothy that he needs to be ready in season and out of season. Question: What did Paul mean when he told Timothy to be ready to preach the word in season as well as out of season? What he meant is that Timothy needed to be prepared to share the truth of God's word at any time, whether it was popular or whether it was not. In other words, he needed to be prepared to share the truth of God's word(s) when they were accepted or when they were not. But do you know something, my fellow truth seeker? This same scenario goes for anyone who claims the name of Jesus Christ. You need to be prepared to share the truth of God's words whether they are accepted or whether they are not, and that's why it's so vitally important to be born again of God's Spirit and to know God's word. Why? Well, the answer to that question is found again in the words of Paul when he was mentoring Timothy found in 2 Timothy chapter 2. In this chapter, Paul is teaching Timothy about the skill of warfare as a soldier in God's army. Paul teaches Timothy that he must be prepared to endure hardship as a good soldier of Jesus Christ. Why? Because true followers of Jesus Christ are in a war, and they need to understand that living by the truth of God's word will more than likely cost them something. In other words, when you live by the truth of God's word, your ultimate goal is to please God and not yourself. That's why Paul tells Timothy in verse 4 of 2 Timothy chapter 2 these words, "No one engaged in warfare entangles himself with the affairs of this life, that he may please him who enlisted him as a soldier." Why? Because just as a soldier is completely detached from the normal affairs of civilian life, so also must the good soldier of Jesus Christ refuse to allow the things of the world to distract him. Furthermore, in the New Testament book of 1 Peter 2:11, we are instructed in God's word to abstain from fleshly lusts which war against the soul. And once again, as we've learned throughout our search for the truth, what are the things of the world? They are those things found in Galatians 5:19-21; they are those works of the flesh that are evident which are adultery, fornication, uncleanness, lewdness, idolatry, sorcery, hatred, contentions, jealousies, outbursts of wrath, selfish ambitions, dissentions, heresies, envy, murders, drunkenness, revelries, and the like.

So in other words, if someone wants to please God, then they must understand what pleases him. And they can please him by eliminating those things of the flesh that are listed here in Galatians chapter 5. But there is a problem, and the problem is a great deal of these works of the flesh is what we war against each and every day of our lives as human beings. Yes, most people don't have all of these works of the flesh evident in their lives, but the secret to pleasing God is to figure out which of these works of the flesh are evident in our own personal lives and then to do something about them. And when we determine which of these works of the flesh are evident, then we go through the process of purging and cleansing our lives into a new lump if you will. Just as the scripture verse we read at the beginning of this chapter says, "Purge out the old leaven, that you may be a new lump. Now a good portion of this process we've already uncovered in our search for the truth (chapter 13, etc.). The whole issue of self-examination and purging has a direct connection to what Jesus Christ instructed true believers to be aware of with regard to being good fruit inspectors. And what is that direct connection? Well, as there is a direct connection to self-examination and fruit inspection and purging the leaven (sin) within our own lives (hearts), there is also another direct connection to overseeing the leaven that is within other's lives as well, especially when those people claim to be followers of Jesus Christ. How so, you ask? Well, as I stated earlier, to get a firm grip on this teaching, it is essential that we place together some pieces of God's word(s). But there is yet another side of this instruction by Jesus that oftentimes get overlooked by multitudes of people. Now I'm telling you this because of a direct responsibility I have in writing this book. I say I have a direct responsibility because it may just be that before you started reading this book, you may have never even given a thought about being a follower of Jesus Christ. Maybe you never gave much thought about your eternal future before. Maybe you've been so in tune on/with the wide path of destruction in this life that you've never really even given a thought about the narrow path that leads to life eternal. But by reading this book,

God has stirred up your heart to the point that maybe you'd like to pursue a personal relationship with him. And it's to this point that I'd like to end our search. I say it's to this point that I'd like to end our search because it's to this point that both Nicodemus and Saul of Tarsus (Paul) had to deal with this topic as well. I say they had to deal with this also because up to the time Jesus exposed both of them to the truth, both of them had religion but they didn't have a relationship with the one true God of the Bible. In fact, they were literally saturated in their religion. They were swallowed up in their religion, but the fact was they were in serious trouble. They were traveling on the wide path that leads to destruction when they thought they were on the narrow path that was leading them to eternal life. But do you know something, my fellow truth seeker? That very same thing may just be happening to you as well. You may have religion, but you don't have a relationship with Jesus Christ (God).

Now you may be asking yourself this question: "What do you mean by having religion versus having a relationship?" Well, for the answer to that question, I'd like to take a look at the parts of God's word that I truly believe bring this together as we begin to draw a conclusion to this book. Now the parts of God's word that I'd like to take a look at are found in the New Testament books of the Revelation chapter 2 and Matthew chapter 7, and in the Old Testament book of Ezekiel chapters 3 and 33. Now I want us to take a look at these specific parts of God's word as we begin to end this book because I believe it's so very important for you to know that as a follower of Jesus Christ, it is important to know that you are accountable for what you do with the word of God. And you say, what do you mean? What do you mean that I am accountable? Well, if you've read this book up to this point, you have come to a point as to whether or not you're going to accept or reject what God has revealed to you by and through one of his watchmen. One of his watchmen, you say. Yes, I said watchmen. You see, the accountability for one's actions is a direct link to knowing whether or not you have religion or whether or not you have a true relationship in/ with Jesus Christ. I say that because of what God has taught me throughout the time I've been a follower of Jesus Christ. Since the time I've been a follower of Jesus Christ, I have learned firsthand that Jesus (God) has some grievances against his church. What are those grievances, you ask? Well, for the answer to that question, it would take a lot more time than we have in our current search for the truth; but as we uncover some of these grievances, it must come through the word "compromise." But then again, please keep in mind, I'm just a forklift operator. After all, what do I know?

CHAPTER 26

Peace
(Be Doers—Not Hearers Only)

Be doers of the word, and not hearers only, deceiving yourselves.
For if anyone is a hearer of the word and not a doer, he is like a man
observing his natural face in a mirror; for he observes himself, goes
away, and immediately forgets what kind of man he was. But he who
looks into the perfect law of liberty and continues in it, and is
not a forgetful hearer but a doer of the work, this one will be
blessed in what he does.
—James 1:22 to 25

IN THE LAST few chapters, we've been uncovering some truths about the Pharisees named Nicodemus and Saul of Tarsus (Paul) and how Jesus Christ exposed them to the truth that they were in some serious trouble with regard to their relationship as supposed representatives of God. We've also learned about how true followers of Jesus Christ are to be watchmen of God's word. We've also uncovered what things please God and what things do not please God. The bottom line to all of what we have discovered with regard to the word of God can be summed up in what these words from the New Testament book of James teaches, "Be Doers of the word, and Not Hearers Only." But then comes the final clincher to what God's words warns people about if they only hear God's word but do not act upon those (God's) words. And what are those words? They are the words "deceiving yourselves." In other words, if you hear the truth of God's words and you do not act upon those words, you will lose out on the blessings of/from God. How do I know that, you ask? Well, take a look at what God's word says in verse 22 of James chapter 1. God tells us if we do what God's word instructs us to do, we will be blessed in what we do. So the key to receiving the best of God's blessings upon our lives is to be doers of his words and not hearers only.

Now to uncover for you just how this teaching first became a reality in my own life, I have to go back once again to the time I was first elected as union steward in the Teamsters union. Now I say I have to go back to my time as being union steward because it was in the time of being an elected official in the Teamsters union that I really began to have my eyes opened to the fact that when you live your life in and for the truth of God's word you will spend much of your life going against the currents of this world (wide path). Just as we discovered in the last chapter with regard to the fish swimming against the strong currents of the water that was in front of them, a true follower of Jesus Christ must learn that the very same thing will happen to them. Like those fish going against the strong currents of water to reach their ultimate goal of releasing their eggs so that life may be established in others, so too is the responsibility of a true follower of Jesus Christ. A true follower of Jesus Christ must know up front that the world (wide path) will place obstacles in front of them, as they release (spawn if you will) the truth of God's word to a world that, for the most part, is traveling on the wide path to destruction. But then again, that's why I used the scripture verse that I did on the front cover of this book. "Narrow is the gate and difficult is the way which leads to life, and there are few who find it" (Matthew 7:14). This takes us back to my time as an elected official (union steward) in the Teamsters union.

Earlier in this book, I told the story of how I was unanimously elected to fulfill the office of union steward in the Teamsters union. Now I'm telling you this because if you remember my story, you will recall that the same year I became a union steward was the same year that I accepted Jesus Christ as my personal Lord and Savior. Now you may be asking yourself, "What the heck does being a union steward in the Teamsters union have to do with being a follower of Jesus Christ? What is the connection?" Well, for me, it was a big connection. How so, you ask? Well, for me it was a time in my life that God used in preparing me for being one of his watchmen, a time of preparation in helping me find the narrow path (way) that would ultimately lead me to finding life. The abundant life that comes to those who adhere to what God's word instructs true believers to carry out in their lives. And what is that, you ask? It is to be doers of the words of God and not hearers only. Now I say that not in the context that by being doers of God's words, that will necessarily give you any favor with God, but for me, being a doer of God's word gives me such an inner peace that it is nearly impossible to describe. But then again, as a true follower of Jesus Christ, I shouldn't have been surprised that by being a doer of God's word and not a hearer only it would give me such inner peace. Now why do I say that? Well, take a look at what Jesus told his followers in the New Testament book of John 14:27 with regard to what Jesus said was his Peace. He said, "Peace I leave with you, My peace I give to you; not as the world gives do I give to you." Also in the Old Testament book of Isaiah 9:6, we read that Jesus Christ is called the Prince of Peace. Now what kind of peace was Jesus speaking about here? Well, for me, the type of peace Jesus is speaking about is the kind of peace that surpasses all understanding. In other words, the inner peace you receive from being a doer of God's word (living in/by the truth) is a divine peace that can only be truly understood by those who are truly in/of Christ and have God's Spirit (the comforter) living within their own lives (hearts). Now I say that because when you live your life in and by the truth, it is imperative that you have the kind of peace that only Jesus Christ (God) can give. I say that because when you become a watchman for the truth of God's word, the spiritual battles that exist between God and the devil will intensify as you become more and more in tune in/to being a doer of God's word and not just a hearer only. But then again, it's within this kind of mind-set that a person's heart will be guarded by Almighty God. And you say, "How do you know that God will guard my heart?" I know it because God's word tells us (me) in the New Testament book of Philippians 4:6 and 7, "Be anxious for nothing, but in everything by prayer and supplication, with thanksgiving, let your requests be made known to God; and the peace of God, which surpasses all understanding, will guard your hearts and minds through Christ Jesus."

Now you may be saying to yourself, "This is all well and fine Joe, but what the heck does all of this peace talk have to do with being a watchman of God's word?" Well, for the answer to that question, we must first take a good look at the word "compromise." Now I say we must first take a good look at the word "compromise" because it was by and through the word "compromise" that God first began to open my eyes to understand how the devil has made his greatest advancements within the area of God's kingdom here on earth. And where is God's kingdom on earth? Well, in a general sense, most people would consider God's kingdom to be a/the church building, but as we learned earlier in our search for the truth, God's kingdom is found within the hearts of those people who truly love His Son, Jesus Christ, and have had their hearts and minds regenerated by and through God's Spirit (the comforter). Jesus said in the New Testament book of Luke 17:21 these words, "For indeed, the kingdom of God is within you." Jesus was saying that God's kingdom is/was found within the hearts of people. But it was also by and through the word "compromise" that I first became aware that if I wanted true peace in my own life, I couldn't compromise the truth that is contained within the word of God. Now there is much to the story of how God first opened my eyes to this truth, but the reality of this story really began when I first took my oath, or promise if you will, to the office of union steward. I say the reality of this truth really began with me being a union steward because it was at that time that I first began to understand that Jesus Christ had some grievances against His/the church. He had some grievances against His church, and He was going to show me what some of those grievances were. It was also at that time that I first began to understand about how God would guard my heart in true peace if I would be a doer of His word and not a hearer only. Now how does this take place? It takes place when you get real with God. In other words, God knows our (your) hearts. He knows when we are genuine, and he knows when we are fake. Far too often, people say they love God/Jesus Christ; but far too often, their actions do not line up with what they claim. They give God lip service, and they think they can get away with it. It's just like the scripture we used earlier in our search for the truth which says, "These people draw near to Me with their mouth, And honor Me with their lips, But their heart is far from Me" (Matthew 15:8). The reality was that those Jesus was speaking to were caught up into what we discovered throughout this book, including our last chapter, with regard to the works of the flesh (sin). Some were caught up in the works of the flesh with regard to adultery. Some were caught up in fornication. Some were caught up in uncleanness, some in lewdness, some in idolatry, some in sorcery, and some in hatred. Some in selfish ambitions, and on and on with regard to all the works of the flesh that are exposed in God's word (Galatians 5:19-21). But do you know what God opened my eyes to, my fellow truth seeker? He opened my heart and mind to the fact that He will guard my (your) heart against these works of the flesh by and through the power of Jesus Christ who now lives in me. That power was the same power that was given to me by Almighty God once I truly repented of my sins against Him and accepted the fact that God's Son Jesus Christ had died for me on the cross at Calvary. In other words, when someone is truly born again of God's Spirit, the power that exists by the Holy Spirit (comforter) will convict that person by and through their conscience (sense of right and wrong) that what they are doing, whether in their flesh or in their mind, are going against the very word (will) of God. Now when this happens, God is actually standing guard over a person's heart and mind so that the deceiving spirits and doctrines of demons (the devil and false doctrine) that exist on the wide path of this world will be eliminated from their heart and mind even as those deceiving spirits are attempting to get a stronghold in their lives/spirits. But then again, that's where the word "compromise" comes into play. It is where the words "chastisement" and "rebuke" come into play as well.

Now I use the word "compromise" and the words "chastisement" and "rebuke" for a very good reason. I say I use the words "compromise," "chastisement," and "rebuke" for a good reason because it is by and through these words that I first learned a very important lesson about my responsibility as a watchman (steward, overseer, ambassador, etc.) for God. I say I learned a good lesson about my responsibilities of being a watchman for God because I learned that as a watchman for God, I had a/the responsibility of proclaiming God's word (truth) to others. But with that being said, it didn't take me very long to learn that when you share what God has called you to share with others (the truth), you will not be very well liked. Now I say that from the perspective that I pretty much expected that that would be the case beyond the walls of a so-called church environment. But what I discovered was that the modern-day church environment of today is pretty much like the religious environment of Jesus' day. The Good Old Boys Club of Jesus' day has once again raised its ugly head. It's raised its ugly head and as a watchman of/for God's word, I am called to take a stand for the truth of his word. But that's not just my responsibility, my fellow truth seeker; it's also everyone's responsibility who wants to follow Jesus Christ. How so, you ask? I say it's everyone's responsibility because as a watchman of God's word, you have the responsibility of sounding the alarm. What alarm, the alarm which has to do with chastisement and rebuke. Why? Because it's by and through chastisement and rebuke that we find the other side of God's love. How so, you ask? Well, let's take a good look at the words from New Testament book of the Revelation 3:19 which come from Jesus Himself. Look at what he says, "As many as I love, I rebuke and chasten. Therefore be zealous and repent." Jesus rebuked and chastised the scribes and Pharisees that included Nicodemus and Saul of Tarsus (Apostle Paul). And why did he rebuke and chastise them? He did it because he loved them. He loved them, and he knew that the devil (world-wide path) had a strong hold on their very lives. In fact, the whole Sermon on the Mount was given to uncover and punch holes in the religious establishment of Jesus' day. But do you know something else, my fellow truth seeker? That very same thing is happening today.

Now as we're beginning to close our current search for the truth, I think it's important for you to know that the word "zealous" has a great deal to do with being a good watchman of/for God's word. I say that because when you're dealing with God's word, you will find that the words "zealous" and "repentance" have a great deal to do with the integrity of God's very character. I say that because when the Holy Spirit takes over your life, you should find that you will be zealous in all that you do. I say that because the word "zealous" is described as such in the dictionary: enthusiastic, keen, passionate, fervent, ardent, fanatical, obsessive, eager, and extreme. Now I mention this because what I have discovered in my own search for the truth has to do with all these words as you work out your own salvation with fear and trembling. Remember what we learned earlier in our search with regard to working out our own salvation. God's word tells us in the New Testament book of Philippians 2:12 that a true Christian is to work out your own salvation with fear and trembling. And why is a follower of Jesus Christ supposed to work out his own salvation with fear and trembling? It is an attitude with which Christians are to pursue their own sanctification. And once again, what is sanctification? It is what takes place within a born-again follower of Jesus Christ's life once God imputes his Holy Spirit into a person's life (heart). The fear in this scripture verse refers to a healthy fear of offending God and a righteous awe and respect for him. In other words, the more zealous you are in repenting of those things (works of the flesh) which offends Jesus Christ/God, the more peace you will find within your own life (heart). But there is the second part of this teaching with regard to God's character. And what is that, you ask? Well, take a good look at what it says in the next verse (13) of Philippians chapter 2, "For it is God who works in you both to will and to do for His good pleasure." In other words, the works, or spiritual fruit, that is being produced within the life of a true born-again believer are actually being produced by and through God's Spirit (the comforter) that inhabits all true believers. Why? Because God wants Christians to do what satisfies him.

Now for me personally, this was an important piece of the puzzle within my own faith journey in finding the narrow path (road). I say it was an important piece of the puzzle within my own faith journey because it was within this specific piece of my own faith journey that I first began to understand about the skill of spiritual warfare. I say I first started understanding about spiritual warfare through God's teaching on peace, because it was by and through this teaching that I first understood how to combat deception. Did I say deception? Yes, I said deception. I use the word "deception" because there is strong evidence in the (so-called) modern-day church today that we are living in a time described in the word of God as the time of the Great Apostasy. And what does the word "apostasy" mean? It means a departure from one's religion. But then again, please keep in mind, I'm just a forklift operator. After all, what do I know?

CHAPTER 27

The Book of Life

He who overcomes shall be clothed in white garments, and I will not
blot out his name from the Book of Life; but I will confess his name
before My Father and before His angels.
—Revelation 3:5

NOW AS WE learned earlier in our search for the truth, Jesus spent
a great deal of time both chastising and rebuking the religious
leaders of his time. In other words, Jesus was scolding them, and he was
telling them off. In fact, Jesus' famous Sermon on the Mount was primarily
directed at the religious establishment of his day, and his teachings from the
Sermon on the Mount were given to show them just how off base they were
with regard to what they held deep within their own hearts. The religious
establishment (the Good Old Boys Club) was very puffed up with pride,
and they needed to repent and turn from their lawlessness (rebellion) and
the way they were misrepresenting God before others. Which takes us to
the words that we left off with in chapter 26 with regard to the time of the
Great Apostasy, and it also takes us back to the word we used at the end
of chapter 25, the word "compromise." It also takes us to the connection
between God's grievance procedure and a true believer's responsibility in
being God's eyes and ears in a world full of lawlessness and people who are
traveling on the wide path that will ultimately lead to their destruction.
That is, if they haven't been born again of God's Spirit. And lastly, it takes
us to a part of God's word that really sums up all that we have uncovered in
our search for the truth. I say it really sums up all that we have uncovered
because it is the part of God's word that really completes all that we have
discovered in our current search for the truth. I say current search for
the truth, because the reality is there is no way that I (we) could possibly
uncover all the truths that the Holy Spirit has revealed to me within the
pages of our current search. In fact, there is a part of God's word that speaks
on this very subject in the New Testament book of John 20:30 and 31 and
John 21:25 which says these words, "And truly Jesus did many other signs

in the presence of His disciples, which are not written in this book [Bible] but these are written that you may believe that Jesus is the Christ, the Son of God, and that believing you may have life in His name." And also these words, "And there are also many other things that Jesus did, which if they were written one by one, I suppose that even the world itself could not contain the books that would be written." Amen.

Now you may be saying to yourself, "This is all well and fine Joe, but what does all of this have to do with our search for the truth?" Well, what I'm trying to solidify for you is the fact that I am also one of Jesus' disciples (followers, believers, supporters, etc.); and just like Jesus' disciples, this book has really been about my testimony (witness) and my walk of faith with Jesus Christ. In fact, the very word "testament" is defined as such: evidence, witness, proof, verification, and authentication. In other words, all the words written within the Bible are really God's testimony to us, and it is by and through the words of truth that we may find the narrow gate that leads to eternal life that God promises to those who truly believe. The whole theme of the Bible is the fact that God has revealed himself to us for a reason. And what is that reason? Well, a great deal of that we have uncovered within the pages of this book but there is a bottom line to all that we have uncovered, and the bottom line really boils down to this one issue. In fact, it is a part of God's word that really sums up what a true follower of Jesus Christ is really searching for as they attempt to find the narrow gate that leads to life eternal. And what is that, you ask? Well, the truth is, it can be found eight times within the word of God, but the one I'd like to specifically take a look at as we end our current search, is the one found in the New Testament book of the Revelation 3:5. Now the words found here are words that come right from the very lips of Jesus himself. And who is Jesus speaking to in this scripture? Jesus was speaking to one of the seven churches that are found within the first three chapters of the book of the Revelation. Now when I say Jesus was speaking to the churches, please keep in mind that he was speaking to the people who were claiming to be his followers. And what does he say to those followers in verse 5? He says to them, "He who overcomes shall be clothed in white garments, and I will not blot out his name from the Book of Life; but I will confess his name before My Father and before His angels."

Question: What did Jesus mean by this? What did he mean by "He who overcomes shall be clothed in white garments, and that He will not blot out his name from the Book of Life?" Well, the white garments Jesus is referring to here are the garments of those who have not defiled themselves as representatives of Jesus Christ (God). The word "defile" means to smear, to pollute, and to stain. Here, Jesus is referring to a person's character, and in this truth Jesus is referring to those who overcome shall be clothed in white garments. In other words, what kind of character did they possess in this life, God's character (narrow path) or the world's character (wide path)? Did they have a godly character, or did they have a worldly character? Did they have religion, or did they have a relationship with God/Jesus Christ? I say that because the white garments Jesus is speaking about here represent the holiness and purity of the redeemed. Those God has chosen to redeem (save) and therefore will possess eternal life (narrow path). They have not smeared God's name. They have not polluted God's name. They have not stained God's name. Now does this mean that they (we) are/were perfect? No way! I say no way because people are not God; we are human beings, and we do/ will make mistakes, but the number 1 objective in a true believer's character is to preserve, to protect, and to defend the very character of God.

And this is where we end our journey. We end our journey with this teaching from Jesus because as we end our time together, it's imperative that we (you) understand that this is what it's all about. It's all about whether or not our (your) name is in the Book of Life. I say that because if your name is not written in the Book of Life, you will be cast (thrown) into the Lake of Fire. And what is the Lake of Fire? It represents hell, the place described in God's word as a place of torture and misery and agony. It is a place you do not want to be in, my fellow truth seeker! Jesus tells us in the New Testament book of Matthew 25:41 these words, "Then He [Jesus] will also say to those on the left hand, 'Depart from Me, you cursed, into the everlasting fire prepared for the devil and his angels.'" Here, Jesus points out that the punishment itself is everlasting. The wicked are forever subjected to the fury and the wrath of Almighty God. The wicked are those who practice lawlessness and in reality are in rebellion against the commands (truths) of God. And who was the first to rebel against God and His word? It was the devil and those angels who followed him in his rebellion in heaven (a topic in itself and you can read about the devil's [called Lucifer] rebellion in the Old Testament books of Isaiah chapter 14 and Ezekiel chapter 28).

In these words from Jesus (Matthew 25:41), He was speaking in reference to the separation of sheep (true believers, who are given God's favor—narrow gate) and goats (unbelievers, who are consigned to the place of rejection and dishonor—wide gate). So in other words, if you have overcome, you will be recognized by Jesus as someone who will possess and enjoy eternal life. Your garment, or your character if you will, has not stained, polluted, or smeared God's character. Your character is recognized by Jesus as holy and pure, and Jesus solidifies that this is true by acknowledging this fact before Almighty God and His holy angels. If this is true, then you've been a good watchman of/for the truth of God's word. You have overcome that which defiles your garment (character). You have found the narrow gate (road) that leads to life, and you have overcome the wide gate (road) that leads to destruction. But we still have a question that remains to be answered. And what is that question? The question is, "Overcome what?" This takes us back to the word of God found in 1 John 2:26 that we uncovered at the beginning of this book with regard to deception. Now I use the word "deception" because within the structure and foundation of this word lies the word "compromise." And it is to this word that the devil has perfected his art of weaponry down through the centuries of humanity; and in my opinion, the devil's greatest weapon is that of deception by and through the word "compromise." But then again that's the lesson that is taught in the scriptures I started to uncover back in chapter 25 with regard to God's word found in The Revelation, Matthew chapter 7, and Ezekiel chapters 3 and 33.

Now to set this in the proper context of what I have discovered in my own faith journey with regard to this very important issue, I have to go back to my time of being a union steward in the Teamsters union. I say I have to go back to my time as union steward in the Teamsters union because it was in my time as being union steward that God first opened my eyes to this truth with regard to the words "deception" and "compromise." Now I say the words deception and compromise because it was through these words that I first learned about spiritual warfare. I also learned about how the word "compromise" has been and is now being used by the devil to keep people on the wide gate (path) to destruction. How did I learn this? I learned this as I started to put the pieces of the puzzle together with the help and guidance of the Holy Spirit (comforter). God's Spirit within me gave me the discernment and the understanding that I needed in my pursuit of overcoming the wiles (tricks, deceit, and allurement) of the wicked one (devil) (Ephesians 6:11). It came by and through my consistent pursuit of abiding in the truth of God's word(s) which led me to being a good fruit inspector. I was free in Jesus Christ. I was free from the bondage of the God of this world, who is the devil and the Antichrist spirit that exists within those who are traveling on the wide path of destruction. It was also a time when God (comforter—Holy Spirit) first started to help me understand about the sword of the Spirit, which is His word (Ephesians 6:17). It was also a time when I first started to understand what Saul of Tarsus (Apostle Paul) was speaking about with regard to putting on the whole armor of God (Ephesians 6:11). It was a time when I began to learn firsthand how I needed all the parts of God's armor to resist the Antichrist spirit that exists in the worldly realm of the wicked one (devil). It was also a time when I first started to understand about the responsibilities I had as a follower of Jesus Christ to open my mouth boldly in making known the mystery of the gospel message. I also learned about my responsibility as a watchman and as an ambassador in chains for the truth of God's word(s). You see, when Saul of Tarsus (Paul) wrote the words found in this section on spiritual warfare in Ephesians chapter 6, he was writing these words while he was in prison. He was in prison for proclaiming to the world the truth of God's word. He was in prison because people didn't want to hear the truth. Here was a man who was once a member of the most privileged and elite religious organization (the Pharisees) of his time, and now he found himself in chains and in prison for preaching the truth of the gospel message found in the Bible. He was one of God's watchmen, and he paid the price because of it.

Now you may be saying to yourself, "This is all well and fine Joe, but what does all of this have to do with our search for the truth?" You see, it has everything to do with our search for the truth because what the Pharisees named Saul of Tarsus (Paul) and Nicodemus had to discover is the same thing that I had to discover myself. I say I had to discover this because it was and is one of the most determining factors in our (your) search in finding the narrow gate (road) to life. I say it's one of the most determining factors because if you're going to be a true follower of Jesus Christ, you must understand right up front that you will face persecution. Saul of Tarsus (Paul) learned this firsthand. Here was a man who was born again of God's Spirit who was being persecuted for his faith; and because of his faith in Jesus Christ, he found himself in chains and in prison. But he knew it would be so and that's why Saul of Tarsus (Paul) exposes true followers of Jesus Christ to these words found in 2 Timothy 3:12, "Yes, and all who desire to live godly in Christ Jesus will suffer persecution." But then again, that's exactly what Jesus exposed people to when He said what He said in our main scripture verse on the front cover of this book. He told those who wanted to find life that it would not be easy, and that's why he said that the way to finding life would be difficult. But then again that's what I first discovered when I served as a union steward. I say I first discovered this when I served as a union steward in the Teamsters union because what I discovered in my time of serving as a union steward was what really molded and shaped me into understanding exactly what Jesus and Saul of Tarsus (Paul) was speaking about. Now I say I started understanding what Jesus and Saul of Tarsus was speaking about because when I first began my time as union steward, I started to see firsthand what persecution was all about. I also started to understand what overcoming and deception was all about. I say I started to understand what overcoming and deception was all about because when I first began to serve as union steward, I really began to have my eyes opened to what was at the heart of/ to finding the narrow gate (way) to life. And what was that, you ask? It was what I discovered in the New Testament book of James 4:6-10 which says, "God resists the proud, But gives grace to the humble. Therefore submit to God. Resist the devil and he will flee from you. Draw near to God and He will draw near to you. Cleanse your hands, you sinners, and purify your hearts, you double-minded. Lament and mourn and weep! Let your laughter be turned to mourning and your joy to gloom. Humble yourselves in the sight of the Lord, and He will lift you up."

You see, my fellow truth seeker, it's all about submitting your life to God/Jesus Christ. It's about cleansing and purifying our hearts before Him, and if we do that, we are given a/the promise that He (God) will lift us up. Question: What does God mean when He says that He will lift us up when we (you) humble ourselves before Him? Well, there is much to the subject of being lifted up by God, but the bottom line to this important subject has to do with putting God first in all that we (you) do. In other words, when a person is truly humble in God's sight, He knows a person's heart, and He knows that they are truly sorry for the way they have transgressed His commandments. He knows that they have a true repentant heart, and that they actually mourn and grieve and yes, even sometimes weep (cry) about those transgressions and their disobedience to His word (truths). Jesus was condemning the pride and deception that is held within the hearts of those who haven't truly repented of their sins. The double-mindedness Jesus is referring to here is like the lesson to the scribes and Pharisees. Jesus exposes them, as well as us, to the fact that there is a direct connection to receiving God's grace as well as His blessings based on one's submission to Him (Ephesians 1:3). The truth was the scribes and Pharisees hadn't resisted the devil, and they had defiled their garments (hearts and minds) before Him and because of that, they had actually created a stumbling block in/to finding the narrow gate (way) to the Book of Life. But then again, please keep in mind, I'm just a forklift operator. After all, what do I know?

CHAPTER 28

Running for the Prize

*Do you not know that those who run in a race all run, but one
receives the prize? Run in such a way that you may obtain it.*
—1 Corinthians 9:24

NOW TO BEGIN to uncover (expose) this part of God's word
for us, it is extremely important for you to know what is going
on in this section of God's word. I say it's extremely important for you
to understand what's going on in this section of God's word because in
a nutshell, this section has a great deal to do with the Great Apostasy we
started to uncover in the last two chapters of our search for the truth. Now
I say we started to uncover this in the last two chapters, but in reality we've
been uncovering the whole apostasy subject since we first began our search
for the truth at the beginning of this book. Why do I say that, my fellow
truth seeker? I say it because of what we've learned with regard to being a
watchman and the responsibilities that go along with it. Now I say that
because of what we learned with regard to overcoming as a requirement
and qualification for having our names written in the Book of Life and
the direct connection of being a good watchman for the truth of God's
word(s). I say that because the overcoming part of what we have been
looking at has a great deal to do with the Great Apostasy leading up to the
second coming of Jesus Christ back to this world.

Now I use the word "watchman" in this scenario because in this section
of God's word, there is also a warning to those He has chosen to be His
representatives (stewards, ambassadors, messengers, etc.). And what is that
warning, you ask? Well for me, this part of God's word began to become a
reality when I first started serving as a union steward in the Teamsters union.
I say it started to become a reality for me because when I became a union
steward, God started to open my eyes and ears to exactly what He means in
His word with regard to overcoming the influence of the wicked one (the
devil) on my life. A great deal of what I have learned with regard to helping
you in resisting the devil I have written within the pages of this book. Now

I started to understand my responsibilities as a watchman for God when I first started to understand the concepts of the grievance procedure as it relates to a/the contract between an employer and their employees (some of this we've already discovered), now when I was first elected to serve in the office of union steward, God started to help me understand that as His representative, I had an obligation to sound the trumpet. Now I know you're probably saying to yourself, "What the heck does that mean, Joe? What the heck does it mean to sound the trumpet?" Well, the whole teaching on sounding the trumpet could take a whole other book in itself, but in a nutshell, it really comes down to this issue. God's judgment is coming, and if you're not prepared, you will face the wrath of His judgment. But then again, that statement is not a very popular statement to make, especially in the days in which this book is written. I say that because in the modern-day world it is not popular to speak about God's judgment. It is okay to speak about God's love, but when you speak about God's judgment, you will be seen as very unloving and very unkind. Now I say that because that was the main reason why God called me out of the darkness of this world back in 1983. He called me to be His representative (watchman) here on earth. I was called to be His eyes and ears to a world that is being controlled by the evil forces of the devil. Much of this we have already discovered within the pages of this book. But do you know what, my fellow truth seeker? If you have overcome the evil forces of the wicked one by being born again of God's spirit, God has made you one of His watchmen as well. God has chosen you to be His eyes and ears as well. But there is one thing I must warn you about, my fellow truth seeker, and that is this: if God has chosen you to be one of His watchmen, the devil is going to make war against you as you make known the truth of God's word(s). Always remember what we've learned throughout our search for the truth: there's a war going on between the devil and the Almighty God of the Holy Bible, and the war is really over the very souls of people. As God wants your name to be written in the Book of Life, the devil wants to make sure your name is not within the pages of that book. And why is that? It's so that you will lose your soul and join him in the Lake of Fire (Revelation 20:15). And so the war rages on. In fact, one of the verses that helped me understand the whole war concept between God and the devil was when I first learned these words in the Bible from the New Testament book of Matthew 11:12 which says, "And from the days of John the Baptist until now, the kingdom of heaven [life—narrow path] suffers violence, and the violent take it by force. Take it by force? What did Jesus mean by this? He meant that you had better be prepared for the battle that will take place in your life and the sufferings that accompany those who are God's watchmen. Just as we learned in the last chapter, Saul of Tarsus (Paul), God's watchman, wrote to warn all who follow Jesus Christ will face persecution (2 Timothy 3:12). In reality, a watchman is actually putting his life on the line as a living sacrifice to and for the integrity of God's truths. Those sufferings Jesus is speaking about may come in the form of physical sufferings. Such as a man by the name of John the Baptist found out when he lost his head for warning and blowing the trumpet to a king named Herod in Matthew 14:1-12. John confronted Herod with regard to his immoral (adultery) behavior with his brother's (Philip) wife (Herodias). He blew the trumpet and confronted the king about his immorality, and because he did so, it cost him his life. In fact, he found his head being served on a platter before Herod and his adulterous partner, Herodias. Likewise, sufferings may come in the form of psychological sufferings. I happen to believe that psychological sufferings in many ways are even worse than physical ones. Now I say that because I personally have never felt the effects of physical suffering as did Saul of Tarsus (Paul) and John the Baptist, as well as many others within the pages of God's word, but I have felt the psychological effects of being persecuted as I have traveled down the narrow path/road of my faith journey in my pursuit of the truth.

Now the whole teaching on warning and blowing the trumpet for God and the persecution that comes along with it first started to become a reality in my life when I first began my responsibilities as a union steward. I say it first began to become a reality in my life because what I discovered as I began my time as union steward were the similarities that came into play with regard to warning and sounding the trumpet as a union steward, as well as warning and sounding the trumpet as a watchman for the truth of God's word. How so, you ask? Well, the first thing you must understand is that when I began my time as union steward, I was very young and immature with regard to the duties and responsibilities that go along with being an elected representative (union steward). Now if you recall what I shared earlier in this book, you will remember that shortly before I was elected to the office of union steward, I accepted Jesus Christ as my personal Lord and Savior and was born again of God's Spirit (the comforter). Now the similarities with regard to being a union steward in the Teamsters union and being a steward and watchman for the truth of God's word began to come together when God helped me realize that my duties as union steward and my duties as a follower of Jesus Christ were very similar in nature. I say they are similar in nature because what I discovered as a new union steward was in many ways the same things that I learned as a new Christian. I say that because as I was very young and immature as a new union steward, I was also very young and immature as a new Christian. And that's where God's Spirit (the comforter) began to open my eyes to not only my responsibilities as a union steward, but also to the responsibilities I had as a steward and a watchman for God's word (truths). Now beginning back in chapter 25, I mentioned some texts of God's word from The Revelation, Matthew chapter 7 and Ezekiel chapters 3 and 33. Now I mentioned these specific texts from God's word (Bible) because it was within these texts of God's word that God really opened my eyes to what I needed to learn if I wanted to be a good steward, both in the Teamsters union, as well as within His kingdom (narrow gate/road). You see, what God opened my eyes to was the fact that once I truly repented of my sins against Him and truly received His Son Jesus Christ into my life, He (God) was free to unleash His power upon my life. Just as He promised He would as we discovered earlier in our search from John 1:12 which says, "But as many as received Him, to them He gave the power to become children of God." God had released His power in/on me, and I had begun to run the race that God would set before me. Now you may be asking yourself, "What the heck are you talking about, Joe? What race are you talking about?" Well, it's the same race that our search for the truth enlightens us to in God's word found in the New Testament book of Hebrews 12:1 which says, "Therefore we [true believers] also, since we are surrounded by so great a cloud of witnesses, let us lay aside every weight, and the sin which so easily ensnares us, and let us run with endurance the race that is set before us, looking unto Jesus, the author and finisher of our faith." Did you hear what God's word says, my fellow truth seeker? The weight that God's word is referring to here is the sin that we carry within us as human beings. In other words, without the power of God being released into our lives by and through the Holy Spirit, we can't run a/the successful race. I say that because God gives us free will. We can either run a/the race He sets before us based on our faith in Jesus Christ (narrow gate), or we can run our own race without faith in Jesus Christ, and that race leads us down the wide path to destruction. The truth is, without the power and faith of Jesus Christ, we can't begin our race because without God's power to endure the devil's snares, it is impossible to even begin to run that (our) race. Saul of Tarsus (Paul) knew this, and he said so in the New Testament book of 1 Corinthians 9:24-27 when he shared these words, "Do you not know that those who run in a race all run, but one receives the prize? Run in such a way that you may obtain it. And everyone who competes for the prize is temperate in all things. Now they do it to obtain a perishable crown, but we for an imperishable crown. Therefore I run thus: not with uncertainty. Thus I fight: not as one who beats the air. But I discipline my body and bring it into subjection, lest, when I have preached to others, I myself should become disqualified."

You see, my fellow truth seeker, Saul of Tarsus (Paul) knew about the race he was speaking about because before he was transformed by the power of God he was running his life under the domain of the devil. His race was being run within the framework of the devil and not for Almighty God. He was God's enemy, and he didn't even realize that he was. In fact, all the Pharisees were God's enemies, and the saddest part of all is that they didn't even realize that they were. What was their problem? Well, much of this we've already uncovered within our search, but the major problem that they had was the same one those who are traveling on the wide path to destruction have. And what is that, you ask? It is found within these words: fortune, fame, power, and pleasure. I say that because these words are really what Saul of Tarsus (Paul) was speaking about when he said what he said with regard to a perishable crown versus an imperishable crown. You see, at the heart of the spiritual battle is the battle within the heart that says, "I am the master of my own life, I am the king of my own domain, and I want to please myself, and I will do whatever it takes to make me happy." You see, what was at the heart of the Pharisees' problem was the same problem that those beyond the boundaries of a godly environment (truth) have; they are running their race to achieve a perishable crown. They are traveling on the wide path of destruction, and they don't even know that they are. They are traveling on a road that the prince of this world (devil) has enticed them to. Saul of Tarsus (Paul) knew that; he knew it, and he knew the remedy for it was found within one word. And what is that word? It is the word "discipline." I say that because without discipline, there will be compromise. Saul of Tarsus (Paul) understood that the key to overcoming the power and influences of the wicked one (devil) was that he must overcome the impulses of the (his) flesh. Those impulses within the heart that says I want fortune (greed, money, material possessions, etc.); I want fame (popularity, recognition, high regard, respect, etc.); I want power (control, command, authority, rule, etc.); I want pleasure (enjoyment, happiness, delight, contentment, satisfaction, etc.). In other words, I want what I want and to achieve what I want, I will do whatever it takes to fulfill what pleases me. But do you know something, my fellow truth seeker? That's where the problem first started for humanity. It started the same way back in the Garden of Eden when Adam and Eve pretty much said those same things. They thought they could be like God. They didn't like the restrictions that God had placed upon them, and the devil enticed them to compromise what God had said. They didn't have enough discipline in their lives to overcome the power of the devil. And do you know what, my fellow truth seeker? That very same thing is exactly the same problem that exists in the world today. People are dealing with that very same problem today, and unless they (you) are running a/the race with their eyes and hearts fixed upon the prize of an imperishable crown that can only be found within the boundaries of a life in Jesus Christ (narrow gate/way), they are in reality putting on the perishable crown of this life, the perishable crown that results from a life of the "me first" mentality. The mind-set (heart) that says, "I am the ruler of my own destiny [soul], and I will fulfill the lust of my own flesh [illicit sex, drugs, booze, etc.], the lust of my own eyes [pornography, filthy movies, TV shows, etc.], and the pride of my own life [pride, arrogant, conceited, snooty, puffed up, a high and mighty attitude, etc.) that says, 'I'm in control of my own destiny [soul] and wherever the chips of this life fall that's where they fall." Eat, drink, and be merry for tomorrow I will die. But do you know something, my fellow truth seeker? That is the same kind of thinking that God's word(s) warns us about in the New Testament book of Luke chapter 12 where Jesus was teaching on hypocrisy and about laying up the treasures of this life (wide gate) instead of the treasures of heaven (narrow gate). Jesus was speaking to a man who had great wealth, and he thought because he had great wealth that he had everything. He thought he was safe and secure because he had put his faith in his earthly possessions. He thought his very soul was safe and secure, and he says so in these words found in verse 19 of Luke 12, "And I will say to my soul, Soul, you have many goods laid up for many years; take your ease; eat, drink, and be merry." And then take a good look at what God (Jesus) says to this rich man in verse 20, "But God said to him, 'FOOL! This night your soul will be required of you, then whose will these things be which you have provided?' So is he [a fool] who lays up treasure for himself, and is not rich toward God." Did you hear that, my fellow truth seeker? Did you hear what God called this man? In God's eyes, this man was seen as a fool. He was a fool because he had run his race (life) within the mind-set of the riches of this world (wide gate), instead of a/ the mind-set of what Jesus said were true riches, the riches of knowing the things of God (narrow gate). But then again, that's exactly what Jesus was saying to those who claimed to be his followers at the end of Jesus' Sermon on the Mount teaching found in Matthew chapter 7. Jesus refers to these people as fools. Why, because like the rich man, they had built their houses (lives) on sinking sand (the world) instead of on solid rock (God). But then again, please keep in mind, I'm just a forklift operator. After all, what do I know?

CHAPTER 29

Sinking Sand or Solid Rock

*Whoever hears these sayings of Mine, and does them, I will liken
him to a wise man who built his house on the rock. But everyone
who hears these sayings of Mine, and does not do them, will be like a
foolish man who built his house on the sand.*
—Matthew 7:24 and 26

I N THE LAST chapter of our search for the truth, we began to have
our minds exposed to how a person lives their lives, whether they live
their lives focused on the riches of this life (wide path) or whether they live
their lives focused on the things of God (narrow path). I say that because
throughout the pages of this book, I've been attempting to open your eyes
to the truth of God's word. Now I say that as one of God's watchman so
that you might have a better understanding with regard to your own search
in finding the narrow gate (road) that will lead you to life. I don't know
what led you to read my book, but I can assure you of one thing: God will
use the words I have shared within the pages of this book for and to His
glory and honor. Now I say that not to be conceited or arrogant, but I say
that within the complete confidence of God's word (truth) that teaches in
the Old Testament book of Isaiah 55:10 and 11, "For as rain comes down,
and the snow from heaven, And do not return there, But water the earth,
And make it bring forth and bud, That it may give seed to the sower And
bread to the eater, So shall My word be that goes forth from My mouth; It
shall not return to Me void, But it shall accomplish what I please, And it
shall prosper in the thing for which I sent it." The word of God produces
its intended results in fulfilling God's spiritual purposes. Just as rain and
snow comes down to provide nourishment to sustain life here on earth,
so too does the word of God nourish and sustain those who have a true
relationship with God/Jesus Christ. When the seed of God's word (truths)
are sown into a person's life, it produces the spiritual food that God uses
in renewing their minds and cleansing their hearts. As that person's mind
(heart) is renewed by the cleansing of God's word, that person begins to be

a watchman of God's truths. When that happens, God is well pleased and there is joy in heaven. God has great joy and rejoices when even one sinner repents and begins to find the narrow gate that leads to life (heaven). He is well pleased because true repentance begins when a person turns from their wickedness and begins to obey God's truths. Now I say that because what we've also learned from being exposed to God's word is that the narrow gate (way) which leads to life is difficult, and there isn't too many who find it. And why don't they find it? They don't find it because they don't search for it. And they don't search for it because it's far easier to compromise with the world than it is to obey God's words. Why, because people don't like to be unpopular. Humans like to take the path of least resistance. People don't like conflict. No one wants to be known as a radical, a troublemaker, and often times even far worse than that by those who are traveling on the wide path to destruction. It's far easier to compromise the truth of God's word on the wide path that leads to destruction than it is to take a stand and obey the truth of God's word. But do you know something, my fellow truth seeker? That same scenario is happening right within the very framework of the modern-day realm of so-called Christianity today. The so-called church has become too much like the world. The church has become too much like the world because the church has compromised the truth of God's word. And how has that happened? Well, for the complete answer to that question, it would take a whole lot longer than we have in this book, but I can tell you this much. Two of the main reasons why the church has become so much like the world are because the church has failed in two major vital areas. And what are those two vital areas, you ask? They can be found within the areas of compromise and discipline, just like it happened in the Garden of Eden when the devil first deceived Eve into eating from the forbidden tree (Genesis chapter 3), the tree that God said was off limits for her and Adam to eat from. God had given a command that the tree of the knowledge of good and evil were not to be eaten from. But do you know what? That command is still in place today. And how is it still in place today? It is still in place today because the whole bottom line issue behind God's command not to eat from the tree of knowledge is really about being obedient to what God says. God gave a specific order to Adam and Eve to leave the tree alone, but they did not listen; and because they did not listen they brought a/the curse upon all of humanity. The curse of/called death. Much of this we've already discovered throughout this book.

Now you might be saying to yourself, "That's all well and fine, but what the heck does this have to do with our search for the truth?" Answer: It has everything to do with our search, my fellow truth seeker. It has everything to do with our search because it is within this command from God that we are seeing a/the falling away within modern-day Christendom. People within the so-called churches of America today are being deceived, and they don't even know it. They don't know it because their eyes have been blinded by the false prophets who have literally invaded the territory known as the church. Christ's church is under severe attack by the forces of evil, and God has come to fight against those evil forces. Now we shouldn't be surprised that God is fighting against these evil forces. I say that because that's exactly what God said He will/would do. Now you may be asking the question, "When and where does God/Jesus Christ say He will fight against those evil forces that have penetrated His church?" Well, to begin to uncover the answer to that question, we must first take a good look at what Jesus said in His word to those followers of Christ within the church as revealed in the last book of the Bible written in The Revelation 2:16. Now if you know anything about the book of the Revelation, you will know that this book is a book about the end times of civilization. It is a book written to open the eyes of people about what is going to take place at the end of time as we know it. You will also know that a great deal of this letter is written to the churches who are supposed to be representing Jesus Christ (God) here on earth. Now the church is supposed to be the eyes and ears of Jesus Christ (God). The church is supposed to be God's representatives here on earth. In a world full of wickedness and evil, the church is supposed to be the very conscience to a world that is being seduced by the devil. The church is supposed to be a collective body of believers who live and stand up for the truth of God's word. They are supposed to be those who have been chosen by God and have had their hearts and minds renewed to new life by being born again of God's Spirit (the comforter). But there is a problem. And the problem can be found within the verses of God's word that I said I wanted to end this book with.

Now as we begin to uncover the problem God's word reveals to us, we must first take a good look at what is taking place at the beginning of the Revelation in the first three chapters. Now within these chapters, Jesus has laid out a whole list of grievances that He (God) has set forward in His word. A list of things that those in the church have done right as well as a list of things they have done wrong. But the main theme of all of these grievances really boils down to this one issue. And what is that issue? It is the issue of repentance and overcoming, the same issue that we started to uncover back in chapter 27 with regard to the Book of Life and defiling one's garments. Jesus had laid out specifically those grievances that He has against those who were supposed to be representing Him within the framework of His body, the church. Now as I stated earlier, this is such a huge topic to uncover that there is no way I could begin to uncover all that is involved within the framework of this subject in our current search, but I will tell you this much. The bottom line to all that is revealed to us in this part of God's word is exactly what had transpired within the framework of the scribes and Pharisees that we uncovered earlier. I say that because if you recall, the Pharisees actually started out as a good organization with good intentions. They started out on the right foot. They started out as representatives of the one true God of the Holy Bible, but somewhere along the line, they went astray. They veered off course. They took their eyes off the main goal of their faith in God and allowed the devil to infiltrate the walls of their hearts and minds. But do you know what, my fellow truth seeker? That very same thing has happened within the structure of the modern-day church today. Like the Pharisaic system of Jesus' day, the very same thing is taking place within the church today. The Great Apostasy that took place in Jesus' time is alive and well today. It is alive and well, and this is the issue Jesus is referring to in these letters to His church. Many in His church had defiled their garments. But there were a few who did not. They had not defiled (corrupted, dishonored, stained, spoiled) Jesus' name and were considered as worthy of not having their names blotted out of the Book of Life (Revelation 3:5). Jesus knew them, and He knew they were worthy to have Him confess them before Almighty God.

Now as I see it, a great deal of what Jesus is exposing to these people in His church line up with the great falling away that must take place before Jesus comes back to earth (Matthew 24:3, 27, 30, 37, 39, 48; 2 Peter 3:10; etc.). The falling away of Christ's church that we discovered earlier in our search found in 2 Thessalonians 2:3. I truly believe we are in the falling-away period that will usher in the tribulation period revealed in God's word. The time of the tribulation that will lead up to God's final judgment, the time when all of those who are not found within the realm of Jesus Christ (born again) will feel the effects of His righteous judgment. But then again that's why God called me out of the darkness of this world to be His watchman. I've been called to open your eyes to the fact that you might just be being deceived yourself. You may be sitting under the authority of a false prophet (minister, pastor), and you may not even know that you are. I say that because a great deal of what Jesus was speaking about is directed toward His church and to those who are being deceived here in the book of The

Revelation. Now I say that because I first became aware of this situation when I first started serving as a union steward in the Teamsters union. Now I'm not going to get into all the details of how God first started to reveal this to me, but I will tell you this much. As a new steward, I came to understand that the connection between my responsibilities as a union steward and as a watchman for God were pretty much the same. Now I say that in this context. As I had a responsibility to enforce the terms agreed to in a collective bargaining unit agreement between the employer and the employees, I also have the responsibility of enforcing God's word as it relates to the truth of His word, not only within my own life (sanctuary, tabernacle, heart, mind) but within the lives of others as well. Just as I as a union steward had an obligation to expose a violation that was taking place within the framework of a collective bargaining union agreement, so too does a watchman of God's word (kingdom) have an obligation to expose a violation of God's contract as well. Now how does this take place? It takes place within the wording of a contract known as a/the grievance procedure. A procedure that spells out a course of action that is to be followed when and if there is a violation within that collective bargaining unit agreement (contract). Now you may be saying to yourself, "Okay Joe, this is all well and fine, but what the heck does this have to do with me and my search for the truth in finding the narrow gate [path] to life?" You see, it has everything to do with you finding the narrow path to life because whether you realize it or not, you are either living your life within the contract of Jesus Christ (narrow path) or you are living your life within the contract of the world (wide path). You are either living your life within the contract of God's word, or you are living your life within the contract of the devil's deception(s). And do you know another thing, my fellow truth seeker? You will be held accountable for the words (truths) that are written within that contract. If you have lived your life within the words of the contract with the devil, you will hear these words from Jesus found in Matthew 7:23 which says, "Depart from Me, you who practice lawlessness!"

Now why are these words spoken from the mouth of Jesus so important? They are important for this reason. They are important because there's a direct connection to the words found in Matthew chapter 7 as well as to the words found in the first three chapters of the book of The Revelation. The connection lies in the fact that Jesus was speaking to those who were in His church and claimed to be His followers. But there is a difference! There is a big difference! And do you know what that big difference is, my fellow truth seeker? The difference is the ones He was speaking to in the first three chapters of The Revelation still had a chance to repent. They still had time to overcome. Overcome what? Overcome the fact that if they didn't repent, there was a good chance that their names would be excluded from the Book of Life, unlike those who Jesus was speaking to in Matthew chapter 7 who were doomed and condemned for practicing lawlessness. They were sent away from the presence of Jesus Christ (God). Why, because they didn't obey the word of God. They built their houses (lives) on the sinking sand of this world instead of the solid rock of the word of God. They were self-deceived because they thought they were traveling on the narrow path to life when they were actually traveling of the wide path to their destruction. They were deceived because they thought they had built their lives on faith in Jesus Christ, but the truth was they had religion, but they didn't have a relationship with Jesus Christ. They had a form of godliness, but the truth was Jesus was disgusted with them. And that's why Jesus said to those supposed followers of His, "Depart from me you workers of iniquity [evil, sin, and wickedness], I never knew you." But wait a minute. Listen to what they said to Jesus in trying to plead their case. In verse 22 of chapter 7, we read these words from the lips of those who Jesus said He never knew. They said to Him, "Lord, Lord, have we not prophesied in Your name, cast out demons in Your name, and done many wonders in Your name?" In a nutshell, what they were saying to Jesus was, "What are we doing here at the judgment of the wicked? After all, we preached Your word, we cast out demons in Your name, and we did many wonderful things in Your name." But do you know what, my fellow truth seeker? They did all those things under false pretenses. Their religion was nothing but a charade and a farce. Do you know why their religion was a charade and a farce, because they hadn't dealt seriously with their sin, just as the scribes and Pharisees of Jesus' day. They had given their allegiance to the worldly system (sinking sand). Their faith in God was phony, and Jesus knew it was so. They hadn't built their lives on the solid rock of God's word (obedience). They had a form of godliness, but their hearts were actually far from the one true God of life. You see, they thought they could fool Jesus (God), but in the end, they found out one of the first things we learned in our search for the truth. And what was that, you ask? Well, we discovered it in the New Testament book of Galatians 6:7 and 8, which says, "Do not be deceived, God is not mocked; for whatever a man sows, that he will also reap. For he who sows to his flesh will of the flesh reap corruption, but he who sows to the Spirit will of the Spirit reap everlasting life." These people were deceived, and they reaped the benefits of what they had sown. They thought they were wise when in fact, they were fools. They had built their faith on a false foundation, just like the Pharisees. They had religion on the outside, but their hearts were far from God (Jesus). Their hearts were far from God, and they never found the narrow gate to life. But then again, please keep in mind, I'm just a forklift operator. After all, what do I know?

CHAPTER 30

Sounding the Trumpet

Now it came to pass at the end of seven days that the word of the Lord came to me saying, Son of man, I have made you a watchman for the house of Israel: therefore hear a word from My mouth, and give them warning for Me.
—Ezekiel 3:16 and 17

NOW I'VE SHARED with you a little bit about how God first started to open my eyes to the truth of his word when I was elected to serve as a union steward in the Teamsters union. It was also a time that I first began to understand that if I was truly going to live and obey the truth of God's word, I was going to have to get used to leaving the comfort zones of my life. What I mean by comfort zone is the areas of my life that I had grown comfortable in, those areas of life that I had grown accustomed to, those areas of life that the worldly system (wide path) will draw you into if you're not extremely careful. The worldly system that has the devil at the controls of your life, and if you don't have God's Spirit living within you, you are doomed. You are doomed, and God has sent you a lifeline to open your eyes to his truth. And what is that lifeline? It is the shed blood of His Son Jesus Christ. Much of this we have already discussed, but there is one last thing that I must disclose before I end this book.

Now you're probably saying to yourself, "What the heck Joe, you've been saying you're going to close this book for quite a while now." And do you know what? You're absolutely correct. But the truth is when you live your life being guided by the Holy Spirit, you learn to trust and obey whatever God wants you to do. One of the first verses I ever learned from God was this one found in Proverbs 3:5 and 6, "Trust in the Lord with all your heart, And lean not on your own understanding; In all your ways acknowledge Him, And He will direct your paths." Since the time I've been a follower of Jesus Christ, I have learned just how true this scripture is and that's one of the reasons why this book has taken so long to finish. Every time my flesh wants to close out this book, the Holy Spirit (comforter) keeps giving me more to share.

Now I've exposed a great deal about the fact that a true follower of Jesus Christ must learn that they are to be God's eyes and ears in a world that is separated from Him. Likewise, Jesus Christ established His church in such a way that the church is supposed to be His eyes and ears in the world as well. The church is supposed to be a place where fellow believers come together to worship the one true God of the Bible and to live together in the fellowship and companionship of God's Spirit (the comforter) in a hostile and wicked environment. I say hostile environment because those who are blinded by the prince of this world (devil) and are traveling on the wide path to their ultimate destruction will not like the message that true followers of Jesus Christ is trying to get across. In fact, what I have discovered in my time of sharing the gospel message is that people oftentimes may think that you might have a demon. How do I know that, you ask? I know it because it says so in the word of God. That very same thing happened to both Jesus and John the Baptist when they confronted those who thought they had it all together with regard to a relationship with God (John 8:48, 49, 52 and Luke 7:33). Both John the Baptist and Jesus were thought to have a demon in them because what they were teaching didn't line up with what the so-called religious establishment of their day believed was the truth. But then again, please don't be surprised by this at all. Why? Because if a person doesn't understand the true things of God and doesn't have the mind of Christ living within them, they will more than likely reject what you are sharing with them, such as it was with the established religious leaders of Jesus' time.

If you do your homework, you will discover that the word "eyes" are used 478 times in the Bible, and the word "ears" is used 139 times. Also as we've discovered, a church is not just a building but a/the true church is made up of the souls of those who have been born again of God's Spirit. Now I mention that because as we discovered in the last chapter, just because someone claims to be a follower of Jesus Christ doesn't really mean that they are. I like to use this illustration to drive home this point. I can claim to be a car sitting in a garage, but that doesn't make me a car, just as I can claim to be a follower of Jesus Christ sitting in a church building, but that doesn't necessarily make me a Christian. Just like it was for those people who heard the words from Jesus in Matthew 7:23, "I never knew you; depart from Me, you who practice lawlessness!" Now when I first had my eyes and ears opened to the truth of what had transpired here in this particular scripture, it really began to get my attention. It got my attention because after all, these were people who were supposed to be people of God. They claimed to be followers of Jesus Christ. They were supposedly the pillars of the church. Why do I say that? I say it because look once again at the words they spoke as they pleaded their case before the very Son of God. They said, "Lord, Lord, we prophesied in your name, we cast out demons in your name, and we did many wonderful things in your name." In a nutshell, they thought they were the epitome of what a true follower of Jesus Christ should be. They thought they had all the qualities of what a true follower of Jesus Christ should have. More than likely, many of them were the leaders in their churches: pastors, elders, deacons, etc. Many of them probably led Bible study and sang in the church choir and did many other things that are associated with the realm of Christendom. They preached the word of God, and according to what these words convey, they more than likely even performed exorcisms (a religious ceremony in which somebody attempts to drive out an evil spirit believed to possess a person or place). Why, they even did many wonders in Jesus' name. But even though they did all of these things in Jesus' name they were doomed (lost). Which got me to thinking, if these people couldn't find the narrow gate to life, what could possibly make me think that I would ever find it? Answer: It came through the verse I used from one of God's watchman named Ezekiel. God used Ezekiel as one of His messengers. God told Ezekiel that he was to warn people about their wickedness. Ezekiel was a man who was deeply concerned and was grieving because the people of Israel had become impudent and hard-hearted toward the things of God. Ezekiel was commanded to give the people a warning. And what was that warning? The warning was the same one that exists within the world of Christendom today. The warning that God had told Ezekiel to share is the same one that exists today. And what is that, you ask? It is with regard to the house of God. Those who claim to be God's people in Christ's church today have in many ways lost their way in the wilderness of the modern-day world in which they live. Many so-called churches today are nothing more than breeding grounds for the prince of this world. The devil and his angels have so penetrated the walls of Christ church today that God is sounding a modern-day trumpet of warning to/for those who are caught in the devil's evil snare of deception and trickery. How do I know this, you ask? I know it because of what God first opened my eyes and ears to when He called me out of the darkness of this world. I, like Ezekiel, was called to warn people that God is not a happy camper. He is not a happy camper, and as Jesus states in the New Testament book of The Revelation 2:14 that He has some things against those who claim to be part of His church. He has some things against them, and in verse 16, He commands them to repent of those things or else, He will come and fight against them. And what is the weapon He uses? Well, look at what it says at the end of verse 16. Jesus says that He will fight against them with the sword of His mouth. And what is the sword of His mouth? Well, if you remember what we learned earlier, you will remember that we were exposed to this in the New Testament book of Ephesians 6:17 with regard to spiritual warfare. In this teaching by Saul of Tarsus (Paul), he exposed us to the fact that the sword of God is His word.

But there is yet another issue. And that issue is the one that God warned Ezekiel about. And what did God warn Ezekiel about? He warned him that the people would not listen. He warned Ezekiel that they would not listen because they were a rebellious house (Ezekiel 2:5). They were a rebellious house because they did not obey the word of God. God told Ezekiel that He was sending him to warn them of their transgressions and offenses against Him, but God warned Ezekiel that the people would not listen. They would not listen because they were, as God tells us in Ezekiel 3:4, impudent and stubborn children. But then again, that was the same kind of warning that God placed within my own heart when I was first exposed to the truth of His word as well. God warned me that I too was an impudent and stubborn child, and I needed to repent of my transgressions against Him as well. And so I did, and many of the results of that repentance I have shared within the pages of this book. When I truly repented of my transgressions and offenses against God, He began the process of cleansing my heart and life as a true follower of Jesus Christ. I cried out to God, and He had mercy on me, and He began the process of blotting out the transgressions of iniquity and sin that lay deep within the very foundation of my soul. Just as it says in the Old Testament book of Psalms chapter 51, "Have mercy upon me, O God, According to Your loving kindness; According to the multitude of Your tender mercies, Blot out my transgressions. Wash me thoroughly from my iniquity, And cleanse me from my sin. For I acknowledge my transgressions, And my sin is always before me."

You see, Ezekiel was given a command by God. God spoke to Ezekiel and gave him a command to go to the people of Israel and warn them that they had transgressed His commandments. God's laws were being violated, and because God's chosen people were violating His laws, they were seen in God's eyes as being a rebellious nation (Ezekiel 2:3). But then again, that shows the mercy of God. God has compassion on/for people. He has so much love and compassion for people that He came to earth to die for our transgressions against Him. He has so much compassion and love for people that God even warns people when they get out of line with His will. But the problem lies within us. The problem lies within us as human beings, because of our sinful nature. We don't always see a/the warning sign from God because we are more in tune with the things and influences of this world (wide path) than we are with the things of God. But then again, that's what redemption/salvation is all about. It's about seeing and hearing the warning that God places within our hearts and minds if there is true repentance. God knows what lies within our (your) heart. Have we (you) truly repented of our transgressions against Him, or are we (you) just giving God lip service, such as was the case of the scribes and Pharisees that we learned earlier in our search for the truth (Matthew 15:8)?

Now you may be saying to yourself, "This is all well and fine Joe, but what does all of this have to do with me being a watchman for God especially with regard to the scripture you used at the beginning of this chapter?" After all, this scripture verse had to do with the nation of Israel and Ezekiel being called by God to warn the nation Israel way back in 593 BC (before Christ). Surely this teaching has nothing to do with me and/or the day we live in. And to that idea, I would respectively use the words of a repentant sinner by the name of Ebenezer Scrooge as a big "Bah, humbug!" I say that because God's word teaches in the Old Testament book of Isaiah 40:8 these words, "The grass withers, the flower fades, But the word of our God stands forever." In other words, God's word is timeless, whether God spoke these words to Ezekiel way back in his time or whether God is speaking to your heart today. The truth of God's words stands forever, and no matter what the prince of this world (devil—Ephesians 2:2) tries to do to usurp (take over) His word, God's words do not change. And as a watchman, having eyes to see and ears to hear God's truth, you have a/the responsibility to share and expose others to the truths of God's words as well. How do I know that, you ask? I know it because of what God said to Ezekiel in verses 18 and 19 of chapter 3 and also in a/the parallel verse(s) found in Ezekiel chapter 33. Here, God teaches about warning people as like sounding a trumpet. As a watchman of his word, a true follower of Jesus Christ has an obligation to warn others. Why, because if they don't, there is a consequence involved in not obeying God's command to sound the trumpet. And what is that consequence? Well, look at what God says to Ezekiel with regard to Ezekiel warning the nation of Israel to turn from their wicked ways.

Now there's much to this teaching, but the bottom line to all of what God was telling Ezekiel boils down to this. God holds people accountable for warning others about their need to repent, to turn from their rebellion against Him (God). In other words, there is a sword coming. And the word "sword" represents God's judgment. We (you) can read about the word "sword" throughout the Bible (384 times). In this scenario, the word "sword" is used in Ezekiel 33:2 as a guide to help steer us (you) in the right direction with regard to what the responsibilities of a watchman are. In this word of God, it is clear that a watchman's responsibility was to sound an alarm when an enemy was approaching so that people could protect themselves and their families from their enemies. Now as I said, there is much to this teaching but the bottom line to all of this comes down to the fact that God's judgment is coming, whether you or I like it or not. Oh, we (you) may not like it, but God's word is crystal clear that every person that has ever lived will be judged. They will be held accountable for their actions. We are exposed to this truth in the New Testament book of Hebrews 9:27 which says, "And as it is appointed for men to die once, but after this the judgment." This is true for both those who have repented of their sins toward God (true believers), as well as for those who have not repented of their sins (unbelievers) as well. The difference is those who have truly repented of their sins toward God and have been born again of God's Spirit (comforter) will not face the same kind of judgment as those who have not truly repented of their sins and transgressions toward God. The true believer will be judged and receive their heavenly rewards for not worshipping the beast (devil), while the unbeliever will be judged and then spend eternity in hell, which is one of the reasons why God sends a watchman to sound a/the trumpet. But then look at what it says will happen if a/the watchman doesn't sound the trumpet and warn the people. In Ezekiel 3:18 and Ezekiel 33:6, it says that if the watchman doesn't sound the alarm and warn the people of their wicked ways toward God, their blood will be held against the watchman because he didn't sound the trumpet and warn them of the coming sword of God's judgment. And that, my fellow truth seeker, is one of the reasons why I wrote this book. I was called to sound the trumpet. I say that because there are multitudes of people today who hear about God's love, but seldom do they ever hear about God's coming judgment (sword). But then again, please keep in mind, I'm just a forklift operator. After all, what do I know?

CHAPTER 31

The Oath

(Evil flourishes when good men do nothing)

Moreover he must have a good testimony among those who are
outside, lest he fall into reproach and the snare of the devil.
—1 Timothy 3:7

NOW THE WHOLE concept of me sounding the trumpet and
warning people about God's coming judgment (sword) began to
unfold in my life when I was first elected as a union steward in the Teamsters
union. God took my time as an elected representative to open my eyes and
ears to what I needed to know about how to represent Him for His glory
and honor. Now I say glory and honor because as we've learned throughout
our search when you're representing God (Jesus Christ) you must never
forget that you are representing His integrity and His honor. But you see
that was the same truth that I first learned when I was a representative
in the Teamsters union. I say I first learned this truth when I served as
a union steward because when you become a member in the Teamsters
union, you take an oath. And part of the words of that oath is with regard
to the word "reproach." It says in the Teamsters oath these words, "I will
conduct myself at all times in a manner as not to bring reproach upon my
union." Now what does that mean? What does it mean when it says that
the one taking the oath will not bring reproach upon the union? Well, I
guess the answer to this question would be in the eyes of the beholder. In
other words, what will/would constitute a reproach against the union as
seen in the eyes of the one(s) who may/might determine that someone had/
has committed a reproach, or a violation, upon the oath that that person
took when they joined the union?

Now the word "reproach" is defined in the dictionary as criticism,
censure, reprimand, blame, accusation, reproof, scolding, rebuke, etc. So
in other words, when you take the oath and say these words, you are at
least in the mind-set of those administering the oath (usually the elected

officers in/of the union) saying, "I won't criticize, scold, rebuke, or say anything negative against the union." Whether I agree or not, I will not criticize or disapprove of anything the union is doing. I will not harm my union by putting, what some may see as a negative view (spin) on what I may not agree with. Now this is what some may think. But for anyone who may embrace that type of thinking, I would once again use the words of Mr. Ebenezer Scrooge as a "Humbug!" I say this is a humbug because what I discovered in my time of being in the Teamsters union was in fact; the very ones who were supposed to be living by the words of the Teamster oath they were administering, were the same ones who were in many ways bringing the most reproach upon our/their union. The problem was they didn't even realize that they were! Now there is much I could share with you with regard to what I discovered in my time of being an elected official in the Teamsters union, and I will refrain from doing so because it is not my intention to embarrass or humiliate anyone. I wrote this book to simply share with you what I have discovered from my walk with God in my search of finding the narrow gate/path to life. I will however share with you that what I discovered along the journey of my time as union steward and trustee in the Teamsters union was exactly what I discovered is happening in Christ's church as well. Now I say that from the standpoint that what I saw happening in the Teamsters union in many ways parallels the same thing I see happening in Christ's church as well. And what are those parallels, you ask? Well, from what I have discovered as both a representative in the union as well as the church, is there is a lack of leadership within both. Now I say that in the spirit that not all the leaders of those two organizations are lousy leaders. I'm simply stating that from what I observed in my thirty years of being a member in the union, as well as my nearly thirty years of being a member in/of Christ's kingdom (church), there are some major leadership issues going on. And what are some of those leadership issues? Well, to answer that question, it would take a lot longer than we have in our current search, but I will share this much with you. From what I have observed in both my time as an elected official in the union as well as my time in a/the church environment, the Good Old Boys Club mentality is alive and well within both of these organizations. Now what do I mean by that? Well, for the answer to that question, let's take a good look at what the word of God says at the beginning of this chapter. Now the key word to focus in on here is the word "reproach." And why is the word "reproach" such an important word in our search? Well, look at what the context of the word "reproach" is referring to in this teaching from Saul of Tarsus (Paul) in 1 Timothy chapter 3. Here Saul/Paul is mentoring his fellow believer Timothy about the importance of having a good testimony. And how can someone achieve a good testimony? Well, for the short answer to that question let's just say that without the help of the Holy Spirit (comforter) it is nearly impossible. I say it is nearly impossible to achieve a good testimony because unless you're living a life based on the truth of God's word(s) (Bible), it is almost impossible to achieve a good testimony among people. And why is this so important? It's important because if you do your homework and study God's word (Bible), you will discover that the word Saul/Paul was teaching Timothy in this chapter was about the qualifications set forth in God's word with regard to an overseer.

Now if you knew the whole truth about my time as an elected official in the union, you might possibly think that some of my remarks are not very kind. In fact, if you knew anything about my trials in the union, you might think that my remarks are being said with a "sour grapes type" attitude. If you knew the whole story about my time as an elected official in the union, you would know that I was ultimately removed (railroaded) from my office as a trustee. I say I was removed (railroaded) from office because that's exactly what happened to me. Now there is much to the story of how I was ultimately removed from office and the circumstances that led up to me being removed. But if I were to sum up and reveal the whole truth (story) of what ultimately led to my being removed from office, you would understand exactly why and how I was removed, which takes us back to the word "reproach." I say it takes us back to the word "reproach" because with regard to the Good Old Boys Club system, I had brought reproach upon the union. Oh, they would never come out and publicly announce that I had brought reproach against the union, but among themselves, I had done exactly that. I had brought reproach upon my union because I would not compromise the integrity of the office that I had taken an oath to oversee. In a nutshell, when I accepted the office of overseer as both a union steward and a trustee in the Teamsters union, I was agreeing to be the eyes and ears for and to the members who elected me to that office. But in many ways, my being elected to the office of overseer (steward/trustee) in the Teamsters union is the same as my being elected to the office of overseer in God's kingdom. How so, you ask? Well, when God elected (choose) me (John 15:16) to become one of His children; I had the responsibility of overseeing His kingdom. And with that responsibility came the responsibility of not bringing reproach upon His kingdom as well. You see, that is one of the major issues that Jesus had confronted the scribes and

Pharisees about. The truth is they had brought reproach upon the integrity and honor of God Himself. They had actually blasphemed the very nature and character of God and Jesus knew it, and that's why Jesus confronted the religious establishment of His time. Jesus confronted them, and his message to them was to repent and turn their wicked hearts back toward the truth and character of God's word(s). But did they listen? No, they didn't! Just as God had told Ezekiel would happen when God commanded the watchman Ezekiel to warn the nation Israel of their wickedness, as we discovered in the last chapter (Ezekiel 2:7).

Now with regard to the word "reproach," there are a number of opinions as to what defines a reproach. And according to what we learned is the definition of the word "reproach," someone or somebody could feel as though you are bringing reproach upon an organization should you express any concern or criticism of that particular organization or person. And that's exactly what happened to me when I was removed out of being an overseer in the Teamsters union. I was removed from office because I had, in the minds of the Good Old Boys Club, the audacity (courage, boldness, bravery, nerve) to engage what I determined were evil practices that were taking place within the realm of what I was elected to oversee within the union. In fact, one of the key conditions that I was given to help me in my decision as to whether or not I would accept the office of trustee in the first place was indeed just that. The leaders in the Good Old Boys Club said they wanted to get away from that reputation. And that's one of the reasons why they wanted me to come on board as part of their team. They said they wanted to do away with the Good Old Boys Club. Now you're probably saying to yourself, "Did you say evil practices?" Yes, I said evil practices. I say evil practices because with regard to these types of situations, an overseer (steward, trustee, watchman, etc.) must be a good discerner of the truth, which takes us back into the fruit-inspecting part (chapter 11) of what God calls us to as followers of His truth/word. This also brings back into play the oath that I had taken with regard to not bringing reproach upon my union.

Now if you go back to the introduction of my book, you will remember that I shared with you that much of our lives are based upon people's opinions. Now within the pages of this book, I have shared my opinions with you. They are my opinions, but those opinions are based upon the truths of God's words. Now I'm sure that there are those who are not going to agree with what I have shared within the pages of this book. And do you know what, my fellow truth seeker? That's okay. It's okay because it doesn't really matter if they (you) agree with me or not. I say it doesn't really matter whether anyone agrees with me or not because in the end, the only thing that really matters is whether or not God agrees with what I've shared in our search for the truth, which again takes us back to whose opinion matters. The oath of office in the Teamsters union was in many ways the same oath that I took when I became a follower of Jesus Christ. I say they are in many ways similar because just as God's word states in the scripture verse we used at the beginning of this chapter, a follower of Jesus Christ's testimony must be based upon how they have conducted their lives within the framework of God's truths/words. Notice what it says, "He must have a good testimony among those who are outside, lest he fall into reproach and the snare of the devil." Question: What did Saul of Tarsus (Paul) mean by this? Well, if you take a look at the verses that precede this verse (1 Timothy 3:1-6), you will understand that Saul (Paul) was referring to the qualifications of an overseer. The he here refers to those who desire to be in a leadership role within the realm of God's affairs (business). But you see that's where many who claim the name of Jesus Christ don't make the connection. They don't make the connection to them being an overseer of God's truths because when they're dealing with those who are outside God's kingdom (unbelievers, those on the wide path, etc.); their testimony becomes a stumbling block instead of a good testimony. Why? Well, take a good look at what God's truth says. It says, "Lest he fall into reproach and the snare of the devil." And what was the reproach that the devil had brought upon himself? It was his pride! He put himself ahead of God, and because he did that, God condemned him to eternal punishment (verse 6). But then again that's where God taught me the importance about having a good testimony. And that's where we get back to the words "opinion" and "oath." In the Teamsters union, I had taken an oath; and in God's kingdom, I had taken an oath. The question was "Which oath was more important: my oath to the union or my oath to God?" Do you know what I learned, my fellow truth seeker? The answer to my question was both! My oath to not bring reproach upon the union was the same as my oath to God. Why, because of my testimony. When I put my trust and faith in Jesus Christ and repented of my sins and transgressions against God, the covenant relationship between God and me was consummated. I was married to Jesus Christ, and now I am a slave and servant to the truth of God's word. And what is at the very core of God's truth? It is a/the battle between good (God) and evil (the devil) (Much of this we have already discovered earlier in our search).

JOSEPH TRAVER

But there were some problems that I had to come to grips with. And what were those problems? The problems lay in the fact that I had to make a determination as to whether or not what was happening before my very eyes was evil. Another thing that I had to take into consideration was if I exposed this evil (wrongdoing), would I be bringing a reproach upon the testimony that I was obligated to maintain as a follower of Jesus Christ? And do you know what I discovered, my fellow truth seeker? I discovered that if I didn't expose the evil before me, I would indeed be bringing reproach upon my testimony. The other perspective I had to consider was that if I exposed what was taking place within the union, chances are it would more than likely lead to me being removed from office, and therefore it would more than likely be the end of my career as a representative in the union. So I had a decision to make. Do I take a stand against what I had determined to be an evil, or do I say nothing and possibly further myself and my future which could lead to a rather prosperous and lucrative career. At that time of my faith journey in finding the narrow path to life, I remember hearing a saying that goes like this, "Evil flourishes when good men do nothing." I also remember what God taught me from his word found in Matthew 6:24 that says this, "You cannot serve God and mammon." Here mammon represents earthly treasures and especially money.

Now as I stated earlier, there is much to the story of how I was ultimately removed from office, but what I saw happening before me was nothing short of an evil. I say it was evil because one of the things I discovered was that thousands upon thousands upon thousands of dollars were being drained from the general funds of the local union that I was an overseer in/ of. Now as both a member and a trustee of that local, I felt obligated to do everything within my power to reverse that practice. Why? Well, first of all, it was the right thing to do. I decided that if I didn't do anything to reverse the trend that was taking place within our local, it could possibly lead to the demise of that local, and I was determined that that was not going to happen on my watch. I also truly believed that by taking no action at all, I would be allowing evil to flourish and that the "Good Old Boys Club" type system would further diminish the integrity and honor of the union that I loved, a union that both my father and my brother before me had served in. I made a determination and saw what was happening to/in our local as a personal attack, not only on my integrity as a representative, but also on the membership and the labor movement as a collective body. But do you know something else my fellow truth seeker? It was a time when God began to open my eyes to what was happening in His church as well.

And this is the last thing that the Holy Spirit has taken so long to expose us (you) to in our search for the truth. You need to know that there is a/ the "Good Old Boys Club" type system that is alive and well within the modern day church movement today. There is a "Good Old Boys Club" mentality, and the results of that mentality has a direct connection to the falling away that must take place before Jesus Christ can return (rapture) for His church (born-again believers). I mentioned this earlier with regard to the Great Apostasy found in 2 Thessalonians chapter 2.

Now what I discovered in my time of trial in facing the Good Old Boys Club system was this. At the very heart and core of that system is the word "deception." I learned firsthand about the skillful art of deception and how it thrives on those who don't even realize that they are being subjected to its influence on/in their lives. But do you know what, my fellow truth seeker? That's what this book has been about. It's been about the fact that you may just be being deceived yourself, and you may not even realize that you are. And that's exactly how the Good Old Boys Club system is designed to operate. It is designed to deceive the unsuspecting and the uninformed. And that's one of the saddest things I can see happening within a great deal of the modern-day church movement today. People are being deceived, and they don't even realize that they are. They are taking oaths to be followers of Jesus Christ, but they are being led astray by the Good Old Boys Club mentality that has penetrated Christ's church. The oaths they are taking are being administered by many of those who are being deceived themselves. And how are they being deceived, you ask? They are being deceived because many of those who are in a/the leadership positions of those organizations do not meet the criteria or qualifications of what God's word requires. Oh, they meet the requirements and the standards according to what the Good Old Boys Club has been able to get established within their particular organization(s) by and through traditions, etc. But within the realm of God's standards (words), they do not meet the requirements. They do not meet the requirements because they have not been ordained by God. They have been ordained by men who are part of the Good Old Boys Club. They are the modern-day Pharisees that have been established by and through the skillful art of deception of/by the devil. And how has much of this come into the church? It has come right through some of the very words of Jesus Himself as he spoke to his body, the church. A great deal of this can be found in the first three chapters of The Revelation (some of this we've uncovered earlier in our search). Now if I were going to compare what I discovered was happening within the Teamsters union with what I see happening within the modern-day church today, I would have to say the key word can be found in the third chapter of the Revelation verse 4. And what is that word, you ask? It is the word "worthy." But then again, please keep in mind, I'm just a forklift operator. After all, what do I know?

CHAPTER 32

Worthy

(He who overcomes)

You have a few names even in Sardis who have not defiled their garments; and they shall walk with Me in white, for they are worthy.
—Revelation 3:4

He who overcomes shall inherit all things, and I will be his God and he shall be My son.
—Revelation 21:7

WE'VE BEEN BUILDING up to the conclusion of our search for the truth for quite a while now, and I know that the Holy Spirit (comforter) has taken us through many curves and rough terrain along the road of our search. And though the Holy Spirit has taken us through many curves and rough terrain along the road of our current search for the truth, we have only touched on the surface of what God has opened my eyes to since I made my decision to be a truthful follower of Jesus Christ back in 1983. Some of the things that I would have liked to share in our current search I didn't, because those things are not as relevant as some of the things that I have uncovered in this book. I say they are not as relevant because in the totality of a person's regenerative state (born again), the things I have uncovered in this particular search are things that must first take place in a person's life (heart) before they can fully comprehend what they're (you're) up against as they (you) search to find the narrow gate which leads to life. In other words, in a/the chronological order, the things we have uncovered in our current search for the truth are the priority things that a person must be aware of before they can comprehend many of the other issues I would have liked to share but simply did not. Things such as the history of the country I live in and how this country (the United States of America) was founded on the advancement of the Christian faith and the glory of the God of the Bible. How do I know that, you ask? Well, if you do your homework, you will discover that one of the first declarations by the founding fathers (pilgrims) of the United States were these words from a historical document known as the Mayflower Compact in the year 1620, having undertaken for the Glory of God and the Advancement of the Christian faith. It is an expository search into how this country is collapsing from within its walls primarily because the church has compromised the truth of God's words and has embraced a worldly mind-set more than a Godly mind-set, just as some of those churches did in the first three chapters of the book of The Revelation. They have defiled God's character.

Now you may be saying to yourself, "This is all well and fine Joe, but what does this have to do with the United States of America and a/the church of Jesus Christ? After all, isn't there a clear definition of a separation between church and state written in the constitution of the United States?" Answer: It has a great deal to do with the connection between both of them. I say it has a great deal to do with the connection between both of them because there is a mind-set in the United States today that is promoting a/the false understanding that the God in which the United States was founded on should be excluded from the public arena. In other words, the secular world is trying to push the God of the Bible out of any public interaction and in the process is forcing that God to pour out his judgment on the very roots in which the very foundation of this country was founded on. And what were those roots? They were exactly what our founding fathers had declared in their words: for the Glory of God and advancement of the Christian faith. Now why is this an important piece to the puzzle as we conclude our current search for the truth? It is an important piece to the puzzle because it has a great deal to do with what's happening within the boundaries of the United States as well as the church in America today. You see, the one true God of the Bible used those founding fathers (pilgrims, etc.) faith in Jesus Christ to establish a body of believers that would be a light for others to follow in a world that is full of darkness. The United States of America was used by God in the same manner as the nation of Israel was used in the Old Testament. The difference is the nation of Israel was primarily a Jewish nation, while the United States is primarily a Gentile nation. I truly believe that as God placed His hand on the nation Israel, He also placed His hand on the United States of America as well. God used the faith (Christian) of our founding fathers as they risked their very lives and their futures in being faithful servants for the Glory of God. Question: Did they succeed? Did they succeed in bringing Glory to God? I believe they did. I also believe it was not just a coincidence that the United States has become the most prosperous and powerful nation in the history of mankind. Our founding fathers had their priorities straight with regard to the God of the Holy Bible and because they did, I am a recipient of the effects of our founding fathers' faith in Jesus Christ. Because of their obedience, God has blessed the United States into becoming the envy of the world. But there is a problem. And what is that problem? The same problem that came upon the nation of Israel is now starting to take root within the boundaries of the United States as well. And what is that problem, you ask? It is the rejection of the Son of God who is Jesus Christ. The nation of Israel rejected Jesus Christ and from what I have learned in my time of being a follower of Jesus Christ, the very same thing is happening within the boundaries of the United States of America as well. And how is this happening, my fellow truth seeker? It is happening from within the very walls of the church itself. Now you may be saying to yourself, "What the heck are you talking about, Joe?" After all, there are churches in every area in America. Why, in the towns and cities of America today there are churches on almost every corner. And you know what, my fellow truth seeker? In many cases, that is absolutely true. But the question that I'd like to end our current search with is the same one that I've been trying to uncover in our journey up to the end of this book. And that is this. What kind of churches are they? In other words, what is going on within the walls of those churches that are found within the borders of the United States of America?

Now I ask that question with this in mind. If you remember the question I asked back in chapter 17 of this book, you will recall that I asked that same question with regard to Mr. Ebenezer Scrooge after he was visited by the three ghosts on Christmas Eve and ultimately repented of his transgressions. It had to do with what the church is supposed to represent in a world full of darkness. It is supposed to be a light for others to see as they pursue and connect with the God of this universe by and through the true light of the world who is Jesus Christ. If you recall the questions I asked in that chapter, you will recall that one of the questions was this: "What did God think of the church Scrooge went to?" In other words, after Scrooge repented, one of the first things he did was he went to church. Now I wanted to bring this out into the open because the bottom line to our current search for the truth really wraps itself around these particular questions. Have you truly repented of your rebellion against God, and if you have done that, you really need to find a church body that will help you as God continues to purify you in your new life in Jesus Christ. But the question for you is twofold. First, what church body do you connect to/with; and second, what does God think of the church body you're considering going to? And that, my fellow truth seeker, is a great question! And do you know why it is a great question? It is a great question because if you're reading this book and you're within the boundaries of the United States of America, you really need to do some serious fruit inspecting and discernment as you consider what church body you want to hook up with in your search to find the narrow gate to life.

Now why do I say that, my fellow truth seeker? I say it because as we close our current search, I want to conclude our search with this. It is from the words of the Savior Himself. The Savior of the world, Jesus Christ, found in the verse I used at the beginning of this chapter. And the question that needs to be asked and answered is this: "Are you worthy? Are you worthy enough to be seen through the eyes of Jesus Christ [God] as wearing a white garment? Are you worthy enough in the eyes of Jesus to have Him confess you as being worthy before His Father in heaven?" (The Revelation 3:5) Now I know you're probably saying to yourself, "What does he mean by a white garment? And what does a white garment and being found worthy have to do with me?" Well, one of the things that God showed me in my time of being a representative in the union versus my time in His kingdom is this. No matter where I travel down the road of my faith journey as a follower of Jesus Christ, there will always be battles to be fought. There will always be battles in this life because no matter where I go or what I do, the influences of the world, the flesh, and the devil will always try to disrupt the truths of God's word and therefore try to get me to defile my garments (character) in my search in finding the narrow gate to life. This was true for Ebenezer Scrooge, it was true for Saul of Tarsus (Paul), it was true for Nicodemus, it was true for me, and it is also true for you, my fellow truth seeker. But not only is it true for individuals, it is also true for a/the collective body of Jesus Christ which is supposed to be the church. Just like Jesus warned five of the seven churches about in the first three chapters of The Revelation. And that's why it's so important for you to do some serious fruit inspecting to see what God thinks of the church you're considering attending. I say that, my fellow truth seeker, because I have done some serious fruit inspecting with regard to the modern-day church system of today, and I am not impressed with what I have discovered in my own personal fruit inspecting. Now how did all of that take place? Well for the answer to that question, you have to consider a great deal about what I have shared within the pages of this book.

Everything I have shared is a tribute to what Almighty God has allowed me to go through as He opened my eyes in my personal pursuit of the truth. I happen to believe that God took me through the trials and tribulations of my time as a representative in the Teamsters union to allow me to see what's happening in the modern-day church system today. Remember what I shared with regard to what I discovered about the Good Old Boys Club within the union? From what I've discovered, those very same things have worked their way into the modern-day church movement today. Not all churches are the same, but from the fruit inspecting I have done in my own personal faith journey in finding the narrow gate to life, that mentality is alive and well; and I would strongly urge you to be extremely aware of it as you determine as to what church body you want to hook up with. I say that with this in mind. Just because a church building might have the appearance of being a church doesn't really mean that it is. Just because a church has a cross on it or has a nice marquee with God's words on it doesn't necessarily make it a true church. Just because a church has the aroma of being a/the body of Jesus Christ doesn't necessarily mean that God is well pleased with what's going on within the environment of that church. What I discovered in my own personal time of being a representative within a church environment is in many ways the same problem I discovered in my time in the Teamsters union. The problem within both organizations is that there is poor leadership within both, and many of those who are in the leadership positions in both the Teamsters union as well as the church have no business being in those positions. Many of them are not qualified to be leaders, and many have come up through the Good Old Boys Club system themselves and quite frankly have no business in those positions of leadership. And do you know what I have also discovered, my fellow truth seeker? It is because of this very reason that I truly believe that both the unions as well as the church in America today are feeling the effects of that truth. What effects, you ask, the effects of dwindling membership in both. And that, my fellow truth seeker, could be a whole other search in itself.

Now before you started reading this book, you more than likely never gave this much thought at all. In fact, much of what we have uncovered in our search for the truth may just be the instrument that God will use to open your heart to what you needed to hear in assisting you in finding the narrow gate to life. God may use this book to begin to prick your heart and mind into the understanding that a changed heart in Jesus Christ is the only way of ever finding the narrow gate that leads to life (eternal). Just as we learned in our search with regard to the people who thought they were followers of the one true God of the truth (narrow gate), when in fact they were following the devil (wide gate) by and through the hardness of their hearts. They thought their desires and their motives were of God when in fact they were not. The reality was with regard to those supposed followers of Jesus Christ that we discovered earlier in our search in Matthew 7:21-27; they had defiled their garments (character) and had brought reproach upon the name of Jesus Christ and His church. But you see, that's exactly what Jesus was warning people about in the first three chapters of the book of The Revelation, and that's where I want to end our current search. I say I want to end our search at this point because up to this point, I have shared many things with you. I have shared these things because of what I have been taught by my teacher, the Holy Spirit. Most of these things I have shared have been formulated in my life over a period of nearly thirty years of diligently seeking after the very heart of Almighty God (Jeremiah 29:13). Always remember that you can know the very heart of God if you remember what His words teach us and then obey what you are taught.

Well, let's put our search in a/the proper context. In this word of God, we learn from Jesus that those who were supposedly following Him in the framework of His bride, the church, were in fact defiling their garments, which meant they were not seen in Jesus' eyes as being pure and holy. They had defiled His character and what His church was supposed to represent in a world that is controlled by the devil. Now why is this an important issue? I say it's an important issue for this reason and this reason only. One of the things I've learned along the narrow road of my faith journey as both a representative in the Teamsters union as well as a representative in Christ's kingdom (church) is this. God uses people for his glory and his honor alone. Our lives are supposed to be in tune with that understanding. God established the church to be in tune with that understanding in mind. But God also knew one thing. He knew that once He gave us the new life in Jesus Christ (born again), our lives and our eternal future will/would never be the same. He also knew that our lives would be full of the trials and tribulations that go along with the territory of being a follower of His Son Jesus Christ. He knew that we would be in a constant conflict between good and evil. But you see, that's one of the problems, just as I stated earlier in our search, these words from Jesus Himself found in Matthew 6:24, "You cannot serve God and mammon." I say it's a problem because the human heart is more in tune with the treasures of this life (material things) than they are of the treasures to come. People get too caught up with the things (treasures) of this life that are temporary instead of the things that are eternal (everlasting). In these words of Jesus, we hear a warning about attempting to serve both God and mammon. Now the Bible depicts mammon as the personification (characteristic) of wealth portrayed as a false god. Now there is much to discuss with regard to whether a person is serving the God of the Bible or the god of mammon (false god), but I will tell you one thing and that is this. It's not just about serving the god of mammon that gets people into trouble; it's about what happens to the lives of those who surround the people who are caught up in that form of serving mammon as well. Again, my friend Forrest calls it the ripple effect. The ripple effect here would be with regard to all those who are affected by those who are serving the god of mammon instead of the God of the Bible. The bottom line of all of this is that these kinds of people are actually serving an idol, and in most cases, they don't even realize that they are. And do you know what I have discovered in my own personal pursuit of the truth, my fellow truth seeker? Mammon worship is one of the key elements at the heart of what is happening in the United States of America today. The idol worship of money (wealth) has such an evil grip on this country (United States) that the devastating ripple effects of its destruction are being felt throughout the world as well. But do you know something else, my fellow truth seeker? The so-called churches of today are literally jam-packed with that kind of worship as well. But I'm not surprised by this at all because Jesus Christ taught that this would take place within some of His churches when He spoke on these issues with regard to His church in the first three chapters of The Revelation. Likewise, Saul of Tarsus (Paul) referenced this portion of God's word when he spoke on this in the New Testament book of 1st Timothy 4:1 with regard to the deceiving spirits and doctrines of demons that will be in place in the end times before Christ returns. I know of at least three of these doctrines of demons that have begun to manifest themselves within the modern-day church movement today. They are those referenced by Jesus as the doctrines of Balaam, the Nicolaitans (Nicolas), and Jezebel (If you do your homework, you will discover what kind of seducing spirits were at the heart of these three people—i.e., money, sex, and rebellion [disobedience]).

Now you may be asking yourself, "But what the heck does this have to do with me?" Answer: It has a great deal to do with you, my fellow truth seeker. I say it has a great deal to do with you because in the process of you working out your own salvation with fear and trembling (Philippians 2:12), you must be aware that these types of church environments are in place today. They are in place today, and you must be extremely watchful for these kinds of church environments. Why? Because if you're not extremely careful, you could find yourself within the structure of this type of church environment yourself and not even realize that you are. I say that because if you get caught in this kind of environment (snare/trap), you may just be in jeopardy of feeling the effects of what we spoke about earlier with regard to what Jesus said to those who thought they were following Jesus. But then again, that's why we are to be soldiers and watchmen in God's kingdom, to teach and expose others about what's happening around them (Matthew 5:19). But then again, that's why Jesus stated numerous times within the Bible to have eyes to see and ears to hear what He is saying to His church. And once again, who is the church? It is found within the hearts of those who have been born again. The true church starts with the invisible condition of a/the regenerated heart(s) that God has called out and the effects of those regenerated hearts are then manifested into the visible and/ or physical church building if you will. The church building is where the called-out ones (John 15:16) come together to share each other's burdens and to grow together in the love (truth) of Jesus Christ, just as Jesus stated in Matthew 5:14, a Christian's life should be like a ray of light that draws people toward the one true light of the world, who is Jesus Christ. Now I say that because what I have discovered in my pursuit in finding the narrow gate (road/path) to life is that when you follow Jesus Christ, there will always be a cost in doing so. When you live your life within the truth of the gospel message, you will be in the direct crosshairs of the devil's sights. He will always use his arsenal of weapons to try and throw you off course in your pursuit in/of finding the narrow gate to life. At the forefront of his arsenal is the weapon of deception. I say deception because if you recall, it was the word "deception" that was at the forefront of what the devil used to deceive Eve in the Garden of Eden which led to the fall of the human race (Genesis chapter 3). The battle was on and the spiritual warfare had begun, which takes us to the word "worthy."

As we uncovered in this scripture verse from the book of The Revelation 3:4, there were those within the church in Sardis who had not defiled their garments (character) before God. We also uncovered that God considered those who did not defile their garments as being worthy. We also discover in this word from God that he uses the word "few." Does that word sound familiar, my fellow truth seeker? Where have we heard that word before? Well, if you remember one of our key verses on the front cover of this book, you will recall Jesus refers to the word "few." Jesus describes a specific number of those who will find the narrow gate that leads to life, which also parallels what is found within the first three chapters of the book of The Revelation as well as the seventh chapter of Matthew. How so, you ask? Well, if you remember what we discovered earlier, you recall that Jesus is talking to those who claimed to be his followers. They had claimed their faith in Jesus Christ, but they had a problem. They had a big problem. And what was that problem? They had a double standard. They were living a double life. They had a double standard in their lives, and Jesus was trying to get their attention. But then again, that is always what happens to those that God loves. How so, you ask? Well, if you recall what God's word says to those whom he loves, you remember what he's urging these churches to open their ears to. They were defiling their garments, and they were offending Jesus. Jesus was drawing attention to the fact that they were not right with Him (God), and He was actually scolding and warning them to change their ways by and through the act of a zealous heart of repentance (Revelation 3:19). Jesus was counseling and pleading with them to repent and turn their hearts back to the things of God. Why? Because Jesus knew that if they didn't listen to what he was warning them about they were in serious jeopardy of having their names blotted out of the Book of Life (Revelation 3:5). Why, because they were polluting Christ's church by and through the blasphemies of a/the worldly mind-set. The influences of the world (devil) had penetrated the walls of people's hearts within the church, and they were profaning the truth of what they were supposed to be revealing to people. Question: Did they heed Jesus' warning? Did they listen to what Jesus had warned them about? Well, according to what we discovered earlier, many did not. How do I know that, you ask? I know it because of what Jesus says in verses 22 and 23 of Matthew chapter 7 where He tells those who thought they had been Jesus' followers to depart from Him. Why did Jesus tell them to depart from Him? Well, I happen to believe that this part of scripture lines up with what Jesus told those that thought they were part of His church at the end of The Revelation 3:16 where He tells them that He was going to vomit them out of His mouth. He meant He was disgusted with them. Why was He disgusted? He was disgusted because they didn't heed Jesus' warning to persevere the commandments of God. In other words, they compromised their faith in Jesus Christ to be popular with the things of the world. They had a form of godliness, but their hearts and lives were more in tune with the things of the world instead of the things (commandments) of God and remember what we learned earlier in our search where God's word says that friendship with the world makes us enemies of God (James 4:4). God knew their hearts, and He knew that they had compromised the truth of God's word(s) to be popular with the world. They had defiled their character (garments), and in reality, they were in serious jeopardy of feeling the effects of God's wrath.

Now you may be saying to yourself, "Okay Joe, this is all well and fine, but what the heck does all of this have to do with me, and what does this have to do with me finding the narrow gate to life." Answer: It has everything to do with you, my fellow truth seeker. It has everything to do with you, my fellow truth seeker, because the summation of all that we have discovered in our current search for the truth really boils down to this one reality of life. Have you overcome the world? Have you overcome the influences and deception of the world (the devil), and are you seen in the eyes of Jesus as being worthy enough to have Jesus confess your name before the God of the Bible (The Revelation 3:5)? These are serious questions, my dear friend. In fact, it is one of the most important questions you will ever make in this life! Now at this point, I don't know who will read this book nor do I know what God will do with the words I have shared within the pages of this book. What I mean by that is I don't know where your heart is at this point. Are you still an enemy of God, or are you His friend? Have you truly repented of your transgressions (sins) against Him, or are you still in a rebellious state of the influences of the world (wide path—i.e., the devil)? Have you overcome the world? Perhaps you believe that you have. You believe that you have because you may be reading this book, and you may claim your faith in Jesus Christ. You may be a member in the so-called church in your community. You may be in the church choir or praise band. You may be leading a Bible study. You may be an elder or deacon in the church. You may be a pastor or something else that is associated with the church. But you know what? You may just be in the same category as those who were vomited out of Jesus' mouth as well as those who were told by Jesus to depart from Him because he never knew them. Now as I stated, I don't know where you are in your relationship to God/Jesus Christ. But there is one thing that I do know for sure and that is this: you can't fool God! I know it because of what God's word says in The Revelation 2:23, "I am He who searches the minds and hearts. And I will give to each one of you according to your works." Here, Jesus is speaking to those who were in His church. He knew what was in their hearts, and He knew the blasphemies that were being committed within the collective hearts and minds of those who were associated with His church.

Now I'm sharing all of this with you, my fellow truth seeker, because anytime you are called by God to share what I have shared within the pages of this book, there is a responsibility that goes along with it. I say there is a responsibility that goes along with it because just as we learned earlier with regard to the prophet Ezekiel, there is an accountability that goes along with being a watchman of God's words. Now that accountability is two fold. I say it is two fold from the standpoint that if God has called you to be His messenger then you have a/the responsibility to be a faithful servant and deliver His message (words). But the question remains. Will the people who hear the words you're sharing just listen, or will they listen and repent of their transgressions toward God? But you see that's where you come into this scenario, my fellow truth seeker. I say you come into this scenario because what I have shared within the pages of this book is what God has shown me as one of His messengers. I was called out of the darkness of this world to be used by God as one of His lights. Just as we learned in the beginning of Jesus' Sermon on the Mount these words, "Let your light so shine before men, that they may see your good works and glorify your Father in heaven" (Matthew 5:16). I was transformed out of the darkness of this world to be a light for Jesus Christ, a light that will/might point others to a true relationship with the Savior of the world, who is Jesus Christ. The truth is, my fellow truth seeker, if God hadn't called me out of a world of darkness (wide road), this book would have never been written. Why? Because everything that is written in this book was unknown to me before God saw my repentant heart and found me worthy of being a servant in/for His kingdom. But the question in our current setting is this: Are you worthy? Are you worthy of having Jesus' seal of approval put on you? You see, just because someone claims to be a follower of Jesus Christ doesn't necessarily mean that they are. Such as was the case of those who thought they were representing Christ's church in our search, and this is my final word to you. Just as Saul of Tarsus (Paul), and Nicodemus, and all the scribes and Pharisees, as well as many in the church thought they were representing God, the fact remained that many were not. The message I leave you with is this, my fellow truth seeker: Repentance is the key to salvation. And if you truly wish to find the narrow gate to life, you must begin with true repentance. Cry out to God and be truthful with him. Plead with Him to come into your heart and mind and use you as a true light in a world full of darkness. Ask Him to find you worthy of having His Son Jesus Christ confessing your name as being worthy before His Father. But also remember the wicked one is our (your) enemy. The truth is the devil is always trying to disrupt the truth of God's word. His goal is to disrupt the truth of God's word and God's true character. Will he succeed in your life, my fellow truth seeker? Will he keep you from being an over comer in finding the narrow gate to life. Will he succeed in having Jesus say to you, "Depart from Me you worker of iniquity, I never knew you? Or will you find the narrow gate to life and have your name confessed by Jesus as being worthy before His Father (God)" (The Revelation 3:5). It is my solemn prayer that what I have shared within the pages of this book will serve as a compass to guide you in your personal search in finding the narrow gate that leads to life. As for me, I have shared the words God has called me to share, just as God had said to the watchman Ezekiel as he shared the words God had called him to speak to the nation Israel; Whether they hear or whether they refuse—for they are a rebellious house—yet they will know that a prophet has been among them (Ezekiel 2:5). How about you, my fellow truth seeker? Is your heart rebellious toward the things I have shared within the pages of this book? Those things God has called me to share with others. Only God knows for sure. But then again, please keep in mind, I'm just a forklift operator. After all, what do I know? What do I know? I know how to find the narrow gate that leads to life. But do you know something else, my fellow truth seeker? I am also known as a "gatekeeper" and do you know what a gatekeeper is in God's word? A gatekeeper is in charge of the house of God (1 Chronicles 9:26). It is an entrusted office, and they are keepers of the entrance (gate) to the camp of the Lord. They are also responsible for making sure that no one who is unclean will enter the house of God. And where is the house (church) of God? It is found within the sanctuary of the heart!

POSTSCRIPT

WHAT YOU HAVE just read is a compilation of the things God has revealed to author Joe Traver as God has renewed his heart and mind as one of his faithful servants (Romans 12:2 and Titus 3:5). Joe also has a personal ministry that he began in the year 1996. The story of how he was called by God and the circumstances that led to the beginning of that ministry is one that he has shared throughout the area in which he lives. The title of his message is called "Leaving Our Comfort Zones." One pastor has called Joe's ministry a unique ministry, and another pastor has said that the message Joe shares is one that everyone who claims the name of Jesus Christ needs to hear. Joe's ministry is a unique ministry from the standpoint that his ministry is a warning ministry. God called Joe out of the darkness of this world (wide path) to open the eyes of those who are caught in the snare of the devil's deceptions. If you or your faith group (church body) may be interested in connecting with Joe and his personal ministry entitled Ministry of Sharing, you can do so. But there is one thing that you must be aware of before you make that decision. Don't plan on having your ears tickled. The itching ear mentality of 2nd Timothy chapter 4 that is breeding in much of Christendom today is not in Joe's spiritual DNA. Just as the words of the prophets of old were not well received in their time the words of Joe's ministry may not be well received as well. But then again, that's one of the reasons why God chose a man like Joe to share his truths with others. The time is growing extremely short, and this may just be the final chance that God is giving mankind to repent of their wickedness before He unleashes His wrath (judgment) upon this world. In fact, you may just be caught up in the apostate church movement that Joe spoke about in this book, and God may just be using the words Joe shared in getting your attention to what's taking place within the corporate body of the church today. Joe is proud of his ministry because there is a big difference between his ministry and many of the ministries that are in place today. Many of the ministries of this modern age are ministries that have been formulated by and through the ordination of men while Joe's ministry has been formulated and ordained directly by God (1st John 2:27). Joe is a minister who has been trained solely by the Holy Spirit and is not part of any of the Good Old Boys Club systems that have been established within the realm of modern-day Christendom today, which goes to the heart of what a gatekeeper's responsibilities is/are within the treasures of God's kingdom. Those treasures Joe has been sharing with others since God first called him to his personal ministry. Those treasures have been shared not only within the walls of a so-called church environment but beyond the walls of the so-called established church environment as well. In fact, you may just be caught in the snare of a/the false church environment yourself, and you may not even realize that you are. Just like the many Jesus spoke about in Matthew 7:21-27 who were caught in that same trap themselves. The fact is the Bible speaks about the end time false church in God's word and that Antichrist false church spirit is beginning to find its way into the churches of today. Some of those facts are confirmed within the first three chapters of The Revelation (some of these facts were uncovered in this book). The fact is there is a storm cloud forming over the earth, and there are many who are not prepared to stand against the force of that storm. The storm cloud that's forming is the wrath of God's judgment and the signs are becoming clearer and clearer that God is slowly removing His hand (hedge) of protection from the United States of America (Ecclesiastes 10:8, Isaiah 5:5, Micah 7:4, Mark 12:1). Why? Because just like the nation Israel of old, the United States have forgotten the truths of God's word (statutes) and if the church (collective body of believers), which is to be the conscience in/of the United States (world) does not heed the warnings of God's modern-day gatekeepers/watchmen their future is not going to be a very pleasant one at all. The United States needs a true revival that turns people's hearts back toward the truths of God's words. The United States, led by the true remnant church (born-again believers) of Jesus Christ, must confront the evil forces of this time and get the church back on the right track of true repentance before Almighty God. The great deceiver himself has blinded the eyes of multitudes of people, and the God of the Holy Bible is calling His modern-day prophets and gatekeepers/watchmen in sounding the alarm to those who are asleep and caught in the snare of the devil's wicked, perverse (rebellious), and abominable spirit. There is reference to this in God's word known as Mystery, Babylon the Great, the Mother of Harlots and of the Abominations of the Earth (Revelation 17:5). It is the false religion (Antichrist spirits) of our time, and the devil and his demons are fully engaged in this movement (deception). The devil is behind this movement, but the one true God of the Bible loves people enough to send His messengers in helping them open their eyes to His truths before it's too late for them and those who surround them. This book has been written with that in mind. God's grace is available to all who call upon the name of Jesus Christ. The Lord (Jesus Christ) is not willing that any should perish, but that all should come to repentance (2nd Peter 3:9). Time is running out, and just as Jesus said to those who were staining their garments (character) within the churches in the first three books of The Revelation,

> Behold, I stand at the door and knock. If anyone hears My voice and opens the door, I will come in to him and dine with him, and he with Me. To him who overcomes I will grant to sit with Me on My throne, as I also overcame and sat down with My Father on His throne. He who has an ear, let him hear what the Spirit says to the churches. (The Revelation 3:20-22)

How about you, my fellow truth seeker? Is the God of the Bible speaking to your heart today? Do you hear His voice? Do you have an ear to hear what God's Spirit is saying to you? God is standing at the door (gate) of your heart right now. He is recruiting your service today. He is looking for soldiers and watchmen and stewards and ambassadors that will fight against the evils of our time. Do you hear Him knocking? If you do, then I urge you to answer the door and let Jesus Christ come into your life and begin to have a relationship (dine) with you right now. Let Him begin to purge and cleanse your life so that He can present you as being worthy before His Father in heaven. The author of this book did, and his life has never been the same since. Knowing that you've found the narrow gate to life is a joy that you can carry with you throughout your life here on earth and then into eternity. Always remember these words and carry them within the very depths of your heart and soul:

> "Soon this life on earth shall pass,
> the only thing's done for Christ will last!"

I pray that this is the desire of your heart today.
Thanks be to God. Amen!

INDEX

D

E

F

G

H

N

Nicodemus (Pharisee), 78, 100, 102, 105–6, 109–10, 114, 116–17, 119, 144, 149, 173–74, 182–85, 188, 192–93

Nicolaitans, 240

nothing, 59

P

pain, 114, 117, 119, 167

parables, 73–74, 142

Patmos, 67

Paul the Apostle (*see also* Saul of Tarsus), 22, 69, 74–77, 94, 173–74, 182–86, 190, 192–93, 204–5, 208–10, 223, 227–28, 230, 237

Pentecost, 67

persecution, 186, 204–5, 208

perspective, 57, 60, 63, 77, 153, 165

Peter (apostle), 108

Pharisees, 62, 71, 76, 78, 94, 99–100, 102, 105–6, 132, 144–47, 153, 170–85, 204–5, 210

Pharisees (modern-day), 94, 171–73, 176–77, 232. *See also* ravenous wolves

Philip (brother of Herod), 208

Pontius Pilate, 11–12, 61

pride of life, 22, 107, 141, 150

priests, 81, 83, 126–27

Prince of Peace. *See* Jesus Christ

prince of the power of the air, 22, 37, 56. *See also* Satan; devil; ruler of this age; god of this world

prophets, 41, 44, 59, 64, 74, 84–85, 95–96, 142

false, 84, 95–97, 100, 177, 215–16 *See also* gatekeepers; watchmen

purge, 188

Q

qualifications of a good steward, 154

R

ravenous wolves, 84, 96, 100, 172, 176–77. *See also* Pharisees (modern-day)

rebuke, 117, 197, 226–27

repentance, 42–43, 70, 102, 117, 121, 198, 215, 223, 242, 244

reproach, 226–31, 239

required, 164

Revelation, 67, 83, 117, 166, 188, 209, 215, 217–18, 232, 235, 237, 239–40

ripple effect, 240

root, 55, 57

ruler of this age, 38, 49. *See also* Satan; devil; prince of the power of the air; god of this world

S

Sadducees, 94, 99–100, 102

salvation, 27–29, 56, 60, 75, 93, 110–11, 118, 138, 142, 169, 183, 198, 224, 240

sanctification, 91, 112, 198

sanctify, 69

sanctuary, 86, 89, 129

Sardis, 234, 241

Satan (*see also* devil; ruler of this age; prince of the power of the air; god

U

United States of America, 42, 157, 170, 234–37, 240
unseen world, 82, 108, 139, 156, 162, 168. *See also* spiritual realm

W

watchmen (*see also* gatekeepers; prophets), 7, 184, 192–95, 197, 204, 207–8, 214, 217, 241, 244
Weeping Prophet, 41–42, 46. *See also* Jeremiah (Hebrew prophet)
white garments, 200–202, 237
Wise Men (Magi), 54–55, 70
works of the flesh, 44, 47, 113–14, 191, 196, 198

Z

zealous, 117, 197–98, 242
Zechariah (Hebrew prophet), 85

Edwards Brothers Malloy
Thorofare, NJ USA
May 31, 2012